Land Acquisition and Resource Development in Contemporary India

This book derives from research and fieldwork in the rural and tribal hinterlands of India, particularly in the mineral-rich states. It looks at the nuances of land and resource politics and summarizes the long-standing land acquisition and mining debate. It uses the political economy lens to discuss relevant theoretical frameworks on space and spatiality, uneven development, accumulation by dispossession, public sphere and issues of justice and fairness from interdisciplinary perspectives, and develops an argument through the case study of Singrauli, a resource-rich region in Madhya Pradesh in India that has seen various 'regimes of dispossession' since the 1960s.

It studies the legal and policy arguments around right to property, 'fair' compensation, public purpose, and the resource curse debate around contested 'spaces' (left-wing extremism) and resource–capital relationship in redrawing geographical boundaries. Highlighting the reasons for large-scale land conflicts in India, scale of stalled investments, social movements, and evolution of land acquisition and mining laws, the book also examines what led to the amendments to the Right to Fair Compensation and Transparency in Land Acquisition Resettlement and Rehabilitation Act 2013 and the Mining and Mineral (Development and Regulation) Act 2015.

Shashi Ratnaker Singh is a research fellow in the Department of Geography at the University of Cambridge. His research interests are in critical human geography, political economy, development studies, environmental laws and natural resource management.

Land Acquisition and Resource Development in Contemporary India

Shashi Ratnaker Singh

CAMBRIDGE
UNIVERSITY PRESS

CAMBRIDGE
UNIVERSITY PRESS

University Printing House, Cambridge CB2 8BS, United Kingdom

One Liberty Plaza, 20th Floor, New York, NY 10006, USA

477 Williamstown Road, Port Melbourne, VIC 3207, Australia

314–321, 3rd Floor, Plot 3, Splendor Forum, Jasola District Centre, New Delhi – 110025, India

79 Anson Road, #06–04/06, Singapore 079906

Cambridge University Press is part of the University of Cambridge.

It furthers the University's mission by disseminating knowledge in the pursuit of education, learning and research at the highest international levels of excellence.

www.cambridge.org
Information on this title: www.cambridge.org/9781108486927

First published 2020

Printed in India by Thomson Press India Ltd.

A catalogue record for this publication is available from the British Library

Library of Congress Cataloging-in-Publication Data

Names: Singh, Shashi Ratnaker, author.
Title: Land acquisition and resource development in contemporary India / Shashi Ratnaker Singh.
Description: Cambridge, United Kingdom ; New York, NY : Cambridge University Press, 2020. | Includes bibliographical references and index.
Identifiers: LCCN 2020027400 (print) | LCCN 2020027401 (ebook) | ISBN 9781108486927 (hardback) | ISBN 9781108764872 (ebook)
Subjects: LCSH: Natural resources--India. | Land use--India. | Regional planning--India. | Rural development--India.
Classification: LCC HC433.5 .S57 2020 (print) | LCC HC433.5 (ebook) | DDC 333.33/9--dc23
LC record available at https://lccn.loc.gov/2020027400
LC ebook record available at https://lccn.loc.gov/2020027401

ISBN 978-1-108-48692-7 Hardback

Contents

Figures

Maps

Tables

Abbreviations

ADB	Asian Development Bank
ASSOCHAM	Associated Chambers of Commerce and Industry of India
AWC	Anganwadi Centres
BJP	Bharatiya Janata Party
CFR	community forest rights
CHRI	Commonwealth Human Rights Initiative
CII	Confederation of Indian Industries
CIL	Coal India Limited
CMIE	Centre for Monitoring Indian Economy
CPI(M)	Communist Party of India (Marxist)
CSE	Centre for Science and Environment
CSR	corporate social responsibility
DFO	district forest officer
DM	district magistrate
EDF	Environment Defense Fund
EJAtlas	Environmental Justice Atlas
FCRA	Foreign Contribution (Regulation) Act
FDI	foreign direct investment
FICCI	Federation of Indian Chambers of Commerce and Industry
FRA	Forest Rights Act
GBPS	Govind Ballabh Pant Sagar
GDP	gross domestic product
GoMP	Government of Madhya Pradesh
GSI	Geological Survey of India
IMR	infant mortality rate
IPHS	Indian Public Health Standards
LA Act	Land Acquisition Act
LARR Act	Land Acquisition Resettlement and Rehabilitation Act
MoEF	Ministry of Environment and Forest
MoHFW	Ministry of Health and Family Welfare

MMDR	Mining and Mineral (Development and Regulation)
MPGATSVA	Madhya Pradesh Gramin Avsanrachna Tatha Sadak Vikas Adhiniyam
MoPR	Ministry of Panchayati Raj
MoRD	Ministry of Rural Development
MoTA	Ministry of Tribal Affairs
NCL	Northern Coalfields Limited
NDA	National Democratic Alliance
NGO	non-governmental organization
NTFP	non-timber forest product
NTPC	National Thermal Power Corporation
OBC	Other Backward Class
PAF	project-affected family
PAP	project-affected person
PAP Gm	project-affected person – General category – male
PAP OBCm	project-affected person – Other Backward Class category – male
PESA Act	Panchayats (Extension to Schedule Areas) Act
PMKKKY	Pradhan Mantri Khanij Kshetra Kalyan Yojna
PPP	public–private partnership
PSUs	public sector undertakings
R&R	resettlement and rehabilitation
RAP	resettlement action plan
RFCTLARR	Right to Fair Compensation and Transparency in Land Acquisition and Resettlement and Rehabilitation
RTI	Right to Information
SADA	Special Area Development Authority
SC	Scheduled Caste
SEZ	special economic zone
SSADA	Shaktinagar Special Area Development Authority
ST	Scheduled Tribe
TERI	The Energy and Resources Institute
TISS	Tata Institute of Social Sciences
U5MR	under 5 mortality rate
UMPP	ultra mega power projects
UPA	United Progressive Alliance
UPSEB	Uttar Pradesh State Electricity Board
VSTPS	Vindhyachal Super Thermal Power Station
WBCSD	World Business Council for Sustainable Development

Foreword

This book emerges from over a decade of careful observation and analysis of two contradictory developmental processes in contemporary India – the transformation of the economy towards one that celebrates big business and the power of the market and the continued need for governments (at least in rhetoric) to be attentive to the concerns and aspirations of communities exploited, marginalized or ignored by these capitalist forces. The question of land remains central to both these processes and has been subject to contestation throughout India's three decades of economic liberalization since the late 1980s. Over this period, the role of the state can seem almost schizophrenic: on the one hand, enacting progressive legislation that protects India's still predominantly rural population which remains dependent on land and natural resources for livelihoods and subsistence and, on the other, also facilitating the alienation and acquisition of rural assets by local and global capital.

I have had the privilege to work closely with the author, Shashi Ratnaker Singh, throughout this last decade. This book is the fruit of work that contributed towards his doctoral research at Cambridge, but it actually reflects wisdom and insights that both predate his graduate studies and have continued to be developed since. It is being published at a unique moment in Indian – and global – history, with 'normal' life having been suspended due to a pandemic of unprecedented proportions.

At another level, though, what the 2020 pandemic has revealed are the vulnerabilities that lie at the heart of this book, the insecurity of those who have been relegated to the margins of growth and capital accumulation. In this moment of exception, as economic activity is temporarily suspended, it is the dispossessed who suffer most – migrant labourers far from the safety of their erstwhile rural homes, with their livelihoods denied and their humanity stripped away. Having already lost their lands, the precariat are now unable to earn the daily wages that might provide a modicum of dignity and have been forced to return to their villages. To truly understand the processes that have led to this immiserization, we need to study the land question – and there could be no better place to start than this book.

In the context of economic growth and transformation from an agrarian economy to an industrial economy, the land acquisition process in India has come under close scrutiny – from academics, from those who shape public policy, and from civil society and social movements. This book analyses the accumulation process in contemporary India, focusing on land acquisition for resource development projects. It discusses issues related to compensation payments to households and to resource-rich regions, the process of dispossession, and the logic behind reorganisation of space or the redrawing of geographical boundaries. This work is inherently interdisciplinary at the interface of development studies, human geography, political economy and resource economics. In its review of the intellectual landscape as well as its own original research, the book traverses these fields and literatures with remarkable ability.

The book focuses on the complexities involved in compensation payments when local communities are affected by large-scale processes of resource extraction – spatial, economic, legal, social and political. It asks questions about the material and discursive dimensions of 'fairness' in the context of land transactions. In doing so, the book investigates the allocation of resources across different levels and sheds light on processes of concentration, accumulation and the influence of vested interests in the resolution of competing claims. It demonstrates the value of a 'socio-spatial approach' in understanding these processes and also for reflecting on how people associate with space, how they organize their lives and livelihoods, and how they struggle against various power structures.

The case study that the book examines in detail is based in the Singrauli region which is spread across the central Indian states of Madhya Pradesh and Uttar Pradesh. With meticulous detail, the author has conducted primary research which reconstructs the land acquisition and displacement discourses over five decades (1960–2012) with a special focus on the varied socio-economic experiences of displacement and compensation payments on the households in this region. The adoption of 'mixed' qualitative and quantitative methods can, sometimes, be risky, but the author has done this successfully by both the rigour with which he has approached primary research and the innovative ways in which he has adapted his own approaches to deal with the complexity of his field sites. The outcome is a unique in-depth study which documents successive processes of 'development and displacement' in Singrauli in rich empirical detail. Not only does this research contribute to our understanding of these issues in the Indian context but has the potential to impact much wider literatures on similar processes of change that are characterizing the dynamics of economic development in the so-called emerging economies.

While scholarly and meticulously researched, this book also draws on the author's professional experience which has allowed him to engage directly with these issues and to work with stakeholders across a wide spectrum, from resource development businesses in the mining sector to civil society organizations agitating for a fairer deal for those who are often seen as the 'victims of development'. It is unusual to find someone who is equally adept at explaining the intricacies of the Indian land acquisition law to the head of one of India's largest business conglomerates while also working at the grassroots to sensitize and empower villagers to secure their legal entitlements. This varied experience is visible in the empathetic way in which this book is presented and the wide-ranging issues that it seeks to address.

For most governments, there remains a trade-off between developmental opportunities and impacts on local people. This book provides some insights into how to structure mechanisms for land-related conflict resolution that are transparent, equitable and efficient. As economies in the region and around the world seek to 'build back better' after the current pandemic, nothing could be more important to ensure that the new order protects the weakest and the most vulnerable from extreme destitution.

Prof. Bhaskar Vira
Head of Department – Geography, University of Cambridge, UK, and
Director, University of Cambridge Conservation Research Institute, UK

Acknowledgements

I extend my deep gratitude to the Governance and Justice Program of International Development Research Centre, Canada, and St John's College, University of Cambridge, for supporting this research on large-scale land acquisitions in India. As an early career researcher, the research provided me an opportunity for public engagement and policy interventions. The research has also been useful in setting up my comparative work on resource-rich economies.

My supervisor Prof. Bhaskar Vira has been a source of constant support at every step of this research. His expertise and guidance helped me in exploring this complex subject and shape this piece of research. At department of geography, I would like to thank Prof. Emma Mawdsley, Prof. Sarah Radcliffe, David Nally and Chrish Sandbrook for providing useful insights in shaping my initial research. I also sincerely thank the Cambridge University Press India team (Anwesha Rana, Qudsiya Ahmed and Tapajyoti Chaudhuri) for working with me on this manuscript.

I am thankful to Tata Institute of Social Sciences for providing constant academic and institutional support for this research. I would particularly like to thank my mentor Prof. Ashwani Kumar and other senior colleagues, Prof. R. N. Sharma, Prof. Swapna Banerjee Guha and Abdul Shaban, for providing their valuable time in discussing this research.

At Council for Social Development, Delhi, I would like to thank Prof. Harimohan Mathur, Prof. K. B. Saxena, Usha Ramanathan and Balaji Pandey for their rich academic insights and guidance. I am especially thankful to Shri Jairam Ramesh (then minister, 2011–2014, Ministry of Rural Development) for providing me an opportunity to participate in expert group meetings on Right to Fair Compensation and Transparency in Land Acquisition and Resettlement and Rehabilitation Bill of 2011. I am also thankful to Ramesh Chandra Sharma of Ekta Parishad; he has been a source of motivation for my work around indigenous communities. I would like to thank my colleagues at my previous organisation (The Energy and Resources Institute) – Smrithi Talwar for encouraging me to undertake doctoral research; Leena Srivastava and Ligia Noronha for giving rich insights and views on the subject; and Sakarama Somayaji, I. H. Rehman, Vivek Jha, Nilesh Kumar and Jeevan Mohanty for their encouragement and support.

I sincerely thank Prof. Pranab Bardhan, Prof. Nagaraj, Prof. Rob Jenkins and Prof. Sripad for providing academic insights relevant to my research. The paper presented at Political Economy Conference at Indira Gandhi Institute of Development Research was useful in gathering different insights on the subject and I thank all the participants for providing detailed feedback on my research.

At Singrauli, first, I thank all the project-affected families who shared their valuable experiences and took out time for the interview and, second, the entire district administration – Vivek Porwal, District Magistrate (DM); P. Narhari, DM; M. Salvendran, DM; K. K. Tripathi, Subdivisional Magistrate; Vikas Singh, Tehsildar; B. P. Pandey, Land Acquisition Officer; and other revenue officials – for openly sharing their thoughts and experiences. I am deeply thankful to National Thermal Power Corporation for providing all the local support and access during my fieldwork; I thank Neeraj Kapur, Sebastian Joseph, Rakesh Prasad, Badri Prasad, Jaiwardhan and Arjun Chauhan for providing valuable information and giving me access to files and other important information relevant to my research. I thank to my research and field assistants, Jitendra Kumar, Surendra Chaubey, Shailesh Singh and Ram Birah Baiga, for their outstanding support and care during fieldwork and data collection. This fieldwork would have been impossible without their support.

Finally, I am thankful to my family who have been a constant support in this journey and my wife, Kavita, for her continuous encouragement and motivation to complete this book, and I thank her for painstakingly reading through the entire draft and making valuable suggestions.

Part I
Theoretical Framework

1

Introduction

From Colonial Regime to 'Welfare State'?

In India, land policy has been a critical subject of public debate since Independence. Initially, the government adopted a socialist approach (partly) towards the economy and introduced legislation to redistribute land under land reform; however, it could only partially achieve this objective due to the political stronghold of the entrenched landed class in rural areas. Post-Independence, land was also acquired for various developmental projects such as dams, mines, highways, infrastructure and so on and the acquisition of land was justified as serving the 'public purpose' to achieve economic development. Land was acquired under the old colonial Land Acquisition Act (LA Act) of 1894, which was increasingly challenged for its inadequacy to deal with contemporary realities and unjust principles, even though there was little resistance to land acquisition due to low political consciousness and lack of civil society organizations to represent the voice of the people.

In the post-Independence era, land served as a critical means of realizing developmental objectives of the government. Land policies were guided by a socialist view, *zamindari*[1] system was abolished, but redistribution of land was only partially successful, as the government had to strike a balance between its socialist objectives and the interests of the powerful landholders whose political assistance was necessary for electoral support in rural areas. The other factor was that land was a state subject and this prevented uniformity of laws on land, especially because of differences in political dynamics at the state level. Although this was not such a major concern, as the Congress party ruled most states and the Centre's dominance prevailed under Nehru's leadership, state-level politics with its own sociocultural complexities made disagreement unavoidable. The left-ruled states, like West Bengal and Kerala, could implement land reforms more successfully

---

1 *Zamindari* system refers to the system of landholding and tax collection during the colonial period.

than others. Considering the social reality of the farming community, these state governments prioritized farmer's welfare over large-scale industrialization and infrastructure projects.

During the post-Independence period, a significant thrust was given to building dams and large infrastructure projects. But the Indian government continued with the same colonial legislation to acquire land throughout the country. Affected people continuously challenged the principles of compensation under the LA Act of 1894 and approached courts for justice. Considering the gross historical injustice embedded in the LA Act of 1894, the Government of India had significantly delayed the amendment of the LA Act of 1894.

In the post-liberalization period, the opening of the Indian economy encouraged the quest to promote privatization and commercialization. The new model of growth, based on relentless competition implicit in a market economy, created immense opportunities for the expansion of private business and global capital. This has led to the overhauling of industrial licensing, tax concessions to the corporate sector, removal of import licensing, special incentives for the export-oriented industrial sector, encouragement of foreign direct investment and foreign institutional investment, establishment of special economic zones (SEZs), free trade agreements in East and South East Asia, and public sector disinvestment. Market expansion that continues to be supported by these policy changes, however, requires the fulfilment of one of the basic conditions, that is, availability of land for commercial purposes. The penetration of the market in rural or suburban areas requires land – for various purposes, for instance, urban real estate, industries, SEZs, extractive industries, dams, highways and so on – that is primarily being used for agricultural activities. Poor peasants and landless agricultural labourers are completely dependent on such land for their livelihood, and the acquisition of land adversely affects such communities, more so when there are no fair principles of compensation and rehabilitation. Resistance to land acquisition in the post-liberalization period has grown exponentially throughout the country, questioning the role of the state in facilitating land acquisition for private corporations under 'public purpose'. But such measures that have led to massive land acquisition and displacement without fair compensation have not gone unchallenged. Social protests and resistance to land acquisition are relatively more organized, focussed and powerful than what it was in the past decades. Civil society protests, particularly around Singur (Tata), Nandigram (Salim Group), Niamgiri (Vedanta), Jagatsingpur (Posco), Raigadh (Reliance SEZ) and so on, highlighted the regional issues and concerns around land acquisition laws at the national level and compelled the government to revise the land acquisition laws. These protests have brought a sense of realization that the state can no more forcibly acquire land without addressing fundamental issues around land acquisition and rehabilitation.

As discussed, conflicts around land issues in India have grown exponentially since 2006 not only at the country level but also globally (RRI, 2016; Land Conflict Watch, 2019). Environmental Justice Organisations, Liabilities and Trade (EJOLT), an FP7 European Commission–funded[2] global research project, which operated during 2011–2015, represents a global distribution map of the ecological conflicts, resistances and environmental injustices that are mostly located in the Global South. The atlas records local or national-level conflicts on account of nuclear energy, thermal power plants, mining, land acquisition and infrastructure, among other parameters. India ranked first on the list, having recorded the greatest concentration of such conflicts. The first three countries are India, Colombia and Nigeria with 201, 101 and 71 cases respectively. Other countries included in the top-11 list are the United States of America (USA), Brazil, Spain, Ecuador, Turkey, Argentina, Peru and Chile. However, it is also important to note that the number of cases reflected in a country's profile does not imply that the database is a comprehensive one. Due to non-representation, cases from many countries may not be reported at all or may be under-reported in this database. One major reason behind the reporting of Indian environmental conflicts is the presence of an active civil society and a vibrant functional democracy, which encourage stakeholders to voice their opinions. The role of political parties as well as civil society groups in influencing public policies in India became important in the last decade and has brought 'organizational strength and visibility'.

However, there is also a growing perception that these civil societies 'obstruct' the path of development, and the foreign funding that many of the non-governmental organizations (NGOs) receive in India needs to be closely monitored. In recent years, the present Bharatiya Janata Party (BJP) government has been closely monitoring the Foreign Contribution (Regulation) Act (FCRA) of 2010 transactions and many of the NGOs have been kept under observation and asked to present detailed reports of the utilization of foreign funds. Chapters 3, 4 and 5 highlight the Indian policy context with regard to land acquisitions and resource development and discuss some of the critical arguments under this debate.

Land is a non-expandable factor of production and this very finiteness tends to cause competition for this scarce resource between various economic activities. In capitalist societies, the industrial and service sectors, dominated by the bourgeoisie and supported by the state's right of eminent domain, adopt land usurpation and acquisition by hyper 'commercialization' and 'commodification' of land. The land acquisition process in India has come under close scrutiny within the overall

---

[2] FP7 stands for European Union's 7th Framework Programme for Research and Technological Development.

context of economic growth and transformation from an agrarian economy to an industrial economy.

The traditional argument, as posited by the Lewis model (Lewis, 1954), states that economic growth requires structural change in the economy whereby surplus labour in the traditional agricultural sector with low or zero marginal product migrates to the modern industrial sector with high, rising marginal product. This promotes industrialization. The Lewis model necessitates structural change and thus explains the emergence of a dual economy (ibid.). Land becomes a prerequisite for industrialization. It implies that land has to change character from its present use to industrial use. The debate about industrialization and land acquisition is thus about how political, social and economic forces are acting in concert to transform the economy for a better condition. At a more basic level, this problem occurs because the emerging industrial sector usually does not have the level of employment intensity as in the existing agricultural activity. Moreover, affected people are not immediately 'employable' as the only marketable commodity they possess in the absence of skills valued by the market is their labour. This alienates the peasantry from their traditional means of livelihood and, more often than not, results in social turmoil and unrest (Porwal and Singh, 2011).

However, the premise of the Lewis model is based on certain assumptions, and critics (Schultz, 1964) argue that the model assumes that a developing economy has surplus unproductive labour in the agricultural sector and these workers are attracted to the growing manufacturing sector where wages are fixed and higher. It assumes that all profits generated by entrepreneurs will be reinvested, which may not be the case and reinvestment can be in the form of fixed capital or capital-intensive technology that may be labour saving and thus the demand for labour may fall in due course. The assumption that surplus agricultural labour can easily move to the manufacturing sector may not be a smooth transition as it involves investment in skill upgradation and training. And the Indian economy is undergoing this transition where the 'demographic dividend' might become a curse if the country fails to address this challenge in a time-bound manner.

Many developing countries, including India, have been undergoing this process of transformation over recent decades, raising several questions about the true nature of the welfare state and its role in protecting the right to property. In India, the role of the state seems to have got reversed; after Independence, through land reform, the government attempted to create a socialistic pattern of society via redistribution of land, which is now being reversed through increased acquisition of land from small and medium owners for industrialization. Sixty years of 'planned' development in India have also entailed large-scale forced evictions of vulnerable populations, without countervailing policies to assist them to rebuild their lives.

Most of the negative aspects of displacement, such as undervaluation of compensation and its payment in cash, lack of information, failure to prepare in advance a comprehensive plan for rehabilitation, failure to restore lost assets or livelihoods, traumatic and delayed relocation, problems at relocation sites, multiple displacement, lack of participation, lack of social impact assessment study and neglect of the special vulnerabilities of the most disadvantaged groups, result from the existing laws and the policies (Porwal and Singh, 2011). The project developers so far have failed to understand or perhaps consciously ignored the fact that resettlement and rehabilitation (R&R) is a 'project within project' which requires an equal amount of effort and time as does to the project construction and development. So far the experience suggests that the corporations prioritise their project construction timelines and the requirements of the financial institutions over the short-, medium- and long-term needs of the project-affected families (PAFs). It is the responsibility of the state to regulate and monitor both the activities – land acquisition for the project and the resettlement and rehabilitation of the families. But, unfortunately, the Indian state, which prefers its role as the 'facilitator' in the development process, prioritizes land acquisition over R&R.

The vast literature (Fernandes and Thukral, 1989; Baviskar, 1995; Mathur and Marsden, 1998; Parasuraman, 1996; Pandey, 1998; Kothari, 1995; Cernea, 2000b; Baxi, 2008; Padel and Das, 2008) generated over recent decades on land acquisition, mining and R&R issues in the country has largely focussed on recording the detrimental social, cultural and economic consequences of development projects on the lives of local PAFs. Development analysts, civil society and media (ibid.) have pointed to the inadequacy of the current normative and legal policy framework, particularly of the pivotal notion of eminent domain underpinning the LA Act of 1894. This literature has been useful in identifying systemic problems underpinning R&R in India (in addition to eminent domain, analysis from political economists [Bardhan, 2011] points to intractable power relations that nullify efforts to sustainably assist PAFs).

Every year, dams, mining, highways, ports, urban improvements, pipelines and petrochemical plants, and other such industrial development projects globally displace about 10 million people (Cernea, 2000a). Unfortunately, in India there is no updated government estimate of the total number of people displaced by various projects and the only available data that gives an approximate estimate is of the year 2000. In India alone, involuntary resettlement is estimated to have affected about 50 million people in the last five decades (Roy, 1999). Three-fourths of those displaced in India over five decades still face an uncertain future (Cernea, 2000a). The resettlement process has frequently been considered to be complete once compensation is paid to the affected people and they are relocated to a new resettlement site. Resettlement refers to the relocation of the displaced families from their host village to a new settlement site, but rehabilitation is a slow and continuous process, which involves social, economic and cultural rehabilitation of the PAFs. Traditionally, little thought went into addressing the factors that limit the benefits available to PAFs, making a series of rehabilitation action plans unsustainable in the long run.

People displaced by development projects confront a variety of impoverishment risks that include landlessness, joblessness, homelessness, marginalization, increased morbidity, food insecurity, loss of access to common property and social disarticulation (Cernea, 1995, 2000b). If resettlement is not to leave people worse off than before, it must be addressed as a process of sustainable development (Scudder, 1997a, 1997b, 2005; Cernea, 2000b). In India, colonial laws have governed the regime of land acquisition and displacement for six decades until 1 January 2014. During the colonial period, with the objective of expanding trade and industrial manufacturing, land was acquired for various purposes. Land rates were fixed arbitrarily and landowners had to settle over predetermined rates. The colonial government was under no pressure to justify land acquisition for commercial purposes (Chakravorty, 2013: 18). It was not deemed necessary to specify the 'public purpose' as the British government was under no political pressure to legitimize state actions on the pretext of public welfare.

The decisive discursive category here is that of today's oustees who, of course, were the rightful owners of property of yesterday. And a series of cumulative consequences of displacement have been compensated under the LA Act of 1894 for more than six decades through a consolidation of temporalities of many future deprivations (Baxi, 1989). Displacement is a pertinent effect of development and rehabilitation is a pertinent effect of displacement. Unfortunately, in this process of material gains, the oustees have been treated in an unfair manner irrespective of their rights and entitlements. To expect a fair compensation and rehabilitation is not a matter of charity but an issue of their legal right. If displacement is inevitable in the process of development, then it is critical to ensure that the affected communities are not worse off; rather they should be the first beneficiaries and such a project should be perceived as a development opportunity for them.

However, the meaning given to compensation has been dominated by its equation with the market value or the notional value of the land in the market. This treats the displaced person as a willing seller. One of the major problems with the LA Act of 1894 was that it did not propose any scientific methodology to calculate the 'market value of land' in case of involuntary land acquisitions. Land acquisition under the power of 'eminent domain' restricts the conditions of free market and positions the landowner in a disadvantaged situation. Compensation is seen as the means for reducing the injustice inherent in acquisition. The limited understanding of compensation has eroded its moral base. The notion of total compensation being unknown to the law, it is ill-equipped to internalize the immoderation that acquisition may entail (Ramanathan, 1996). Understanding the issue of compensation for land acquisition requires both a multifunctional view of resource and a multidimensional perspective of land as a resource and its significance for communities. The land acquisition process also tends to be individual-centric and compensation is not sensitive to the displacement of communities. The trauma involved in displacement, the fragmentation of communities, the breakdown of support structures, the deprivation of displaced populations and the increased susceptibility to exploitation where protected populations are dislocated are usually neglected by the law of compensation. The only significant reparation for displaced persons guaranteed by law is the payment of monetary compensation for compulsorily acquired individual assets, mainly land or houses. However, the manner in which the law is framed and interpreted ensures that the displaced landowner or house-owner is always at a loss (considering past experiences).

In the context of land acquisition for resource development[3] projects, the local community and the surrounding region experience different kinds of challenges in the short, medium and long terms. The potential impact of resource development in regional development is a subject of debate between dependency theorists, who argue that resource development obstructs a balanced development process, and comparative advantage theorists, who argue that resources can expedite development (Gunton, 2003). The literature suggests that natural resources have the potential to provide a significant comparative advantage relative to other economic sectors by virtue of generating resource rent which is surplus above normal returns to other factors of production. However, there are considerable risks in resource-led growth, including the propensity to dissipate rent, increase community instability and several other negative externalities (social and environmental). There is extensive literature on 'resource curse' that argues that natural resource abundance is negatively correlated to economic growth and there are risks involved in such projects (Ross, 2003a; Collier and Hoeffler, 2000; Atkinson and Hamilton, 2003; Sachs and Warner, 1995; Wheeler, 1984).

Under the land acquisition and resource development debate, there are layers of conflicts between different stakeholders. One layer of conflict is between the Centre and state governments regarding sharing of power and decision-making; the other layer of conflict is between the displaced community and the project developers. In the context of this study, analysing the way federalism plays out in the natural resource sector is very critical at this juncture of the evolution of the Indian political system, given its commitment to a more decentralized system of

[3] The term 'resource development' or 'resource development projects' has been used in the context of mining projects.

governance. In no sector is such an engagement more urgent than in the context of natural resource development, given the sharing of administrative and fiscal powers, along with growing responsibilities at the local government level. A central issue, both from the point of the working federalism and in terms of the impacts that resource development can have on local people, is the monitoring, regulation and enforcement of laws and rules in place. Both the centre and the state collect revenue through different taxes and levies imposed on mineral development under different legislations. In the given precarious fiscal situation of the mineral-bearing states,[4] there is a question with regard to the powers exercised by the Centre vide the Mines and Minerals (Development and Regulation) Act (MMDR Act) on the fixing of royalty rates for a resource that is in principle owned by states. There is also discontent with the manner in which revisions are done by the Centre in terms of their periodicity.

There is a long-standing grievance of the regional governments (of mineral-bearing states) that at present there is no national programme to compensate states for the irreparable damage caused by the mining activities. The royalty that is paid to the state government is inadequate considering the huge loss that the state suffers. The necessity to arrive at a fair royalty is critical for the state and should not be dealt with as merely a commercial activity but should take into consideration the ecological and social aspects of mining. The term 'regional' used in the book refers to the governments at the state and local levels. However, there are contradictions between the arguments of resource-rich states and their pro-investment policies where they are competing among each other to attract investments and are willing to provide several incentives to the private sector in the form of tax benefits or tax holidays. As a result of the long-standing demands by civil society and the state governments, there has been a policy amendment in the MMDR Act of 2015 (Section 9B), which talks about the sharing of royalty with the district mineral foundations. We will examine the implications of this Act in forthcoming chapters.

Developments at the state level and the growing interest in resource projects by national and multinational corporations are giving rise to demand for more compensation by the local community and revenue sharing by resource-bearing states. The lack of clarity about the nature, basis and rationale for compensation and a recognition that the issues relating to 'fair compensation' to individuals and resource-bearing regions are very important in the context of the federal democratic polity of the country are the main motivations for this investigation.

The complexities for resource development policy and, consequently, for compensation issues arise from the 'roles' that resources perform and the 'values' attached to them. Understanding the issue of compensation for resource

---

[4] See Appendix.

development requires a multifunctional view of resources and a multidimensional perspective – spatial, economic, legal, social and political. Such a perspective enables an understanding of the impacts that these projects have on the community and the region, and the need to be attentive to them if resource development is truly to be in the 'national interest'.

The LA Act has undergone a series of amendments in the last five years with different governments imposing different opinions on the subject. The Right to Fair Compensation and Transparency in Land Acquisition and Resettlement and Rehabilitation (RFCTLARR) Bill, 2013,[5] was tabled in parliament by the United Progressive Alliance (UPA) government to amend the LA Act of 1894, and the Act came into effect from January 2014. However, the BJP government that succeeded the UPA introduced the Land Acquisition Ordinance in 2015 to amend some of the provisions of the Act. The issue of land acquisition has been at the centre of political debate under the present BJP regime. The introduction of the land ordinance in the previous RFCTLARR Act of 2013 by the BJP government raised serious concerns over its impact on the lives and livelihood of the farmers. The land ordinance proposed to facilitate the process of land acquisition by relaxing legal norms to exempt the landowners' consent clause and the social impact assessment study in certain sectors (including private sector projects). The ordinance was vehemently opposed by the Congress, the left-winged and other political parties and has provided a basis for the consolidation of opposition forces to question the anti-farmer sentiments of the present regime. Considering the massive opposition to the land ordinance introduced by the BJP government, the government decided to withdraw its amendments to the initial legislation (RFCTLARR, 2013) prepared by the UPA government; the only amendment that was introduced in the second land ordinance was to extend the provision of the RFCTLARR to other 13 central enactments that govern land acquisition specified in the fourth schedule of the RFCTLARR.

The central concern of the land use amendments is the paradox between rapid industrial and infrastructural development that necessitates land acquisition as a prior requirement for such purpose and the displacements, that is, economic and social insecurities that result from such developmental initiatives. State action in this regard is justified on the ground of the trickle-down effect that the capitalist model of development would bring about. Inherent in this argument is the necessity for supporting long-term plans that exact short-term sacrifices. The logic of ascendancy in global market is yet another point of justification for

[5] I would like to indicate that I was invited by the Ministry of Rural Development in 2011 to participate in the expert group consultation meetings on the drafting of the RFCTLARR Bill.

this relentless capitalist or industrial drive. But, from the perspective of justice and fairness, the developmental model as implemented in India so far falls short of the basic minimum standards for its justification.

The main focus of this book is to show how land acquisition processes reflect two contradictory developmental pressures in contemporary India: one that supports a capitalist model of development and envisages an economically powerful nation with large businesses playing a key role in the development and expansion of market forces, and the other that prioritizes the concerns and aspirations of the poor and underprivileged groups for whom land remains the most basic source of livelihood. While the politics of growth and uncontrolled privatization and commercialization justifies land acquisition, the politics of resistance serves as a democratic alternative, by demanding justice and fairness. Thus, the core questions that this book will address are: How do developments in land policy in India reflect the interests of global and local capitalist classes, while the state continues to face resistance against its pro-capitalist and pro-business policies? How is the path towards a corporate-led model of development opposed and contested by those who are displaced, and how does the political process provide support for these marginalized voices? Finally, in a resource-rich area, how can the interests of capital and resource exploitation be reconciled with a fair and just process that recognizes the land-based livelihoods and aspirations of local communities?

The research attempted to assess this debate through a case study analysis of the impact of land acquisition for resource development projects on a regional economy. The objective was to put the theoretical discussion into a historical perspective and argue that it is the inherent tendency of capital to generate uneven development. The purpose of this research was to study the dimensions of land acquisition in case of resource development projects and arguments with regard to resource revenue sharing between the national, state and local levels. The study particularly attempted to analyse the issues related to compensation payments to households and to the region, the process of dispossession and the logic behind reorganization of space or redrawing of geographical boundaries in the context of land acquisition for resource development projects.

The research analysed a case study of the Singrauli region (the 50th district of Madhya Pradesh, carved out of Sidhi district in 2008) which has undergone three phases of land acquisition and displacement between 1960 and 2015. The resource-rich space of Singrauli has undergone massive transformation in the last five decades with more than 0.1 million families having been uprooted from their habitat (Singh, 2015: fieldwork data, 2015). During earlier decades, primarily the public sector undertakings (PSUs) such as state electricity boards, National Thermal Power Corporation Limited (NTPC) and Coal India Limited (CIL) undertook industrial activities in the Singrauli region, with a few private companies (mainly Birlas) operating in a limited capacity. In the last one decade (2008 onwards), the government of Madhya Pradesh received massive private investments in the Singrauli region for coal mining and thermal power generation, and the geographical boundaries of Singrauli were redrawn in 2008 to declare it as an independent district. One reason behind reorganization of the space, which clearly justifies the reorganization, is to facilitate the smooth entry of private capital into this backward region and provide better administrative support to facilitate land acquisition for the corporations.

It is important to highlight that despite the massive discontent with the LA Act of 1894 at national and state levels, Singrauli is perhaps the only district in the country which has been successful in acquiring more than 30,000 acres of land for private corporations (see Chapter 7) with the already challenged, unfair Act. It is important to note that at a time when 804 projects[6] (CHRI, 2015) across India were held up due to land acquisition, environmental clearance, financial irregularities and other issues, Singrauli has been successful in acquiring such massive private land and forestland involving significant displacement of families. Out of the total stalled projects, 78 per cent are private sector projects and 22 per cent are public sector projects (such as central/state governments, PSUs and so on). Perhaps it indicates the reasoning behind amending the RFCTLARR by introducing the land ordinances and making provisions for removing the landowners' consent clause and exempting projects from social impact assessment study.

This book brings together a set of academic literatures that are relevant to this debate but which have previously been discussed independently of each other. This research seeks to build on the existing literature, applied as a set of overlapping intellectual arguments and merged systematically to discuss compensation issues in the resource development debate. The earlier literature of displacement and resource use has tended to see these issues in a disjointed manner. The research adopts a socio-spatial approach to understand social, economic and political processes not only for the analysis of the changing sociopolitical framework but also for reflecting on how people associate with space and how they organize their lives, livelihoods and struggles against various power structures. It argues for a multidimensional approach for determination of compensation in resource development projects. It further identifies the policy gaps in the existing compensation mechanisms and also places the Indian experience in the context of international practices. The book is unique in consolidating the 'development and displacement' discourse of the last five decades of Singrauli and this research contributes to the sparse literature on Singrauli.

---

[6] Data provided by Ministry of Finance in reply to a Right to Information (RTI) application by the Commonwealth Human Rights Initiative (CHRI).

2

State, Space and People

Nature of the Indian State

The Indian state has been evolving post colonisation and has maintained its uniqueness as compared to other neighbouring countries. India's approach towards the state-driven nationalization to the state-driven globalization indicates that such strategy requires a greater control over interest groups, for instance, industrialists, trade unions and farmers. To understand the changing nature and role of the Indian state, some of the scholarship on Indian politics is reviewed and reflected in this chapter. The concept of state was not prevalent outside Marxist literature before the advent of political systems theories in the 1950s and the 1960s. The idea of a political system had been developed consciously in the 1950s as a way of avoiding the ambiguities surrounding the term (Easton, 1981). Considering the literature on reflections on the Indian state, this can be divided into two schools: the liberal and the Marxist. However, it would be more fruitful to redraw the lines of division a bit into the following two groups of theories: political–institutional and political–economy perspectives on the Indian state. In the first group would fall theories which focus on the political institutions and processes as the key to understanding the character of public power in India. Political scientists who hold liberal modernist values usually propose these. The second set of theories regard political economy as holding the clue to the nature of the state. From the social sciences viewpoint, such theories are mostly of Marxist persuasion.

Political–Institutional Perspective

The Indian state, as identified by most liberal theorists, is one ruled by the middle class or by the 'middle sectors'. Myron Weiner, in his studies in the 1950s and the 1960s on Indian politics, contends that the ruling Congress elite represents the middle sectors in urban and rural life, that is, the educated and professional groups, the town merchants and small businessman, and the middle and rich peasantry. He states, 'The Congress Party today is very much the party of peasant proprietors in the countryside and of businessmen in the towns and cities' (Weiner, 1967: 488). This understanding is based on his assessment that 'while business in India is well organised, its influence on central government policy is negligible'. Weiner (1962: 129), however, does not elaborate or clarify how an economically powerful organized force, like big business, can have 'negligible' influence on government.

Nayar (1971) and Jones (1974) have similar views on the character of the Indian state, that the middle class or the intermediate strata rule it. Jones, further, refers to the relationship 'between business and Congress and Government' as a 'triangle [which] according to him was likely to remain in flourishing existence'.

Other scholars like K. N. Raj (1973) saw India as an example of an 'intermediate regime'; the term 'intermediate regimes' has been used to describe governments in which the lower middle class and the rich peasantry could be identified as performing the role of the ruling class. He further explains that due to specific conditions that emerged in many underdeveloped countries, the lower middle class transforms into the ruling class; some specific conditions cited were the numerical dominance of the lower middle class at the time of achievement of independence of these countries, the extensive involvement of governments in economic activity and the availability of credits to them from socialist countries. Given these conditions, the state could, in his view, perform the role of 'dynamic entrepreneurs' and promote a pattern of amalgamation of the interests of the lower middle class with state capitalism.

Kochanek (1974), in his work, had similar views. According to him, initially, the Congress comprised of the elite, highly Westernized professional, middle class interests that also came to include the middle sectors in the rural areas after the party was turned into a mass movement at the initiative of Mahatma Gandhi. Among his broad conclusions was the finding that '... business collectively has not been able to influence the broad outline and direction of public policy in India'.

Myrdal (1968) in his classic, *Asian Drama*, characterized India, like other South Asian countries, as a 'soft state' for its failure to perform on the front of mass poverty. The term was meant to highlight the severe limits to the scope of public power in India, the inability of the state to enforce policies and to place obligations on the people.

Rajni Kothari's (1972) work has been the most innovative attempt to understand the nature of public power in India in the liberal framework. According to him, the Indian state had the following attributes: autonomy in dealing with demands and pressures, a high degree of legitimacy and authority, an elaborate institutional edifice, and the capacity to perform. In his study, it is contended that neither interest groups nor political parties 'have taken on a "class character" ...' (1972: 217).

'Significant interest articulation in India is not in respect to social and economic interests in the modern sector but it was in respect to antecedent structures of Caste and Community in the large and pervasive traditional sector' (ibid.).

In the state structure, a coalition of urban caste (mainly Brahmin) elites with the local rural elites dominate. Because of 'the large and pervasive traditional sector', 'trade and business associations, farm lobbies, [and] even trade unions' are not considered legitimate bases for political bargaining. In Kothari's model of Indian politics, the question of modern interest groups, particularly business lobbies playing a major role in shaping government policy, does not arise. In his work, Kothari (1987) views the Indian state as having lost its autonomy to the narrow interests of the neo-rich and their allies who control and manipulate the state.

Political–Economic Perspective

Most of the analytical theories on the Indian state are from the perspective of political economy. They sensitize the analysts to the systematic linkage between the operation of public power and the dominant interests of the society. The classic Marxist study of Indian society was written by the British Marxist Rajni Palme Dutta. According to him, the leadership of government and the state vested in the hands of 'the national bourgeoisie', which sought to pursue independent capitalist development (Dutta, 1970). His evaluation of the 1944 Bombay Plan, whose authors included important Federation of Indian Chambers of Commerce and Industry (FICCI) leaders, namely Purshottamdas Thakurdas, G. D. Birla, Kasturbhai Lalbhai and Shri Ram, makes clear his belief that 'top-rank' industrialists enjoyed a major share of political power (632–635).

Charles Bettelheim (1968) deals quite explicitly with the relationship between Indian capitalist organizations and the political leadership. According to him, the big capitalists and other bourgeois factions control the Congress and through it the functioning of the government. Thus, according to Bettelheim, the Congress 'by [its] social and economic policies has satisfied the majority of the bourgeoisie, while being of particular advantage to big capital'.

Desai (1975) seeks to demonstrate that despite contrary appearances, the state in India is a capitalist state. C. P. Bhambhri allows for conflict within the ruling classes and the consequent weakening of the state, but the latter is seen simply as a vehicle of capitalism. Kurien (1975b), after a brief survey of the increasing concentration of production and capital in the monopoly sector, going together 'with foreign finance capital' and the failure of land reforms, observes, 'The state in India is an organ of the class rule of the bourgeoisie and landlords, led by the big bourgeoisie which is increasingly collaborating with foreign finance capital in pursuit of the capitalist path of development' (117).

Mitra (1977) and Patnaik (1972) argue that a coalition between the bourgeoisie and large landowners, or in Mitra's words, 'a duopolistic arrangement between the rural oligarchy and the industrial bourgeoisie', forms the basis of state power in India. Mitra suggests that the rural rich play a crucial role in state power because they control the majority of votes. They are especially strong in state legislatures while the big bourgeoisie enjoys greater power and influence at the centre. This formulation, expressed by other writers more graphically as 'the strangulating embrace' of rural oligarchy and industrial bourgeoisie, is close to that of the Communist Party of India (Marxist) (CPI[M]). The CPI(M) line says, 'The present Indian state is the organ of the class rule of the bourgeoisie and the landlord, led by the big bourgeoisie who are increasingly collaborating with foreign finance capital in pursuit of the capitalist path of development.' However, the Communist Party of India's (CPI) viewpoint slightly differs from the CPI(M), and they believe that the national bourgeoisie is the ruling class and the state can hence resist pressure from the big bourgeoisie and landlords to play a progressive role.

Pranab Bardhan (1984) identified three proprietary classes in India – the industrial capitalist class, the rich farmers and the professionals in the public sector. He views the Indian state as an autonomous actor in that it acts neither at the behest of nor on behalf of the ruling classes; it plays a catalytic role in industrial–technological transformation and is an important part of the economic base itself. The conflict within the heterogeneous ruling classes is such that this autonomy is reflected more in the regulatory than the developmental functions of the state. Bardhan considers the industrial bourgeoisie as the dominant proprietary class and the principal beneficiary of the state policies in India. This class, under the leadership of the top business houses, supported the government policy of encouraging import-substituting industrialization, of instituting quantitative trade restrictions providing automatically protected domestic markets and of running a large public sector providing capital goods. Budhadev Bhattacharya asserts that the transfer of political power was from the imperialist rulers to the newly constituted ruling party representing the interests of the Indian capitalist class as a whole and mediating and reconciling between the functions of this class (Chatterjee, 2004).

Not all political economy arguments are from the point of view of Marxists. Francine Frankel (1978) gives the impression of the Indian state in the sense of an actual organization controlling territories and people. Her theme is that India's public power is a 'paradox of accommodative politics and radical social change'. According to her, interests of both groups – rural elite and big bourgeoisie – do seem to have been generally favoured by the actions of the state, but not unfailingly so; political exigencies make the modern Indian state a very imperfect instrument of the interests of the economically dominant classes.

Rudolph and Rudolph (1977) have presented an elaborate and in some ways an innovative argument in their work. In their view, India is a paradox of a 'weak-strong state', for, in the past four decades, the Indian state has alternated between autonomous and reflexive relations with the society. Drawing strength from various historical legacies, the state acts as the 'self-determining third actor', independent of both capital and labour, and has served at different times the capitalist, socialist and liberal-constitutional objectives or sometimes its own partisan interests. Highly mobilized albeit fragmented social forces are its sources of weakness. The paradox is reflected in the realm of economic policy in the alternation between two models: 'command polity', when the state makes authoritative allocation, or 'demand polity', when the state surrenders to popular sovereignty and fulfils societal interests and values.

Role of the Indian State

The aforementioned selected review of literature highlights the nature of the Indian state and its role over a period of time. The political economy literature has been useful in identifying the systemic linkage between the capitalist class and its influence over state policies. With the opening of the Indian economy and with the entry of foreign capital, the state–capital relationship has come under scrutiny and role of the state is in question. In a neoliberal era, it is becoming critical to investigate the role of capital in driving state actions, nature of public power and its influence on public policies.

Empirical data gathered from the research site – Singrauli – highlights the initial discourse on the Indian polity and state relationship with the industrial bourgeoisie (national capitalists) and its role in facilitating private capital. It also highlights the state power of 'eminent domain' to acquire millions of hectares of land in the name of 'public purpose' to benefit a few capitalists. With the opening of the Indian economy and entry of foreign capital, the state–capital relation has been reorganized and aggressive capitalism has led to the withdrawal of the state from several spheres and left the state to act as the 'managerial workforce for the bourgeoisie'. The redrawing of geographical boundaries of Singrauli substantiates the inherent tendency of capital in using the 'space' for a particular 'need'.

Theoretical Framework

To summarize the present research, the study adopted a political economy framework and drew theoretical inputs primarily from the literature on space and spatiality, uneven development, accumulation by dispossession, justice, land acquisition, resource development and displacement to study and analyse

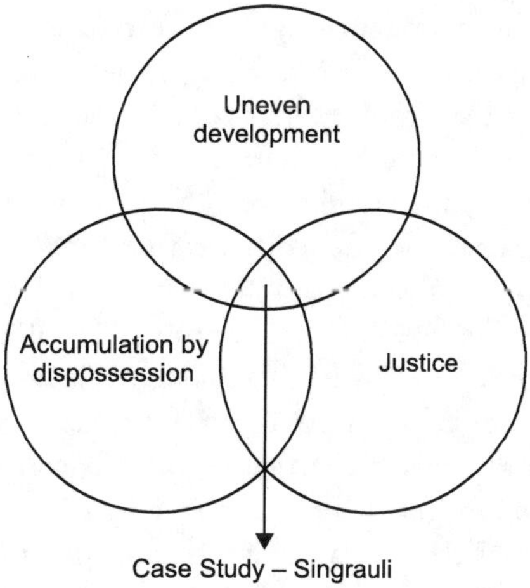

Figure 2.1 Case study

Source: Author.

the case study selected for the research. (See Figure 2.1 – this is a conceptual framework developed and used by the author to analyse and produce empirical evidence through the case study of Singrauli.) The case study selected is unique in its features, such as resource abundance, multiple displacement of households and uneven geography (geographical isolation and backwardness of the region).

Space and Spatiality

Scholars from different disciplines have been raising issues about the relevance of geography and geographical praxis in studying and analysing contemporary issues related to society, economy and environment. Research in the social sciences is increasingly using space and spatiality as key theoretical constructs to articulate the link between social and political processes, between the state, people and issues of their everyday life. On the one hand, this opens up the potential of linking social processes with their respective spatialities from various angles, while on the other it calls for a more comprehensive understanding of 'space' and 'spatiality' as key constructs in social, literary and cultural theories. Poulantzas (1978) offered a comprehensive understanding of a socio-spatial dialectic and argued, building in part upon Lefebvre's (1974) works, that for establishing a primary material framework for social life, both spatial and temporal matrices were logical priorities.

Until the early twentieth century, the term 'social' was generally separated from the 'spatial' – a profoundly Kantian dualism (Gregory and Urry, 1985) and despatialization of social process was evident in sociological researches (Durkheim attempted to secure a niche for sociology) that carved out a distinct identity for sociology in explaining social processes with the help of social structures. This prevailed until the 1940s and worked on a complete separation of spatiality from social theories. On the other hand, in human geography, space was considered as epiphenomenal, a mere codification of social structures. The culmination led to two distinct directions: conception of social life, first, in the realms of interpretative sociology and humanistic geography and, second, in the realms of structural functionalism (ibid.). The question of integrating spatial structures with social processes remained quite non-essential to both these deliberations. Further attempts at refining explanations of spatiality through quantifications and formal techniques intensified this process of distancing that reached its climax in the 1950s. The quantitative revolution brought about by introducing scientific methods in spatial theories established a notion of spatial studies as functioning science that, according to Peet (1977), became instrumental in the search for a philosophical perspective in human geography in the 1960s.

During the 1970s, through series of work from human geography and other social science disciplines, society and space started getting juxtaposed with logical explanations and the imperative to embed space in critical social theory. It culminated in a critical understanding of space with a bearing on the dynamics of its production and reproduction. The related interpretations and analyses ushered in a philosophical revolution projecting the ontology of spatiality (Harvey, 1973; Massey, 1973; Peet, 1977; Bunge, 1977; Lefebvre, 1974; Pickvance, 1976; Castells, 1977; Poulantzas, 1978; Gregory, 1978) and a precise understanding of space–society integration. While Lefebvre (1974) conceived space as a material product, often supported by ideology, reflecting an integrative relationship between social and spatial, Poulantzas conceptualized a 'spatial matrix' of state and society embodying the relations of production and challenged the prevailing idea of spatial structural analysis as a derivative exercise, inferior to the analysis of social structure. Massey showed how spatial, neoclassical accounts of industrial location got fundamentally disrupted when spatial dimensions were addressed. Harvey, on the other hand, explained in a systematic manner the conceptualization of space under capitalism, which remained his main concern and became critical for his later works on space–time compression, commodification of space and time, and the neoliberal globalization process. For Harvey, space is produced within capitalism and expresses the system's inner contradictions.

The discourse in the 1980s emphasized on the conceptualization of the structuring of human life and practices in diverse social forms. Giddens (1984) considered 'structure' and 'agency' as its foremost elements, Gregory focussed on the subjective notion of actors and Massey emphasized the significance of the component of 'space' in it. Subsequently, scholarship in the social sciences started articulating that sociocultural, economic or political context has spatial expression which indicates that social relations are both constituted through and constrained by space, giving rise, in the process, to a socio-spatial dialectic (Soja, 1989; Dear and Flusty, 2001). From the 1980s, human geographical thinking got reoriented towards the aforementioned dialectic with an increasing number of researches focussing on the relationship between nature, space, society (Harvey, 1982; Smith, 1984), economy and uneven development, moving towards the theorization of space.

During the 1990s, there has been significant research on space as a component of social theory and political economy (Harvey, 1996; Guha, 1992; Smith, 1993) in the light of post-Fordist, postmodern and neoliberal constructions, bringing in the process dimensions of gender, nature and environment. In the recent decades, researches in the social sciences, including human geography, are found to have got intermixed with studies on spatiality, uneven development, geopolitics, gender, culture and social theory, to mention a few (Nilsen, 2010; Lahiri-Dutt, 2001; Guha, 1997). The scholars provide explanations of spatial patterns and structures of everyday life that are integrally connected to social and political processes.

The understanding of space as a material social and political construct is progressively becoming significant, focussing on issues of spatiality, intermixed with uneven development, contemporary globalization and the prevailing geopolitical order. The need for a socio-spatial approach in understanding the present-day social and political processes thus has become important not only for the analysis of the changing sociopolitical framework but also for reflecting on how people associate with space, how they organize their lives, livelihoods and struggles against various power structures. In the last 100 years of capitalist development, due to drastic redrawing of economic and political boundaries based on newer political economic relations, discussion on space has become more important. Consequently, globalization is being theorized as a reconfiguration of superimposed socio-economic spaces that operate on multiple geographical scales, interconnecting societies and economies of a large number of nation-states within the network of an anomalously developed interdependence. The spatiality of the above process is further shaped by the geographies of cultural forms and practices in countries and regions and hence may vary from one spatial framework to other (Banerjee-Guha, 2011).

Space can be absolute, relative, relational or all together depending on the ongoing process (ibid.). The absolute space on the basis of its elements (such as natural resources and people, forming a part of a contextualized spatiality) can simultaneously become an area of material practice as well as an object of imagination of communities that possess an organic connection with regional elements through historically evolved spatial practices. But, the absolute space, as discussed, can be completely disregarded through a process of multiple construction by the state through territorialization and re-territorialization with specific economic, political and cultural objectives (Banerjee-Guha, 2011). Such conceptualization often leads to practices of an absolutely conflicting nature vis-à-vis the perceptions of the locals such as land acquisition or expropriation of natural resources. In India, the unjust expropriation of land and natural resources in the rural and tribal hinterlands of Jharkhand, Madhya Pradesh and Odisha, for setting up SEZs, are at complete opposition to the imagination or objectives of the locals with regard to the economic and cultural aspirations of such areas. The relational concept of space suggests that both space and time are embedded in processes and vice versa; nothing exists in dissociation. For instance, social protests against land acquisition and environmental conflicts in India have to be seen in a larger global context. Tension and conflict, however, are seen to arise over the use of space for individual or social purposes (often termed as 'public purpose' or 'national interest') or its domination by the state and other forms of class power. Definite patterns of praxis that emerge out of such uses are an integral part of the socio-spatial dialectic of every region. Underlying such spatialities, one thus can find a complex material framework of social relations, power structure and discursive methodologies of the common people (Banerjee-Guha, 2011).

'Space' and 'place' are key geographical concepts, which have different connotations. Literature suggests that scholars studying the relationship between people and physical landscape have used a variety of terms and different ontological and epistemological perspectives to describe this phenomenon. For instance, Low and Altman (1992) used the term 'place attachment' to refer to the phenomenon of human–place bonding. While they stressed that 'affection, emotion and feeling are central to the concept' (4), they also indicated that these emotional elements 'are often accompanied by cognition (thought, knowledge and belief) and practice (action and behavior)' (4–5). Researchers working within a naturalistic paradigm have stressed the subjective nature of the sense of place construct. For example, Tuan (1977) distinguished between space and place by suggesting, 'What begins as undifferentiated space becomes place as we get to know it better and endow it with value' (6). In describing his interpretation of sense of place, Steele (1981) also referred to people's subjective perceptions of their environments and their more or less conscious feelings about those environments.

Uneven Development

Uneven development, as a necessary aspect of capitalism, comes from Volume I of Marx's *Capital.* Marx stated that a major contradiction of capitalism is the simultaneous emergence of concentrations of wealth and capital for capitalists, on the one hand, and poverty and oppression for workers, on the other. Among Marxist scholars (Emmanuel, Amin, Frank, Mandel, Harvey), uneven characteristics of capitalist development have drawn significant attention. However, Neil Smith's (1984) work on uneven development is one of the comprehensive and systematic inquiries about the geography of capitalism. Smith's work on uneven development not only explains the origin and pattern of the geography of capital but also helps in understanding its objective of how 'the production of space has contributed to the survival of capitalism' (1984: 96). Smith advances his argument that capitalism does not merely generate uneven spatial patterns as a side effect, but rather the production of space is critical for its own development. Smith (1984) presented his thoughts in three major sections: the production of nature, the production of space and particularly the geography of capitalism or precisely the 'relationship between the production of nature and the unevenness of capitalist development' (66). This approach sets the premise for understanding the capitalist spatial expansion and the resulting capitalist landscape.

In general terms, uneven development can relate to differential growth of sectors, geographical processes, classes and regions at the global, regional, national, subnational and local levels. 'Uneven development' hence refers to uneven rates of growth between different sectors of an economy or between different regions of a country, reflected in the persistent disparity in skills, wage rates, investment and circulation of capital, life cycle of economic activity, productivity, income, welfare and so on. In spatial terms, unevenness is associated with processes of unequal exchange forming innumerable cores and peripheries and continuous shifting of positions.

The last hundred years of capitalist development have involved the production of space on an unprecedented scale. The renewed importance of geographical space in recent times is reflected in the increased attention paid to issues such as centralization and decentralization of industry, selective industrialization of the developing countries, deindustrialization, urban redevelopment and gentrification, fast mobility of capital through international financial institutions, and redrawing of geographical boundaries and spatial restructuring (Harvey, 1985; Smith, 1984). Any geographical space is the totality of spatial relations organized into identifiable patterns, which are themselves an expression of the structure and development of mode of production. A 'space' is a container of a built environment, which contains various elements interacting with each other (Smith, 1984). There is an intricate link between the whole and the part and any change in a constituent part affects the whole, and the parts themselves cannot escape the modification made in the whole at the macro level.

It is commonplace now to recognize that the national and international restructuring of capital is producing rapid and dramatic changes in regional economies. Social processes take place over space in a geographically differentiated world which affects their operation. According to Massey, understanding the spatial organization of society is crucial, and it is central to his understanding of the way in which social processes work. One of the most striking characteristics of the process of capitalist development, as it has appeared historically across many different countries over a long period of time, is the phenomenon of uneven development. Specifically, the process is marked by persistent differences in levels and rates of economic development between different sectors of the economy. Relevant indicators which identify the phenomenon include the level of labour productivity in different sectors, the level of wages, occupational and skill composition of the labour force, the degree of mechanization and production techniques, rates of profit, rates of growth, the size and structure of firms and so on.

The regional implications of restructuring of capital can be extended to encompass, in a more explicit way, land, property and rents as well as capital, employment and all forms of work and local and national government actions (Pahl, 1985) that are organized and juxtaposed. Unevenness becomes relevant to the process of juxtaposition at a regional level within national economies as well as at a global scale between different national economies. While the relative position of particular sectors may change from one period to another, there is, nevertheless, always a definite pattern of such differentiation. Uneven development, in this sense, is an intrinsic or inherent property of the capitalist mode of production. Far from being merely transitory, it appears to be a pervasive and permanent condition.

Harvey argued,

> Historical-geographical materialism entails a consideration of the process of unevenness in more general ways. The fulcrum of geographical unevenness is the differentiated return on investment that creation and/or destruction of entire built environments and the social structures that accompany them offer to different kinds of investors with different time horizons. Different spaces compete endlessly with one another to attract investment. In the process they tend to intensify unevenness, allowing capital to play local or regional or national class configuration off against others. (1996: 295)

Uneven development theories also describe how capitalist competition generates a landscape of constant change and of simultaneous growth and decline, producing uncertainties in the life of the people. Uneven development produces a mosaic of expansion and decline for production complexes immobilized in places not only by fixed capital but also by the availability and quality of natural resources that enter the production process. Uneven development generates a dynamic resource base, and resource-rich spaces constantly compete among each other to attract private investments. Resources expand and contract and the people who depend on them become subject to the changes and instabilities that accompany change. Political struggles over natural resources arise over who will appropriate the gains and who will share the losses. These struggles are the core of many natural resource conflicts around the world (Rebecca and Jaque, 1992).

The role of the state becomes significant at this conjuncture because it sets the rules and jointly determines the external conditions within which firms operate. Legal, financial, educational and state administrative systems, together with built environments, transportation and urban systems, are arranged in support of the circulation of capital. The emergence of growth centres, unevenly scattered over space and yet connected, is a reflection of this underlying process. It is a consequence of the effort on the part of many firms to create or to rush into those spheres in which a margin of profitability exists that allows them to capture new profit and growth opportunities (Harvey, 1985). It is this constant flux – consisting of the emergence of new growth centres, their rapid expansion relative to existing sectors and the relative decline of others – which shows up in the economy as a whole as uneven development.

Disparity among societies and individuals and the aggregation of such disparities between different places have become a significant aspect of human geography and development studies in the present day. The present study seeks an explanation for the aforementioned spatial inequality and unevenness that has been obtained in the identified space in the light of contemporary policies. The study attempts at investigating the uneven allocation of resources across different levels and regions and tries to understand the process of concentration, accumulation and the vested interests therein. Finally, it attempts to identify the regions that remain neglected and the repercussions of such spatial differentiations.

Natural resources and their presence in diverse geographical locations are critical to the process of uneven development and have become a cornerstone of the geographical perspective on environmental problems. The tragedy of the commons has become a core theoretical issue for the analysis of natural resource problems (Rebecca and Jaque, 1992). Some of the insights on geographic ideas can be drawn from the long-standing engagement in human geography with the people–environment relationship, the functional theory of resources developed by Zimmermann (1951) and critical perspectives based on Marx's recognition of the role of human appraisal in the construction of nature (Peet, 1989). These insights provid strength in analysing the resource–human interactions.

Accumulation by Dispossession

The research draws theoretical insights from the work of Marxist geographer David Harvey and analyses the case selected for the purpose of this study. The concept of accumulation by dispossession as discussed by Harvey defines the impact of neoliberal policies across the world resulting in centralization of wealth in the hands of a few private individuals by dispossessing the larger public of their wealth, particularly land. The central argument is that land acquisition, resource development, resettlement policies and their flawed implementation need to be studied within the context of accumulation by dispossession that occurs at various spatial and temporal scales. Accumulation by dispossession or accumulation by encroachment (as termed by Patnaik, 2005) has been prominent in various waves of expansion by capital. Marx's argument on 'primitive accumulation' perceived this process as a beginning point in the transition to capitalism, since the process created ownership of land and capital on one hand and a class of dispossessed labourers on the other. However, Harvey (2003) and Patnaik (2005) advance this argument that it often reoccurs throughout the various phases of capitalism and becomes prominent during phases of global expansion due to various tensions and contradictions; capitalists tend to explore a 'spatial fix' by shifting capital outside their home countries. It is the way of expansion of capital. Accumulation by dispossession is not just an original condition that sets capitalism in motion. Periodically, capital requires a fund of assets outside itself to confront periodic pressures of over-accumulation. Financial capital and the international credit system were the major levers 'opening' up the remaining common property regimes throughout the world to accumulation by dispossession. A number of scholars (ibid.) have noted that the privatization of public or common property assets has restored the rates of profit in both core and emerging economies. The recent wave of privatization, although globally uneven, includes

> ... the commodification of land and forceful expulsion of peasant populations; the conversion of various forms of property rights into exclusive private property rights, the suppression of rights to the commons, the commodification of labor power and the suppression of alternative forms of production and consumption, neo-colonial process of appropriation of assets; and monetization of exchange .... (Harvey, 2003: 43)

The commodification of land, minerals and forests has now affected populations that were earlier among the more isolated due to their geographical location. The commodification of 'common property resources', since they had no monetary price to begin with, are being released to capital at very low or no cost. And it is the people who live in these spaces who bear this incremental cost of 'development'.

Harvey (1996) has argued that imperialism in the age of neoliberalism has rediscovered 'the original sin of simple robbery'. Global capitalism continues to recreate, preserve and extend itself through an ongoing process of primitive accumulation. In Harvey's exposition, this process of 'accumulation by dispossession' is actively promoted through the neoliberal agenda. Harvey's accumulation by dispossession explicitly recognizes that dispossession is driven by an advanced form of capitalism.

Levien's (2017) thesis is built over Harvey's work and suggests that accumulation by dispossession advances the arguments under primitive accumulation. Levien argues empirically with the case of contemporary land grabs in India, particularly the large-scale land acquisitions for the SEZs. It is important to analyse these discourses from multiple viewpoints as the role of the Indian state has significantly changed from 'regulator' to 'facilitator' of the development process. He argues that contemporary land grabs are not primitive accumulation, rather it should be seen from the viewpoint of political economy of dispossession. While discussing the Indian case study, he further argues that the contemporary land grabs may be considered accumulation by dispossession but we must understand this as a political process of state redistribution and not as a functional response to over accumulation. The Singrauli case study presented in this book (Chapter 6) substantiates this argument as it has gone through different regimes of dispossession and it has witnessed both state-led industrial developments and private-led dispossessions, affecting lakhs of families.

However, in the process of land dispossession, it is critical to emphasize that it is deeply political and the state legitimizes the transfer of wealth (land) from one class to another. Although Harvey (2003: 154) recognizes that state force can be central to dispossession, his overarching argument includes several factors, including those like finance capital that has an indirect influence on the state force; he does not explicitly incorporate the state into his theory. Hence, Harvey's framework misses the critical feature of accumulation by dispossession as it applies to land – its fundamental dependence on the state force and distinctive politics of dispossession. As a process of transparent and coercive redistribution, land dispossession is a political process whose outcome is determined by class struggle and not just circulation of capital (Brenner, 1977, 2006; De Angelis, 2007; Levien, 2011, 2012).

In the context of land dispossession, it would be relevant to analyse why capitalists need the state to act on their behalf for land dispossession rather than purchasing through market. Dispossession requires a state that is willing to facilitate investment and use its monopoly of the means of violence to acquire land from one class of people to benefit others. The reasons behind capitalist preferences for the state to acquire land on their behalf are to overcome barriers such as fragmented landholdings, outdated land records, possession of unencumbered land and so on. In India, the colonial state acquired land for railways, industries, extractive industries and so on to serve the motive of the British government; post-Independence, the Nehruvian state acquired land for the public sector undertakings and infrastructure; and the neoliberal state dispossesses land for all forms of private accumulation, including real estate. Undoubtedly, the quantum of land dispossession is increasing with the institutions of neoliberal economic policies, but it is unclear if the over-accumulated capital in the Global North is the only reason; for instance, significant capital for India's SEZs has come from India itself (Levien, 2012). It is important to understand why states restructure themselves at different time periods to dispossess land for different purposes (often termed as 'public purpose') for a particular class.

Justice as Fairness

From the political economy viewpoint and in the context of the land acquisition debate, it is important to analyse the discourse through the lens of justice and how justice is experienced and perceived by different stakeholders and its consequences.

Rawls' View

Rawls argues that basic institutions of society must be regulated by two principles of justice: the liberty principle and the difference principle. He attempts to solve the problem of distributive justice by utilizing a variant of the familiar device of social contract. Distributive justice concerns what is just with respect to the allocation of goods in a society. Social contract is an implicit agreement within a state regarding the rights and responsibilities of the state and its citizens. The liberty principle holds that each individual must have a maximum individual liberty compatible with like liberty for all. The difference principle has two parts: the distribution of economic advantages and the distribution of social positions. The difference principle states that these must be arranged so as to be to the maximal advantage of the least disadvantaged. In particular, the need is to find fair principles that are able to act as the least common denominator which allows for a plurality of values and modes of life to coexist in peaceful and stable societies.

Rawlsian Theory of Justice Follows This Tradition

> The contract doctrine assumes that the rational individuals who belong to the society must choose together, in one joint act, what is to count among them as just and unjust.... A veil of ignorance prevents anyone from being advantaged or disadvantaged by the contingencies of social class and fortune; and hence

> the bargaining problems that arise in everyday life from the possession of this knowledge do not affect the choice of principles. (Rawls, 1993: 75)

Consensus is a reasonable requirement for a normative theory that describes the social legitimization of claims, and the Rawlsian veil of ignorance is a useful instrument that permits moral debate without reference to specific personal circumstances.

Sen's View

Sen's (2009) work on justice (*The Idea of Justice*) focusses on reason, objectivity and impartiality and raises many interesting questions in relation to the Rawlsian and other approaches. The key point for Sen is that there is an overriding need to 'focus on actual realizations and accomplishments' rather than only on the establishment of what are identified as the 'right institutions and rules'; this is a point he relates to the dichotomy between an 'arrangement-focused view of justice' and a 'realization-focused understanding of justice'. The former proposes that justice should be conceptualized in terms of organizational arrangements, that is, 'some institutions, some regulations, some behavioural rules the active presence of which would indicate that justice is being done' (7). This is a vital point; Sen is primarily concerned with the necessity not to restrict the analysis of justice to 'getting the basic institutions and general rules right' but with the need to examine what emerges in a society, including the kind of lives that people can lead, given both the institutions and rules, and also other influences, including behaviour, that would necessarily affect human lives.

Sen is on strong ground in arguing that 'transcendental theory' simply 'addresses a different question from those of comparative assessment ... [and] is of no direct relevance to the problem of choice that has to be faced' (17). This is because what is required is agreement, based on public reasoning, on rankings of realizable alternatives. He sets this in the context of a distinction drawn from Indian legal thought between *niti* and *nyaya*,[1] where the former refers to organizational propriety and behavioural correctness, while the latter 'stands for a comprehensive concept of realized justice'. For *nyaya*, institutions, rules and organization, although they are important, have to be assessed in a broader context 'which is inescapably linked with the world that actually emerges, not just the institutions or rules we happen to have' (20). A focus on *niti*, as Sen defines it, would be prone to building elaborate institutional frameworks that might do little to reduce actual suffering or

[1] *Niti* and *nyaya* are Sanskrit words meaning law and justice.

injustice. Against this, Sen puts forth the idea of *nyaya*, he defines as representing 'a comprehensive concept of realized justice'. When justice is conceived in terms of *nyaya*, Sen believes, it must be concerned with the actual lived experience of individual people. *Nyaya*, with its emphasis on the social conditions in which people actually live, is far preferable to the more narrow institutional focus of *niti*.

This focus on realized justice is essential to Sen's approach and to his rejection of any kind of prior requirement for objectivity and the principles of justice. Sen agrees with Habermas and Rawls in so far as they link objectivity in ethical and political convictions to the ability to survive challenges from informed scrutiny from diverse quarters; however, he differs sharply in strongly asserting, 'The principles that survive such scrutiny need not be a unique set' (45).

The theorization about the ideal arrangement of a just society, which Sen refers to as 'transcendental institutionalism', is neither necessary nor sufficient as an approach to actually promoting justice in the real world. In its place, Sen proposes a comparative approach to justice, in which political philosophers engage in public reasoning to identify the most just choice among a set of feasible alternatives – always aware that there may be more than one reasonable viewpoint on any given issue.

In the context of compensation debate, it was useful to use some of these principles in analysing the allocation of resources at different levels and the issue of fairness in the land acquisition and resource development process, particularly in the case of multiple displaced families at my case study site, Singrauli. In this empirically grounded research, it was relevant to analyse how 'just' compensation is experienced and perceived at the household level.

Public Sphere and 'Participative' Democracy

In the context of the land acquisition debate, it will be relevant to posit the theoretical arguments under 'public sphere' and understand how the process has evolved in India. This section tries to locate public sphere and its relevance and scenario in India. It briefly highlights the concept of public space, and thereby tries to understand public sphere in India by drawing parallels with what Habermas in Western Europe conceptualized as 'public arena'. It will be followed by an analysis of public hearings in case of land acquisition projects, where we shall see how public sphere has failed to generate 'social good', but rather furthers marginalization and exclusion. It highlights the concern that the public sphere in India does not take into account the plurality of cultures. In the second section, an effort is made to look at the role of civil society in the public sphere. Civil society is supposed to emerge as a representative platform for the people and is the third partner in the development process along with the state and the market. It becomes extremely crucial to analyse the role of civil society in the public sphere and also its manifestations.

The public sphere as conceptualized by Habermas is a bourgeois institution that had emerged in Europe as a 'discursive platform' to engage in critical discussion and deliberations with the idea of delivering the 'common good'. The concept was used as a counterweight to absolutist states and it aimed to mediate between 'society' and the state by holding the state accountable to 'society' through 'publicity'. In general, this means information about state functioning is made accessible so that state activities would be subject to critical scrutiny and the force of 'public opinion' (Fraser, 1990). This institution has been replicated in many countries, including India. But the institution as a whole has inherent assumptions – that of the social structures of a bourgeois society. The platform that is supposed to generate the 'common good' is transforming into the one which is almost bringing together socially unequal cultures whereby the language of the dominant overrules the subordinate. There is no sociopolitical safeguard to the pluralism of the masses, and hence the 'common good' is decided by the motivations of private interest in place of public interest. Therefore, it becomes crucially important to relook at the present structure of 'public sphere' in the Indian context to see how far the institution itself is democratic to deliver the 'common good' to the society (Singh, 2009).

It has been understood over a long period of history that institutions of change are the manifestations of human experiences. There have been several attempts to rationalize these experiences in order to understand the individual's existence in the existing political and social order. The public sphere as an institution had emerged in Western societies not only to understand the processes of governance or administration vis-à-vis 'maladministration' but also to conceptualize and concretize the idea of 'state of society' and its nature and functioning. It may be pointed out that historicity and social location of any category structure its experiences and perceptions of institutions. But the public sphere attempts to problematize the matter a little more and is supposed to concretize and crystallize the experiences into opinions and thus make an effort towards a 'desired' social change (ibid.).

Habermas' (1962) concept of the public sphere developed with the emergence of bourgeois society, conceiving the 'market' as a meeting place of 'equal' members of an informed bourgeoisie who engaged in critical, rational and enlightened discussions ultimately aimed at formulating the 'common good'. In his views, a public sphere was conceived as a space for the communicative generation of public opinion, in ways that were supposed to assure (at least some degree of) moral–political validity. Thus, it matters who participates and on what terms. In addition, a public sphere is supposed to be a vehicle for mobilizing public opinion as a political force. It should empower the citizenry vis-à-vis private powers and permit it to exercise influence over the state. Thus, a public sphere is supposed to correlate with a sovereign power to which its communications are ultimately addressed. Together, these two ideas – the validity of public opinion and citizen's empowerment vis-à-vis the state – are essential to the concept of public sphere in democratic theory. Without them, the concept loses its critical force and its political point (ibid.).

In the context of India, the emergence of the public sphere dates back to the period of British colonialism and the national movement that arose against it. But with the passage of time, it is important to take a look at this tool of participatory democracy (Ali, 2001). The idea of the 'common good' to be generated by the public sphere is now contested. In this regard, it becomes crucial to rethink the present-day public sphere in India.

The Public Sphere in India

The public sphere as a concept has received several criticisms, especially with respect to developing countries. Habermas (1962) contrasted various forms of an active, participatory, bourgeois public sphere in the heroic era of liberal democracy with the more privatized forms of spectator politics in a bureaucratic industrial society in which the media and the elite controlled the public sphere. The aforementioned introductory remarks on conceptualization of the 'public sphere' by Habermas and its relevance, more so in developing societies, have been the focus of an intense debate by leading scholars, such as Peter Dew. Habermas (1962) stated that the public sphere reached its zenith in the mid 1800s and subsequently degenerated to an arena of competing private interests. The logic of reason similarly became subjected to manipulation and negotiations that created inequality and degraded citizens to a mass of consumers.

The public sphere designates a theatre in modern societies in which political participation is enacted through the medium of talk. It is the space in which citizens deliberate about their common affairs, and hence an institutionalized arena of discursive interaction. The arena is conceptually distinct from the state; it is a site for production and circulation of discourses that can, in principle, be critical of the state. The concept of the public sphere permits us to keep in view the distinctions among state apparatus, economic markets and democratic associations (Fraser, 2003).

One of the assumptions of the public sphere is that it is possible for interlocutors in a public sphere to bracket status differentials and to deliberate as if they were social equals. The assumption ultimately signifies that social equality is not a necessary condition for political democracy. The net outcome is inequality within the public sphere as well. Egalitarianism as an element is absolutely absent from the public sphere in India. The systemic inequalities are such that only the elite preside over the public sphere. Public sphere in India can be best understood in terms of the public hearings that are held with respect to land acquisition projects and their impact on people, their lives and the environment. Public hearing is supposed to provide a 'discursive platform' to different stakeholders. The stakeholders constitute the company, the state and the people. The very assumption of social equality is violated as the participants of the public sphere are neither socially nor economically equal. So, whatever the members of public sphere deliberate and discuss, they do so under the curtain of a false notion of social equality.

In most of the backward regions of India, especially regions pertaining to backward states such as Madhya Pradesh, Jharkhand, Bihar and Odisha, the 'social preparedness' for a relevant discourse in their interests is extremely low. Therefore, in most of the instances of public hearings,[2] the affected community fails to understand the debates and deliberations that take place. Another common phenomenon of the public sphere that emerges out of participation of 'unequal members' is the lack of proper and adequate communication. Several times, it is observed that the communities are unable to express their voices because they lack coherent communicative skills. So, often their thoughts and opinions remain unexpressed, and hence not taken into account.

Another assumption of the discourse of public sphere is that it should be restricted to deliberations about the common good and that the appearance of private interests and private issues is undesirable. Habermas' public sphere was to be a discursive arena in which 'private persons' deliberated about 'public matters'. There are several different senses of 'private' and 'public' at play here. Public, for example, can mean (a) the state-related, (b) accessible to everyone, (c) of concern to everyone or (d) pertaining to the common good or the shared interest. These stand in sharp contrast to what we call 'private'. The notion of 'private' can mean pertaining to (a) private property in a market economy or (b) intimate domestic or personal life. In the context of the public sphere in India, it cannot be determined whether the outcome of a deliberative process in the public sphere is going to yield a 'common good'. I again cite the example of public hearings in case of large-scale

---

[2] Public hearing conducted by the Orissa Pollution State Control Board at Tikri on 17 October 2006 for Utkal Alumina International Limited (a joint venture of Hindalco and Alcan, a Canadian aluminium giant) faced strong resistance from the local civil society Prakrutik Sampada Suraksha Parishad for a proposed project in the Fifth Schedule Areas for the violation of constitutional protection to tribal land. Public hearing for the Polavaram project in Andhra Pradesh is another case which faced stiff resistance from the local civil society.

land acquisition projects in public and private sectors in India. A market economy is always guided by its motive of private interest or profit. In case of most of these projects, there are consultation requirements with the communities regarding the compensation package, selection of the resettlement and rehabilitation colony site or even alternative livelihood strategies for them. The idea of the 'common good' (which is one of the features of public interest) is contested. Moreover, the idea of participation is defeated. Thus, it can be stated that in the conflict of interests that happens in the deliberative process, the dominant interest emerges victorious. In a neoliberal market economy, the state is restricted to facilitation and regulation by giving market the lead in controlling the nexus of the public sphere. The systemic inequalities keep the oppressed voiceless, providing them a pseudo equal status.

India has a stratified society, that is, a society whose basic institutional framework generates unequal social groups in structural relations of dominance and subordination. Unequally empowered social groups tend to develop unequally valued cultural styles. The result is the development of powerful informal pressures that marginalize the contributions of subordinated groups, both in everyday contexts and in official public spheres. Moreover, these pressures are amplified by the political economy of the bourgeois public sphere. The Indian public sphere does not take into account the plurality of cultures. The deliberations are governed by the voice of the dominant culture. Neera Chandhoke (1994) cites the example of large-scale displacements of tribal communities for the construction of the Narmada dam and reservoir. The government used land ownership (demonstrated by official documents) to determine the amount of compensation owed to tribal households. However, because this concept of land ownership was unknown to tribal communities, the government simply gave no compensation at all. Chandhoke does not elaborate on bureaucratic indifference but instead concentrates on language, seeing the case 'as a story about the collision of two languages and the victory of one at the expense of the other'.

The Indian public sphere thus has no homogenous character of its own. It is not a unitary space, but rather a fragmented space. This can be explained by observing the outcomes of public hearings in case of land acquisition projects.

Civil Society and the Public Sphere

One of the assumptions underlying the bourgeois conception of the public sphere is that a functioning democratic public sphere requires a sharp distinction between the civil society and the state. But a participatory parity is important for the discursive element of the public sphere, and the socio-economic equality is a necessary condition for this parity. The presence of civil society as a distinct entity has become crucial for the modern-day public sphere in India.

Civil society can be defined as an associational activity, which involves individuals. Civil society can also be briefly defined as a certain type of social organization, mode of social behaviour or even political ideal (Kaviraj and Khilnani, 2008). For our discussion, we shall consider civil society as an institution whose entity is in relation to people, although it becomes very important to look at the economic system and sociocultural structures before commenting on the role of civil society functioning in a certain society. Civil society, however, plays a pivotal role as far as grass-root governance is concerned. Its presence and role in many ways govern class relations and power relations. While tracing its evolution, it can be well considered that even during the collapse or withdrawal of other institutions, civil society emerges as a social safeguard. However, in no way shall we try to qualify its role. In many contexts, civil society may have the same structural inequalities and continue to represent a certain power, thus making representation lopsided. A very good example of civil society's 'skewed' representation can be understood by looking at the 'support groups' at water users' associations that exist in some of the Indian states.

But, in the context of the public sphere and participation in it, the role of civil society has transformed or, to put it correctly, has reduced. We shall again consider the case of public hearings in India. The role of civil society as a social and political safeguard for people in public hearings has reduced. This has happened in many ways. In some cases, again in the backward regions, there is a complete absence of civil society during public hearings. The presence of civil society brings about the factors of social accountability, transparency and public disclosures. In such a case, the role of other institutions makes people all the more vulnerable. Civil society can act as a spokesperson for communities when they are unable to express their opinions, grievances and points. Civil society in a way becomes the conjunction in such a scenario. It acts as the connection between the people and other institutions.

Civil society as an institution thus requires being present and offering a position for the community to collectivize and thus participate. The absence of civil society 'retards' the local community from forming a concrete public opinion and thus alienates them. Civil society helps communities to remain informed and also to understand social realities. Communities by themselves are not always competent at these. Thus, most of the time, discussions taking place in the public sphere are rendered useless for the communities. The 'common good' might as well not benefit the people at the end of the day. However, 'non-participation' of the civil society is not a frequently evident phenomenon. While non-participation can be a case, another case could also be that of a participative civil society. But to what extent participation makes a difference is also to be considered.

Institutions of governance have an inherent crisis. The crisis is one of political will. The same reflects in the case of a civil society. The crisis also surfaces when participation is in question. The clear lack of a constructive critic and the mere tendency towards assertion truncates civil society's role in the public sphere. The modern-day civil society which participates in public hearing creates an atmosphere of chaos followed by negotiation. But, most of the time, civil society overlooks fundamental issues of systemic inequalities and oppressive mechanisms. It overlooks the fact that plurality of cultures do not get recognition. In brief, civil societies function towards superficial assertion of their ideas, which are, most of the time, not representative of or relevant to the affected people. Thus, the presence of civil society in a public hearing does not serve the purpose that it aims to achieve. Whether we call it a structural constraint or a functional constraint, civil society does an incomplete job of participation. The current situation is that, even if the civil society is present, its role is such that it subordinates within the 'socially equal member' of the public sphere which are marginalized automatically. The whole idea of public interest is thus never achieved. The manifestation of civil society and its will thus to a great extent determine the association of people in the public sphere.

3

Land, Mines and Minerals

Land Grab

Over the past few years, large-scale acquisitions of agricultural land in Africa, Asia and Latin America have made headlines in media reports, and there is a growing body of literature on 'land grab' across the world. However, dispossession in India and China in the last decade has been primarily for industrial, infrastructure and urbanization purposes, while in Africa and Latin America it is largely for agricultural plantations. The contemporary, global land grab has recently become a key development issue, and there is growing concern that people's connection to their land is being undermined. The term 'land grab' generally refers to large-scale cross-border land transactions that are carried out by transnational corporations or initiated by foreign governments. They concern the lease (often for 30–99 years), concession or outright purchase of large areas of land in other countries for various purposes (GRAIN, 2008). However, there is another view which suggests that this is a new phase of capitalist expansion led by 'private capital' which is also driving local governments to dispossess and displace peasants from their agricultural land to facilitate the entry of private capital. For instance, special economic zones (SEZs) in India have become centres of protest across India with farmers resisting the state's forcible transfer of their land to the private sector.

The global land grab is to a large extent the result of the liberalization of land markets, which became a major policy goal in the course of the 1990s and has contributed to the commoditization of land and other natural resources (Brenner and Theodore, 2007). Along with the spread of the neoliberal model, and with the support of donors, many governments in Asia, Latin America and Africa started to give more priority to creating dynamic, free and transparent land markets (Deininger, 2003). In a globalizing world, local development is increasingly played out in a matrix of links that enable connections to be made between people and places on a world scale. The intensification of worldwide social relations links such distant localities where local happenings are shaped by events that occur many miles away and vice versa (Giddens, 1990: 64; see also Harvey, 1989).

Global Land Conflicts

Environmental Justice Atlas (EJAtlas), an FP7 European Commission–funded project, has, since 2011, documented land and ecological conflicts across the world. According to EJAtlas (2020), there have been 3,108 reported cases of land conflicts across the world (see Map 3.1). These land conflicts vary across different categories of industrial, conservation or developmental projects. In this survey, India was ranked number one in having the maximum number of land conflicts with 328 cases (see Map 3.2) followed by Colombia, Brazil and China. The EJAtlas survey maps the category of projects and nature of conflicts in a particular region. The overall global data also provide a sense of communities' growing concerns over the use of land and natural resources and with the way their lives and livelihoods are being affected. India recorded 328 land conflicts spread across various states and categories of projects. These projects range from mining, dams, and thermal power plants, to industrial corridors, highways, nuclear power and so on. The data clearly reflects the scale of social unrest around land acquisition projects and the level of awareness among people to assert their rights and represent their concerns. Undoubtedly, the vibrant, functional democracy and the presence of active civil societies in India have contributed to reporting these cases and to highlighting these issues to the media, legislatures and the judiciary.

Around the world, there have been strong reactions from states, corporations and civil society groups. Some see land grabs as a major threat to the lives and livelihood of the rural poor and so oppose such commercial land deals. Others see economic opportunity for the rural poor, although they are wary of corruption and negative consequences, and so call for improving land market governance. Of course, between these two positions, there is a range of intermediate views offered by other groups (Borras, 2010).

In India, this process has been driven, in particular, through privatization of resources held in common and state redistribution in favour of capital. Liberalization, for instance, has entailed the active promotion of mining interests in regions of Madhya Pradesh, Chhattisgarh, Jharkhand and Odisha, both through privatization and by opening these regions to foreign capital. Land is taken over, natural resources, including forests and rivers, denuded and exploited by private capital while the local people living in these regions lose their lands and livelihood. Millions of poor families (Fernandes, 2008) are driven out of their land by this relentless logic of accumulation by dispossession. It is time the state stopped justifing land dispossession under the ideology of 'public purpose' or 'national interest', which is often used in the name of 'development'. The social reality demonstrates that these ideological justifications and material compensations prove inadequate considering the large-scale resistance, and the ability of the state to dispossess land is decided by the balance of political forces.

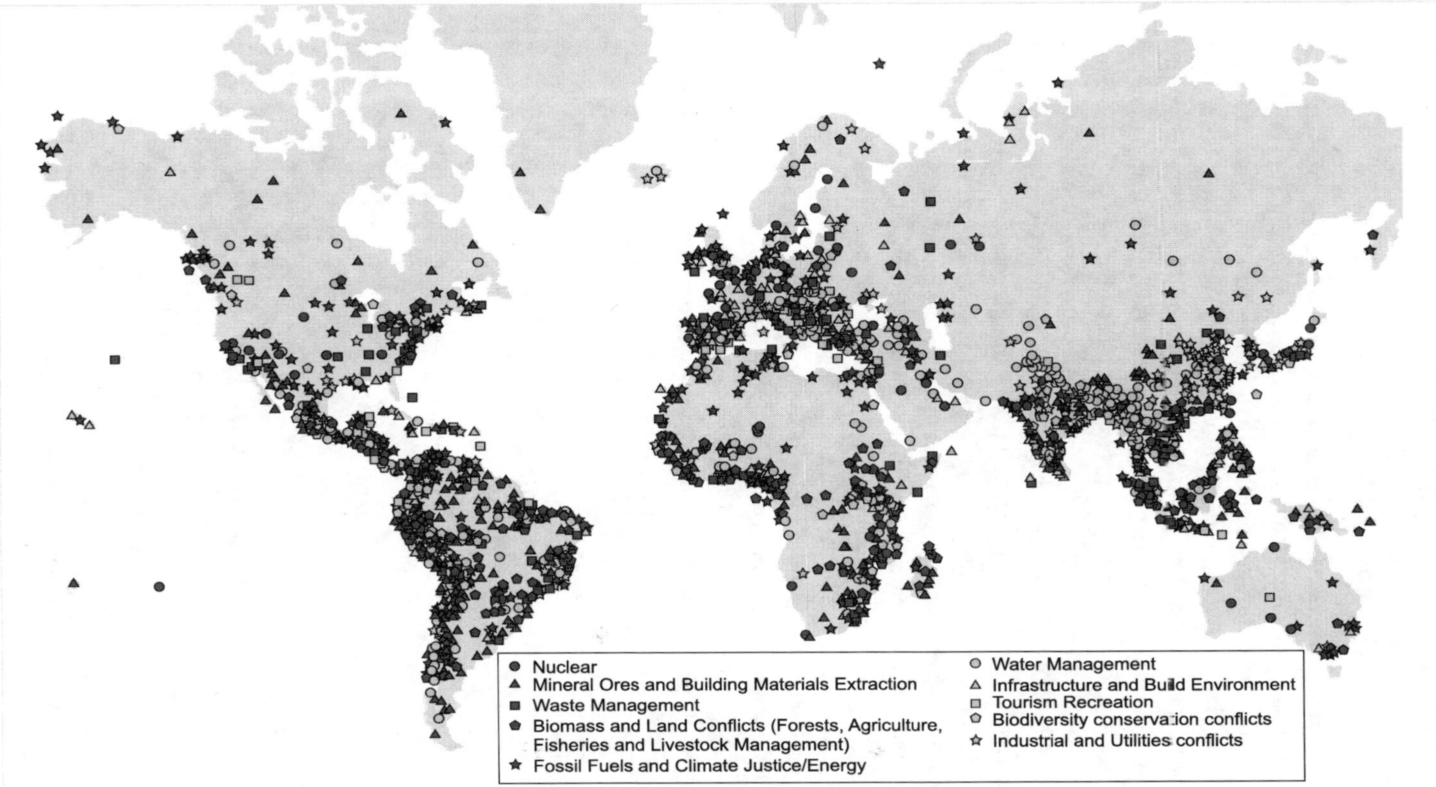

Map 3.1 Land conflicts across the world

Source: Adapted by author from EJAtlas (2020).

Scale of Stalled Investments in India

During the United Progressive Alliance (UPA) regime (2004–2014), the two terms of the government witnessed interesting mobilization of private capital and signing of memoranda of understanding (MoUs) vis-à-vis actual realization of investments on the ground. The first phase of the UPA (2004–2009) saw the creation of an 'investment climate' in the country and the nation did witness extensive signing of trade agreements and global investments in large-scale infrastructure projects, some of the prominent ones being POSCO – signed under the Indo–Korea trade agreement – among others. However, the second phase of the UPA (2009–2014) experienced a sharp failure in actual realization of promised investments and a steep decline in the announcements of new projects (see Figure 3.1), the major reason being large-scale protests across the country around land acquisition issues. This was the decade that witnessed massive protests against projects, for instance, Singur, Nandigram, POSCO and Vedanta SEZs (see Figure 3.2) among others, that grabbed the attention of national media, the judiciary and public at large. Undoubtedly, civil society organizations played a significant role in highlighting the social concerns and organizing social movements. One significant change that has been observed during recent times is that civil society movements are now much more organized, focussed and impactful. The large-scale protests and civil society movements also compelled

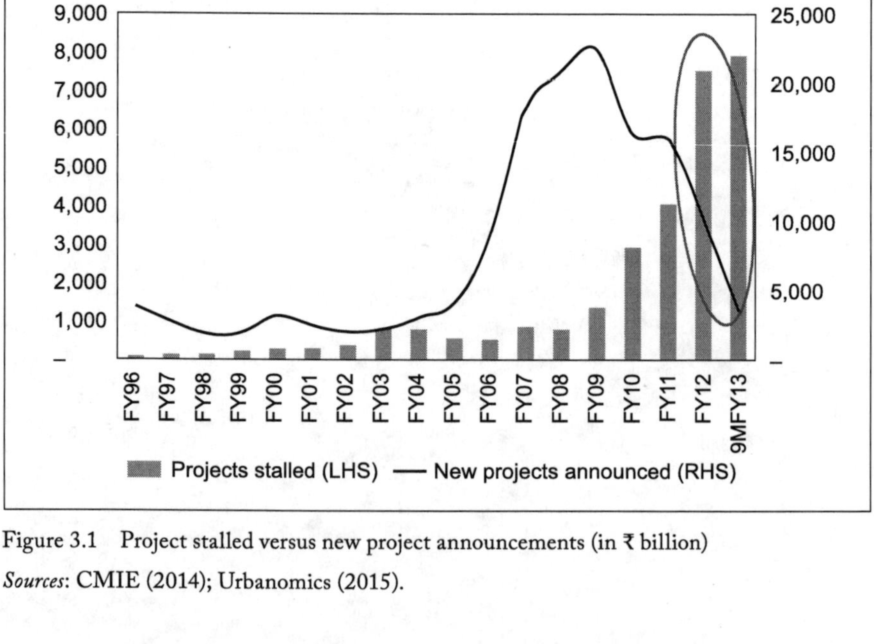

Figure 3.1 Project stalled versus new project announcements (in ₹ billion)

Sources: CMIE (2014); Urbanomics (2015).

Prominent 'Development Projects' that led to land conflicts between 2005 and 2015

- Nandigram: chemical hub, West Bengal (land issue)
- Singur: Tata Motors project, West Bengal (land issue)
- Posco: steel plant, mining, Orissa (land, forest rights issue)
- Vedanta: bauxite mining project, Orissa (land, FRA issue)
- JSPL (steel + thermal): Angul, Orissa (land issues)
- Arcelor Mittal: Jharkhand (land issue)
- JSPL: Tamnar block, Chattisgarh (land and mining issue)
- Reliance SEZ: Navi Mumbai, Raigarh (land issue)
- Reliance Tilaiya UMPP and coal mining (land issue)
- NHPC: hydro, Lohari Nagpala, Uttarakhand (ecological issue)
- Reliance, Adani, Jaypee: Arunachal Pradesh (land, R&R, ecological issues)

Figure 3.2 Controversial developmental projects, 2005–2015

Sources: RRI (2016); EJAtlas (2020); Land Conflict Watch (2019); CMIE (2014).

Note: R&R and FRA stand for resettlement and rehabilitation and Forest Rights Act of 2006 respectively.

the government to amend the colonial law of 1894 (Land Acquisition Act) and address the historical injustice embedded in the Act.

The Rights and Resources Initiative (RRI), a Washington-based advocacy group, conducted a comprehensive study in 2016 to acquire clarity on the number of stalled projects across India and the industrial investments at risk. The RRI (2016) report analysed the 289 ongoing land conflicts across various states, involving acquisition of 1.2 million hectares of land that displaced 3.2 million people across the country. Infrastructure projects account for almost half of the land-related conflicts, and these projects range widely such as thermal power plants, mining, highways, industrial corridors, dams and so on. Another significant finding from the study was that three-quarters of these land-related conflicts involved common lands – either forest or non-forest. This indicates consciousness among non-titled holders to assert their land claims and entitlements that are often ignored during the land acquisition process.

Among 289 projects, 40 per cent of the land-related conflicts involved forestlands as the customary rights of the indigenous communities were not recognized in these regions. This provides an understanding that even 10 years after the enactment of the Scheduled Tribes and Other Traditional Forest Dwellers (Recognition of Forest Rights) Act of 2006, the transfer of land titles (*patta*) to forest dwellers is still an unfulfilled agenda. In 60 per cent of the reported land conflict cases, land acquisition by the government has been seen as the major reason behind land conflicts. And lastly, districts affected by left-wing extremism and Fifth Schedule Areas (that are also rich in minerals) have 1.5 times greater number of land conflicts compared to the national average, and together they

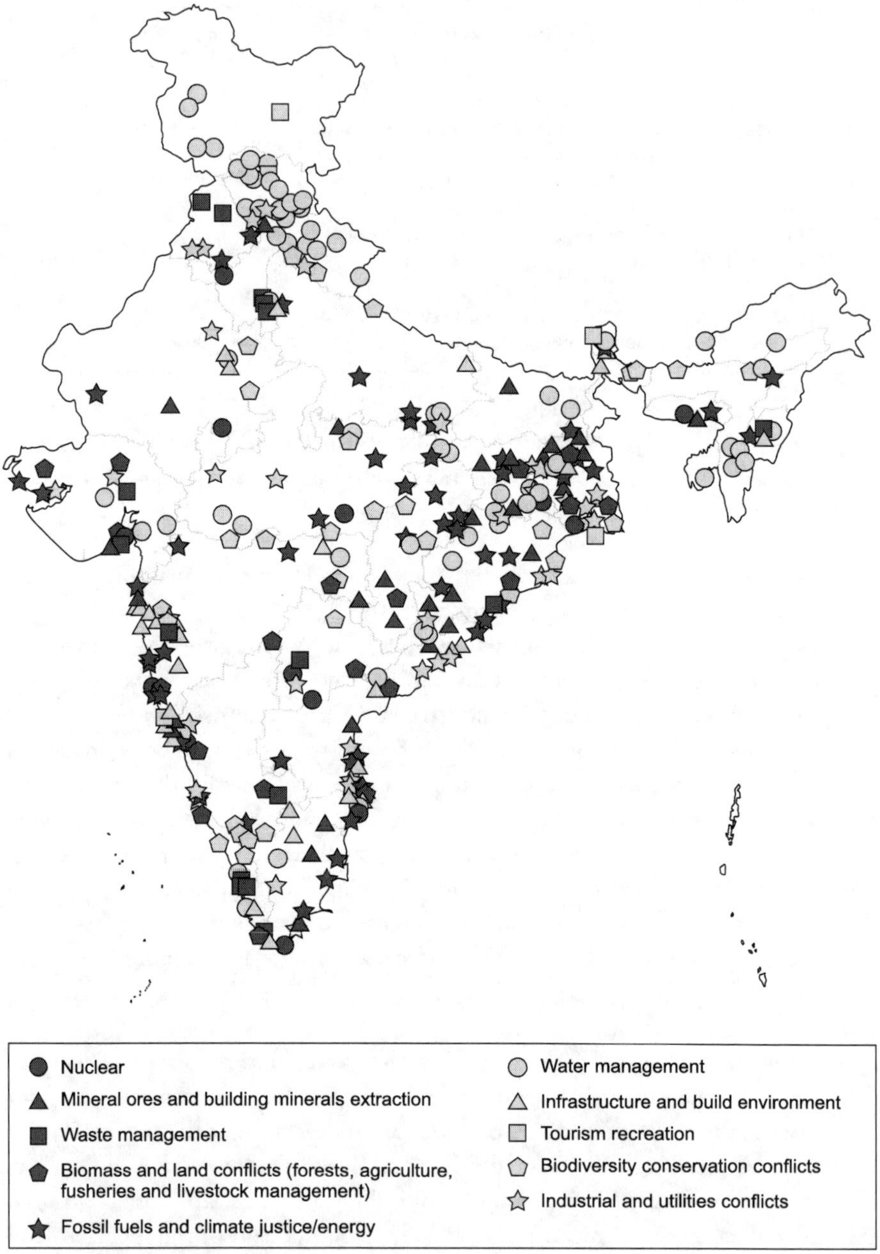

Map 3.2 Land conflicts in India

Source: Adapted by author from EJAtlas (2020).

Note: Map not to scale and may not represent authentic international borders.

account for one-third of the total number of people affected by conflicts. These conflicts are geographically spread across the country, even in the newly formed Telangana. The three major reasons recorded around land disputes have been dissatisfaction with the compensation amount, environmental impact of the projects and expropriation of public lands (the common land). The study reflects that there are several challenges at the institutional and administrative levels, and considering the awareness among people, it will be difficult to realize these investments on the ground until their concerns are settled.

Resource Curse

By the late 1980s, there had been substantial discussion about the existence of the 'resource curse' that 'natural resource abundance increases the likelihood that countries will experience negative economic, political and social outcomes' (Rosser, 2006: 7). Scholars such as Sachs and Warner (1995), Atkinson and Hamilton (2003), Neumayer (2004) and Auty (2001) argue that there is negative relationship between natural resource abundance and economic growth. The analysis reflects that governments of these countries fail to manage large resource revenues in a sustainable manner, which results in uneven development patterns.

There is a body of extensive literature on the 'resource curse' which suggests that regions or economies rich in natural resources are poor in developmental outcomes. Wheeler (1984) found that within sub-Saharan Africa, countries that were rich in minerals grew more slowly than those that were not rich in minerals during the 1970s. Sachs and Warner (1995) examined the experiences of a large and diverse set of natural resource economies between 1970 and 1989 and found that natural resource abundance was negatively correlated with economic growth. Other scholars have presented evidence to suggest that the economic problems of resource abundant countries have gone beyond poor levels of economic growth. Leite and Weidmann (1999) found that natural resource abundance tends to worsen corruption. Finally, Ross (2003a) found that oil wealth and non-fuel mineral wealth are associated with bad outcomes for the poor in terms of poverty and human development levels.

Resource development has associated social, resource, cultural and environmental costs. Mineral development, for example, has the potential to be both beneficial and detrimental to poverty reduction. At a macro level, research suggests that a state's dependence on the export of non-fuel minerals tends to hurt the welfare of the poor (ibid.). At a micro level, while new income and mine-supported social services can help reduce poverty, land alienation and deterioration, loss of access to common property and services, loss of traditional livelihoods, crowding out of agriculture, increased morbidity and mortality from environmental health impacts, human rights infringements and displacement are potential sources of distress and poverty (McMahon, 1998b; Cernea, 2000a and 2000b; IIED and WBCSD, 2002; Warhurst and Hughes, 1998).

At the pre-mining stage, there could be displacement of people, clearing of forests, removal of vegetation and several other impacts due to land acquisition. Apart from the mining activity itself, these impacts are caused by the large-scale in-migration of construction workers and the transport of heavy mining equipment for construction, trial shipment of mine products and bulk samples. The existing infrastructure including roads is often not upgraded to cope with the heavy load. Vehicular emissions and dust contribute to air pollution even before active mining begins. The environmental impacts of mining during the operational phase are likely to be greater than those in the pre-mining phase. These range from the impact on land, groundwater quality and levels, air and water pollution, and solid waste generation. Cropland productivity loss is the outcome associated with the degradation of soil, either due to silting or due to desiccation. This leads to creeping expropriation and a marginalization of farming communities.

The post-mining phase has long-term implications for the ecology of the region. Negligence in planning of long-term water management, safety and stability of mining voids, and final rehabilitation can render the mining area uninhabitable. Abandoned and closed mines are often associated with ongoing groundwater and surface water contamination, which may continue for a long period. The magnitude and significance of impact on the environment due to mining varies from mineral to mineral, the type of mining (for example, underground versus opencast) and also on the potential of the surrounding environment to absorb the negative effects of mining, the geographical disposition of mineral deposits and the size of mining operations.

Capital Resource Relationships

If redrawing of geographical boundaries according to the value of resources is an inherent tendency of capital, then the Singrauli region, from the perspective of political economy, is an appropriate 'space' for analysis. This study is an attempt to analyse the consequences of reorganization of space, resources and dispossession under a capitalist system, in the context of Singrauli. The objective is to put the theoretical discussion into a historical perspective to argue that capitalist development does not occur in a homogeneous and even form, but rather unevenness is the very essence of capitalist development. At the most basic level, the objective of this research is to unravel the theoretical logic driving the creation of the contemporary economic space of Singrauli.

Capitalism perpetually strives to create a social and physical landscape requisite to its own needs at a particular point of time, only just as certainly to undermine, disrupt and even destroy that landscape at a later point in time. The inner 'contradictions of capitalism are expressed through the restless formations and re-formations of geographical landscapes. This is the tune to which the historical geography of capitalism must dance without cease' (Harvey, 1985: 145).

Before positing this 'space' to analysis, it is important to first understand the theoretical premises which are helpful to understanding the subject under study. While the desire to develop is universal, what constitutes 'development' has always been contested. Due to the variety of arguments and plurality of ideas, no amount of definitional reductionism has been able to encapsulate the idea of 'development' in consensual terms, and it remains a debated concept. Development theories differ according to the political position of their adherents, their philosophical origins and their place and time of construction. They also differ according to scientific orientation, ideas which are predominantly economic, sociological, anthropological, historical or geographical (Peet, 1999).

Development has been variously defined as a general increase in total production leading to economic growth, modernization of societies through ideal principles of industrial organization or 'take-off' from agrarian economy to industrial economy through huge financial investment and so on. Such notions have also been challenged in the post–World War II era by many scholars who saw it as an attempt by erstwhile colonial countries to impose their own values on the least developed countries. Dependency theorists, in particular, have pointed out that the world is not a monolithic structure and the development of one region of the world is a direct consequence of the colonial exploitation of many other countries (Frank, 1996). The world as we see it today, they argue, is a consequence of the rise and fall of regions played out through ceaseless accumulation of capital, underlined by long cycles of expansion and contraction over thousands of years of human history.

While the exclusive disciplines of economics, political science, history, geography, sociology, anthropology and environment sciences have attempted to establish a proper conceptual foundation for explaining the nuances of development, the very exclusiveness of these disciplines has hindered them from examining it. Then came the recognition among many theorists and social scientists that since problems of development and underdevelopment constitute a complex matrix of social, economic and political factors, an interdisciplinary perspective of investigation and interpretation was needed which would be both theoretically grounded in political economy and robust enough to handle the evident spatial articulation of 'development'. As the issues involved are more interactional, cutting across strictly economic and political variables, we need to turn to a more dynamic tradition of thinking, that is, the political economy of development.

The Emergence of Contemporary Economic Spaces

As discussed earlier, capitalism does not inherit the world as 'homogenous space'. According to Lefebvre, capitalism survived in the twentieth century 'by occupying space, by producing space' (Harvey, 2001: 376). He further argued that the space ideally produced by capital was abstract – a dull homogenized space – that facilitated the circulation of capital and which was progressively emptied of social meanings that might challenge its hegemony. Its organizing practices are calculative, bureaucratic and violent. Its production is made possible by dispossession (Lefebvre, 1991). It is inserted, grows and spreads within a variegated geographical environment that encompasses great diversity (Smith, 1984). The natural uneven distribution of resources on earth is a barrier to the circulation of capital as long as this unevenness is not organized to facilitate surplus accumulation and free circulation of capital (Smith, 1984). The internal coherence of capitalism is defined by circulation of profit achieved through compression of time and space (Harvey, 1985). To function efficiently, capital needs strong institutional backing of stable physical and social infrastructure like legal institutions and political systems.

Redrawing of geographical boundaries according to the value of resources has been found to be an inherent tendency of capital. In a 'globalizing' India, at the turn of the twenty-first century, a redrawing of the boundaries of the state of Bihar created an exclusively mineral-rich administrative region called the state of Jharkhand. Emergence of Jharkhand was simultaneous with the formation of two other states of Chhattisgarh and Uttaranchal. Creation of these new states, at a time when a neoliberal fervour had swept the economic sense of the country, was not an independent development but a result of historically specific but contingent processes, 'the symptoms of a much deeper transformations in the geography of capitalism' (Smith, 1984). These newly created 'spaces' went through a process of spatial, political and economic restructuring in facilitating a smooth entry of industrial capital and tapping vast mineral resources of these regions.

The creation of these new states was proposed on the basis of administrative efficiency rather than on linguistic principle that has primarily guided state formation in the past. As Mawdsley (2002) argues, this was the beginning of a new era in the political economy of India associated with economic liberalization and regionalization of politics. This also indicated a shift in India's federal ideology, as regional identity and cultural and geographical differences were recognized as valid basis for administrative division and political representation. However, Brass (2012) argued that in a plural and diverse society like India, centralization of power, decision-making and control of resources further aggravates regional and societal tensions. Some of the outcomes have been erosion of the effectiveness of some political organizations, failure of the central government to implement development plans in different states and heightening caste, and regional and cultural conflicts. Mawdsley (2002) further argued that in a new era of liberalization, these pressures have only increased and the states are now permitted to engage directly with external donors and corporate interests and there is growing evidence of the regionally uneven impact that such policies are having within the states as well as between them (Corbridge and Harris, 2000; Nagaraj, 2000; Bajpai and Sachs, 1999; Ahluwalia, 2000). The states' numerous avenues in negotiating their economic futures and liberalization have opened up new political avenues of wealth creation, particularly for certain regions and sectional interests (Jenkins, 1999).

Another recent and significant work on state formation is by Tillin (2013); it is a well-documented study on the formation of Jharkhand, Uttarakhand and Chhattisgarh in 2000. She highlights the popular explanation of the new state formations in terms of popular social movements, electoral calculations, capitalist exploitation of natural resources and professed gain in governance at a smaller scale. However, she also argues, in case of these three states, there was no active mass movement at the time of bifurcation from the larger states of Bihar, Uttar Pradesh and Madhya Pradesh. Tillin does emphasize the factor of capitalist expansion in the case of Jharkhand and Chhattisgarh which are heavily endowed with mineral resources. Redrawing of boundaries of India's richest mineral reserves from larger states with greater civil society mobilization potential against narrow capitalist exploitation in the era of liberalization cannot easily be ignored.

The role of the state is significant at this conjuncture, especially in institutionalizing capital investment. This is because collective means can effectively achieve what individual capitalists cannot. The intricate mediation of diverse economic agents is brought within a common framework of the state. The state also takes on the role of overall manager of the production of social infrastructure, performing fundamental coordinating functions, and employs a whole lot of manpower for preservation and enhancement of such infrastructure (Smith, 1984). The state, thus, acts on behalf of the capitalists. The relation between the state and the bourgeoisie is an objective one. The functions of the state and the interests of the bourgeoisie coincide.

Land Acquisition, Dispossession and Rehabilitation

Land acquisition and displacement of populations can have systemic consequences on the socio-economic structure of the affected community. Resettlement and rehabilitation of affected families is an intricate and elaborate process, which requires tenacious efforts over a period of time to ensure a wholesome post-resettlement life for them. More often than not, R&R interventions are subject to criticism by both observers and beneficiaries, raising inordinate questions on the goodwill of the project implementer. To ensure an acceptable R&R package and to quell criticism, it is essential that the interventions of the project implementer among the displaced community are periodically monitored and reviewed so as to enhance the socio-economic impact on the project-affected families (PAFs). Even though impact analysis of involuntary resettlements have majorly been analysed through a socio-anthropological lens, a socio-economic assessment of resettlement may contribute to a better understanding of the actual impact of displacement on the community as well as the project implementer.

During the post-displacement period, the lives of the PAFs are heavily dependent on the rehabilitation package (compensation) offered to them. While the package is prepared and implemented by the project developers, its impact on the target group (displaced community) is profoundly influenced by the expectations of the stakeholders of the rehabilitation process from the rehabilitation package. The stakeholders would include the government (through its land acquisition policy), the project developer and the displaced community. An ideal rehabilitation package lies at the intersection of the expectations of the project proposer, the affected community and other stakeholders in the rehabilitation process (Cernea, 2000a). A perceptible inability of the rehabilitation package to meet these expectations exposes the community to sociological and economic risks in the post-resettlement life. The concept of risk in post-resettlement lives is posited as a counter-concept to security. Higher the risk, lower the socio-economic security of the displacement populations (Basu, 1996). The social and cultural constructions of risk are often directly perceptible and also measurable (Adams, 1998). The understanding of risks in the lives of the PAFs can be achieved by deconstructing the multifaceted process of resettlement into its identifiable and most widespread threats to socio-economic security. A detailed socio-economic impact of land acquisition and displacement on the PAFs has been studied in Chapter 6.

Rationales and Conceptualization

Following the Scudder–Colson model of relocation (Scudder, 1982), the affected families would face varying amounts of stress at every stage of relocation, that is, recruitment, transition, potential development and handing over/incorporation. In Singrauli, where the PAFs in the third phase of displacement are currently at the stage of 'incorporation', the risks faced by them would be cumulative of all the four stages. Each stage requires social and behavioural changes in the PAFs, coupled with stresses from the economic status of the families. While an attractive resettlement package may account sufficiently for the economic stress, the social and behavioural stress may be overlooked more often than not. To gather empirical evidence, a socio-economic survey of the PAFs was executed at this stage to obtain a holistic picture of their present status by ascribing values to each of these risks which pose a threat to the socio-economic security of the families.

Cernea's (1998) Impoverishment Risks and Reconstruction (IRR) model arose in the 1990s in response to this recognition. In particular, it stresses that unless specifically addressed by targeted policies, forced displacement can cause impoverishment among oustees by bringing about landlessness, joblessness, homelessness, marginalization, food insecurity, loss of access to common property resources, increased morbidity and mortality, and community disarticulation. To these risks, Downing (1999) and others have added loss of access to public services, disruption of formal education activities, and loss of civil and human rights. The model also recognizes risks to the host population, which, while not identical to those of oustees, can also result in impoverishment. Not all of these processes necessarily occur in each case of forced resettlement and not all displaced households are necessarily affected in the same way by each process. Rather, the model notes that when taken together, these processes capture the reasons behind many failed resettlement operations. Aside from distinguishing risks, the IRR model serves several other functions: a predictor of impoverishment; a guide for formulating research hypotheses and conducting theory-led field investigations research; and a compass for risk reversal, advocating targeted resettlement policies such as land-based (as opposed to merely cash-based) resettlement, job creation, health and nutritional safeguards, and social network rebuilding (Figure 3.3).

This conceptual framework provides a snapshot of the dialectic between potential risk and actuality. Understanding the linkages between these social risks and its impact on the PAFs helps in devising risk mitigation strategies by the project implementers. Hence, this framework can be effectively used as an operational guide for effective action to reduce or nullify these risks using carefully planned strategies according to the severity of the measured risks. That is to say that the components of this framework may be manipulated or influenced by careful planning to diminish the impact of the risks mentioned. As a conceptual template, the framework may also be utilized as a backbone of financial planning to mitigate risks faced by the affected communities.

The IRR model has been used as a framework for a number of studies. Mahapatra (1999) uses the model to examine India's experience with involuntary resettlement during 1947–1997, examining each of the IRR risks in turn. Thangaraj's chapter in the same book employs the model to analyse resettlement operations in two Indian projects – the Upper Indravati Hydroelectric Project and the Orissa Water Resources Consolidation Project. Lassailly-Jacob (2001) has looked specifically at land-based resettlement strategies in African dam projects arguing that such strategies must

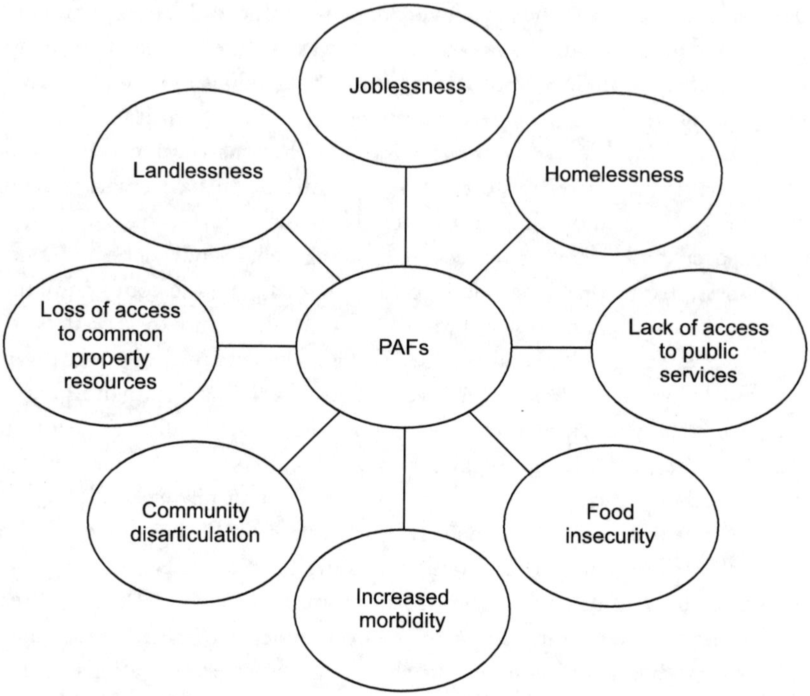

Figure 3.3 Impoverishment risks and reconstruction framework – each spoke represents a risk, with the affected family in the centre – drawn from IRR model

Source: Prepared by author.

include not only land on which to resettle but also the common lands, adequate productive farmland, full title for lands (rather than tenant arrangements) and resettler-directed (rather than top-down imposed) development programmes.

In order to gather empirical data from the selected site, the discussed models and framework were used while designing the survey questionnaire to gather requisite information from the field. The data collected were analysed in order to understand the risks and impoverishments faced by the PAFs. The research did not limit its investigation to any specific model or framework for designing the survey, rather inputs were drawn from the existing literature and were strategically blended with author's own experiences in the subject.

4

Land Acquisition and Resource Development in India

Political Economy of Land Acquisition in India

In the last one decade (2005–2015), land acquisition and dispossession have become central questions in India's political economy. However, according to the last available estimate of 50 million displaced (Cernea, 2000a, 2000b; Roy, 2007; Fernandes, 2008) in the last five decades (until 2000), the scale of land acquisition and displacement has accelerated since liberalization. Entrance of private and foreign capital in several sectors, such as infrastructure development, urbanization, industrialization, real estate, mining and so on, has eclipsed public sector projects and led to aggressive penetration of capital and forceful acquisition of land from farming and tribal communities. While many social movements in the 1980s, notably the Narmada Bachao Andolan, constantly provided a platform for the voices of affected communities against dams and public sector projects, they had little success in stopping or halting such projects. However, they did contribute towards policy advocacy, awareness and concerns around displacement, importance of resettlement and rehabilitation policies, safeguard mechanisms and so on, and the mass movement influenced the central and state governments and public sector undertsakings (PSUs) to conceptualize resettlement and rehabilitation (R&R) policies.

What has changed in the last decade is the magnitude of social protests led by the civil society and its opposition around land acquisition projects and their strength in successfully stalling such projects. According to one estimate, 804 projects[1] (CHRI, 2015) across India are held up due to land acquisition, environmental clearance, financial irregularities and other issues. Out of the total stalled projects, 78 per cent are private sector projects and 22 per cent are

[1] Data provided by Ministry of Finance in reply to Right to Information (RTI) application by Commonwealth Human Rights Initiative (CHRI).

public sector projects (such as central/state governments, PSUs and so on). As per government estimate in 2011, capital investments worth 3 per cent of India's gross domestic product (GDP) were stalled due to land acquisition issues (CMIE, 2012) and the government considers this as a significant cause of India's economic slowdown and a key concern for the state and capital. The Indian state at this point is caught between the land requirements for industrial investments and assertive civil society protests across India.

Land Acquisition Pre-Independence

The land acquisition law has its genesis in the Bengal Regulation Act (I) of 1824, which was formulated by the British to promote their commercial interests in India. With subsequent amendments of 1850 and 1857, the Land Acquisition (LA) Act of March 1894 replaced all previous laws relating to land acquisition and became applicable to the rest of India (Ray and Patra, 2009).

The rationale behind this legislation was unencumbered acquisition of land for public works. The state had to be able to acquire land with ease while minimizing compensation payment, as it was perceived as a drain on the state exchequer. At that point of time, there was a need for large amount of land for expanding the railway network in the country. The colonial law's view was evident in one simple fact: 'public purpose' was neither defined nor elaborated by the law; it was sufficient for the state to declare it to be so (Chakravorty, 2013). In the LA Act of 1894, rules were framed to keep compensation payments to a minimum, and nowhere in the legislation appropriate methodology was indicated to arrive at a fair compensation for determining land value. This Act made the collector's award of compensation final, unless alerted by a decree of a civil court in a regular suit, and it helped speed up the process of determining compensation (Kasturi, 2007). Even after the end of colonial rule, the republican constitution of 1950 did not bring any significant change in the LA Act.

Development Post-Independence

India post-Independence (in the 1950s) was primarily an agricultural economy and the government at that time was grappling with the landlessness and acute poverty that marked its countryside. Abolition of the *zamindari* system and the land reform measures that followed led to the redistribution of surplus land from *zamindar*s to the landless, in various degrees, at the behest of the respective state governments. In this sociopolitical milieu, it was not difficult for the Nehru government to get away with token compensation to a handful of rich *zamindar*s for the land acquired for development purposes (Ray and Patra, 2009).

This was, however, not easily done when land was sought from the small farmers. The national government had, at that time, adopted a policy of heavy industrialization largely under the domain of the public sector, with private companies and multinationals functioning under strong governmental control through intimidating licensing systems. There was an enormous increase in infrastructure development and industrial activities by the state as compared to the colonial period (Chakravorty, 2013). Numerous large dams, power plants, mines, and steel and heavy engineering plants came up on land acquired using the 1894 law, thus causing massive displacement of small farmers, agricultural labourers, landless village workers, artisans and forest dwellers. The issue became complicated when decisions had to be taken on paying the price for the land acquired. The question boiled down to: what would constitute 'fair compensation' to the landowner? At that time, the country was in financial penury and had to begin large-scale industrialization. If the public sector industries did not buy land at cheap prices, they would not be financially viable. There was a very little financial leeway for generous compensation. So, the Constituent Assembly broadly endorsed the LA Act of 1894 (Ray and Patra, 2009).

During this period, land was not only acquired for government projects, but also acquired by the state for private companies on the pretext of public purpose in the interest of the states. So, even in the Nehruvian period, land was being acquired for private industry by state governments. A landmark judgment (*R. L. Aurora vs State of UP*, 1962) of the Supreme Court held that the government could not justify acquiring land for a textile machinery manufacturer as a 'public purpose'. It further declared that 'the Land Acquisition Act did not contemplate that the Government should be made a general agent for companies to acquire lands for them for their private profit' (Kasturi, 2007).

The court judgment might have been an opportunity to revise the injustices of the Act but the Nehru government chose to do the opposite. The immediate response of the government was to amend the law through the LA (Amendment) Act of 1962 to allow land to be acquired for a company which was engaged in or was taking steps for engaging in any industry or work for a public purpose. This was applied retrospectively and superseded the earlier Supreme Court judgment. Thus, the Nehruvian state succeeded in preserving its authority for acquiring land for private industry.

According to Palit and Bhattacharjee (2008), the government from the 1960s to the 1980s played the role of a 'venture capitalist'. The fact of the matter was that the government needed land and just took it, not only by virtue of the LA Act but also by a host of other central Acts, mainly governing petroleum, mines, forests and wildlife. The tracts of land acquired were huge. It was not always for building industries, such as the Durgapur Steel Plant, or for infrastructure projects, such as the Damodar Valley Corporation. Often, it was for building townships such as Bhubaneshwar, Durgapur, Gandhinagar and Chandigarh, all of which certainly entailed large-scale displacement. The very same states (West Bengal and Odisha) where the anti-special economic zone protests have been massive, had ceded huge tracts of land to these townships. Even the largest special economic zone (SEZ) required far less land than the smallest tract of land acquired by the government (ibid.).

New Economic Policy 1990 and Beyond

Under liberalization, the policy climate of the central government went through a paradigm change in the early 1990s. Gradually, the government loosened the controls of the licensing system in a bid to open up and encourage private sector industries. Private investment was invited into diverse economic activities that were previously under the public sector such as generation of power, mining, roads and infrastructure, airports and setting up of SEZs.

With the advent of the new economic policy, a new role was assigned to the state, the task of acquiring large tracts of land from farmers and state-mediated transfer of land to private corporations. A public perception developed that the private corporate, unlike its public sector counterpart, was financially strong and the private sector was both capable of and honour-bound to pay adequate and acceptable compensation. Public outcry erupted as the government used the same legislation to acquire land compulsorily against meagre compensation to the landowners and this land was then handed over to private companies. This phenomenon of 'acquiring land for a public purpose for use by a private industry' (operating with the sole motive of earning private profits) was not acceptable to the public, notwithstanding its legal sanctity (Ray and Patra, 2009). In the post-liberalization period, and particularly during 2005–2015, there have been numerous farmer and public protests across the country, and civil society organizations have been consistently raising concerns around the LA Act and socio-economic and environmental consequences of such projects on the project-affected people. The consequences of financial investments of a few projects in the recent past, which initiated a significant national debate, have been discussed later in this chapter.

Concept of Property in Constitution of India

Right to Property

There has been a significant erosion of the 'right to property' with respect to state takings in India, reflected in a sequence of amendments to the Indian constitution.

There is extensive law and economic literature on takings (Austin, 1966; Berlin, 1961; Cooter, 2000; Epstein, 1985; Miceli, 1997; Ramanathan, 1996; Baxi, 1989), which broadly explains the takings doctrine as a solution to the hold out problem that arises in the context of large-scale land acquisition. The majority of this literature is situated within the American institutional setting – where the American constitution justifies the broad takings doctrine (eminent domain) by stating that takings must be for public purpose and just compensation should be paid for the takings (Singh, 2006). There is a wide range of opinions on how to understand the public purpose – should public purpose be understood as a 'means' (a reaction to the hold out problem) or 'ends' (determining whether the use is for a public rather than a private purpose) (Merrill, 1986; Ulen, 1992), and by asking what is the relationship between political theory and practice with respect to public purpose (Epstein, 1985; Fischel, 1995). The literature also asks, given that a socially justified public purpose is in place for taking, what compensation should be paid out to ensure 'fairness' in the land transaction and resource allocation process.

The Right to Property under Article 19(1)(f) of the Constitution of India was included by its founders in the section of the document that specifies fundamental rights of the nation's citizens. The 44th Constitutional Amendment of 1978 removed the right to acquire, hold and dispose of property from the section of the constitution specifying fundamental rights and retained it as only a simple legal right in Article 300A (Porwal and Singh, 2011). This Article reads as follows:

> 300 A No persons shall be deprived of his property save by authority of law.

After the 44th Constitutional Amendment Act in 1978, the essential protection that remains to be offered to property owners is an entitlement to obtain compensation – that is, a right to receive an indemnification equivalent to the value of the property expropriated (ibid.). The view of the Supreme Court[2] in this regard is reproduced as follows:

> All modern constitution of the democratic character provides payment of compensation as the condition to exercise the right to expropriation: Commonwealth Australia Act, French Civil Code (Art 545), the 5th amendment act of the

[2] The analysis is the reflection of several judicial pronouncements with regard to land acquisition and compensation issues given by the Indian courts at different points in time. Some of the relevant cases referred to are as follows: *State of Bihar v. Kameshwar Singh, AIR 1952 SC 252, State of West Bengal v. Mrs. Bella Banerjee 1954 SC 170, State of W.B. v. Subodh Gopal (1954) SCR 587, State of Madras v. Namasivaya Muralidar (1964) 6 SCR 35, Newcrest Mining (WA) Limited v the Commonwealth of Australia [1997] [HCA].*

constitution of USA and the Italian constitution provide principles of 'just term', 'just indemnity', 'just compensation', as the reimbursement of the property taken have been provided for. As pointed in the Halsbury's law of England that 'when parliament has authorized compulsory acquisition of land, it is invariably provided for payment of money compensation to the person, deprived of his interest in it' (ibid.)

Eminent Domain

Concomitant with this reduced protection offered to personal property rights is the ability of the state to acquire the property of a private person, exercising the power of eminent domain, for public purposes. In India, eminent domain is defined as the power to take private property such as land and associated resources (subsurface) for public use by the state, municipalities, and private persons or corporations authorized to exercise functions of public character (Ramanathan, 1996). The Supreme Court[3] has held that eminent domain is a right inherent to every sovereign to take private property belonging to individual citizens for public use; the limitations imposed upon this acquisition is that such takings must be for public purpose and, finally, that no property can be taken unless the expropriation adheres to the provision for payment of compensation in the manner laid down in the relevant statute. Eminent domain is therefore in the nature of a compulsory purchase of a citizen's property, for the purpose of using this land for a public purpose, against the payment of an equivalent amount of compensation (Lalor, 1899). However, the Supreme Court judgment of 1952 noted that 'the concept of acquisition and that of compensation are two different notions having their origin in different sources. One is found in the sovereign power of the State to take, the other is based on the natural right of the person who is deprived of property to be compensated for his loss.' Natural law has little role in the Indian constitution and the British common law from which the doctrine is drawn precedes the Indian constitution, and hence the doctrine of eminent domain has extra constitutional and pre-democratic moorings in India (Sampat, 2013).

In India, although the term 'eminent domain' does not appear in the onstitution or any of the Acts, the principle of eminent domain is believed to be the underlying principle of Article 31A of the Indian constitution. Under Article 31A of the constitution, the parliament as well as the state legislature can make a law providing for the extinguishment or modification of any rights accruing by virtue of any agreement, lease or license for the purpose of searching for, or winning any mineral or mineral oil, or the premature termination or cancellation of such agreement, lease or license, even though it may be inconsistent with the fundamental rights

[3] *State of Bihar v. Kameshwar Singh, AIR 1952 SC 252.*

of speech and to equality (Singh, 1991). A state legislature is also empowered to enact such a law provided it receives presidential assent. The doctrine is also implicit in legislation on land and natural resources such as the LA Act of 1894, Forest Act of 1927 and Irrigation Acts of certain states.

Doctrine of Public Trust

In contrast to the eminent domain principle is the theory of public trust. Public trust theory (Sax, 1970) is derived from the concepts of common property and open access and is based on the belief that certain natural resources are held not in absolute ownership but trusteeship by a nation, state or community. The doctrine of public trust, a Roman principle, is a part of the law of the land in India. It was founded on the idea that the government in trusteeship with the public held certain common resources such as river, forest, seashore and air for free and unimpeded use. Therefore, such trust property was distinguished from other forms of public property which the government could grant to private owners. According to Joseph Sax (1970), this imposes three kinds of restrictions on government authority: first, that a public trust doctrine should not only be used for public purpose but be made available for use to the general public; second, that such property may not be sold even for fair cash; and, last, the property must be maintained only for particular types of uses.

Whilst affirming that the public trust doctrine is part of Indian jurisprudence, the Supreme Court ruled in 1996 that the state is not an absolute owner but merely a trustee of all natural resources which are by nature meant for public use and enjoyment.[4] The public at large is the beneficiary of forests, running water, air and seashore. It was held that the state as a trustee is under a legal duty to protect natural resources and cannot convert resources meant for public use into private ownership. With the changing needs of society, the types of uses for which a public trust property is normally or traditionally used may also change. According to the Supreme Court, this can be resolved by legislation. 'But in the absence of any legislation', the executive responsible for the administration of the resource or property in question has to act as a trustee. Any legislation enacted for the purpose must take a balanced approach towards preservation of natural resources to provide economic benefit to the greatest number of people (Smith and Sweeny, 2006).

Thus, there is a marked difference between the extent of the control of a resource by the government in eminent domain and public trust doctrines. First, unlike the public trust doctrine, the principle of eminent domain has a legislative and

---

[4] *M. C. Mehta vs Kamal Nath (1997) 1 SCC 388.*

constitutional basis in terms of the LA Act and Article 300A of the constitution. Second, in India, the eminent domain concept has been applied right from its pre-Independence days, while the public trust doctrine developed much later and in the context of an environmental protection regime. In a way, the Supreme Court, to effectively recognize the state's responsibility in terms of its obligation for environmental protection, thereby reflecting the need for the appropriation of natural resources to be balanced by public interest obligations, has applied the public trust doctrine.

Judiciary on Land Acquisition

Compensation

The LA Act provides some degree of participation to the affected people to contest the quantum of compensation and allow the magistrate to determine the final award (Ramanathan, 1996). Acquisition and displacement, with their constitutional implications, have inevitably reached the courts. The petitioners have primarily been the people affected by projects like dams, reservoirs, mining, thermal power plants, industry and other infrastructure projects causing people to lose their assets and their capacity for subsistence, leaving them to face an uncertain future. The courts have given a variety of judgments in this regard, such as scrapping of projects as they are based on a misconception of what is in the public good; halting project work until the displaced are rehabilitated in a manner that does not treat them as a cost of the project; asserting a right to spaces for participation in the process; consideration of equity and infusing into the process of displacement a recognition that there are fundamental rights which are non-negotiable, even where eminent domain and public purpose may be invoked; or for enhancement within the law of compensation which will make the compulsory exchange less inconsonant with justice (Porwal and Singh, 2011). Some important judgments with regard to valuation of land are summarized here.

The courts have given a diverse set of judgments with regard to compensation, for instance, expert opinion can be considered to determine the market value of the land;[5] the collector should not neglect the non-agricultural potential of the land;[6] the Supreme Court suggested a few parameters to assess this,[7] such as nature and location of land to be acquired, present use of land to be acquired, nature of use of nearby lands and their effect on the land under consideration, and capacity

[5] *AIR 1959, SC 429.*

[6] *Bhojraj vs collector of Durg, 1979 JLJ 24.*

[7] *A. Gopalakrishan vs Special Deputy Collector, AIR 1980 SC 1870.*

of the land being acquired; market value should be equal to the price at which a willing seller would give it to a willing buyer;[8] market value of similar land in past should be taken into consideration;[9] if agricultural land to be acquired falls within urban body limits, enhanced compensation should be paid;[10] market value paid for small pieces of land cannot be a basis of land rates;[11] assessment of land revenue can be a good indicator of market value of the land;[12] and under some conditions, prevailing rent or rate of tenancy can be taken into consideration for determination of land rate.[13] In considering the petition of people displaced by the Rourkela Steel Plant, their claim for jobs to the adult population and for a preferential right to employment was rejected by the Supreme Court. The Court found the process of acquisition validated by conformity to the process prescribed in the LA Act. 'Their land', the Court said, 'was taken under LAA. They were paid compensation for it. Therefore, the challenge raised on violation of Article 21 is devoid of any merit.' The government had paid market value for the land acquired. Even if the government or the steel plant did not offer any employment to any person, it would not result in violation of any fundamental right.[14]

It is evident from the judicial pronouncements listed in the previous paragraph that the isolated principles that have been articulated do not create a predictable and consistent template for governing displacement and determination of the market value of land. But they do recognize the problems and inadequacies in the existing legal framework for land acquisition, compensation and R&R.

Public Purpose

The rationality of the law, which supports land acquisition and displacement, is based on the 'larger public good'. It is framed in the name of 'public purpose' with the power essentially resting with the state to determine what constitutes public purpose. Past experiences of land acquisition projects under the umbrella of public purpose have adopted a utilitarian perspective. Utilitarianism is a pragmatic philosophy, advocaing the pursuit of the greatest happiness for the greatest number of people. It does not actually advocate the marginalization of the people who

---

[8] *1964 JLJ 231: 1964 MP Law Journal 299.*

[9] *1961 MP Law Journal 1219.*

[10] *Deep Chand vs State of UP, AIR 1980 SC 633.*

[11] *1970 JLJ 466.*

[12] *Chatarbhuj vs Collector Raigad, AIR 1964.*

[13] *Ramnarain vs State, AIR 1963 MP 35.*

[14] *Buta Prasad Kumbhar v SAIL, 1995.*

sacrifice their lands and livelihoods and get excluded from the benefits of such projects. There are layers of 'public' in this larger 'public purpose': one is the immediate displaced or affected person who is sacrificing his/her livelihood or the local community, and the other is the actual beneficiary of such projects. In a similar pattern, there are competing 'spaces' which leads to 'valorization' and 'de-valorization' of spaces and create geographical unevenness.

The utilitarian mindset is evident from Jawaharlal Nehru's statement[15] during the initial years of development planning in India. It is relevant to bring in the constitutional provisions while dealing with the broader issue of governance. Though theorists, such as John Locke, proclaimed right to property as a 'natural right', which even a social contract cannot do away with, the Constitution of India does not recognize it as a 'fundamental' and justiciable right. The Rawlsian argument[16] of inviolability of certain rights goes against the socialist ideals professed by Indian political leaders, such as Nehru, who viewed large-scale development projects to be 'temples of modern India'. The displacement of the underprivileged few for the construction of large-scale development projects clearly qualifies as 'unjust' in Rawlsian terms.

All across the world, the state is given powers to acquire land for public purpose in lieu of compensation that may be paid to the landholders. However, the definition of the term 'public purpose' and, therefore, the justification for acquiring land vary across countries. The courts have given a variety of judgments at different points in time with regard to public purpose.

Some of the judgments have been summarized as follows.

The courts have ordered that a private textile manufacturing industry cannot be seen as public purpose;[17] the Supreme Court rejected the narrow interpretation of Section 3(f) of the LA Act of 1894 (if a government acquires land, the project automatically becomes one of public purpose; otherwise, it becomes something beneficial to private parties). The project was challenged in the apex court, the key contention being that the Uttar Pradesh government acquired the land for a private company and no public purpose was involved in the project.[18] 'Even if the state acquires land for a company, it could be for a public purpose', said a three-judge bench headed by the Chief Justice of India;[19] it was a case of the state using its power of eminent domain to take land from one set of people and handing it over, for redevelopment, to another set of people. This

[15] 'If you are to suffer, you should suffer in the interest of the country', Nehru.

[16] 'Each person possesses an inviolability founded on justice that even the welfare of society as a whole cannot override', John Rawls.

[17] *R. L. Arora vs State of UP, 1962.*

[18] *Nand Kishore Gupta v State of U.P., (2010) 10 SCC 282.*

[19] *Singur Case: April 20, 2010, SC.*

has to do with notions of opportunity cost. The US Supreme Court, by 5:4 majority, upheld this use of state power.[20]

It is evident from the courts' judgments that acquisition of land for private corporations by the state under 'public purpose' has been questioned on several grounds, and the broad definition of public purpose is a contentious and debatable issue.

Land Acquisition Practices for Determination of Land Price and Procedures

The provisions of the LA Act of 1894 relating to the definition of compensation, the method of its fixation and its disbursement are replete with loopholes that cause many difficulties for displaced landholding households. In this context, neither the existing LA Act of 1894 nor the proposed Right to Fair Compensation and Transparency in Land Acquisition and Resettlement and Rehabilitation (RFCTLARR), 2013, prescribe any appropriate methodology for the determination of rate at which land should be acquired. The LA Act of 1894 uses different terms to denote the sense of 'quid pro quo'. In Section 11(i), it uses the words 'value of land'; in Section 11(iii), the word 'compensation' is used; in Section 15 of the Act, the word changes to the phrase 'amount of compensation'; in Section 23, it switches to the term 'market value of the land'. And nowhere in the Act has any of these terms been adequately defined. Consequently, they have been used interchangeably at the level of field assessment causing great damage to the rights of the landowners (Porwal and Singh, 2011).

In the absence of any clear value for rate of land, different casual (ad hoc) practices, predominantly two, have gained ground. First, rates used in registered sale deeds in neighbouring areas (project notified region) are averaged over three years. Second, the stamp duty rate, known as the collector rate, is taken as market value of the land. The first is more prevalent than the second. However, most land transactions in India are grossly undervalued to evade registration fees.[21] Therefore, the oustee receives a rate which is typically much below the market

[20] *Kelo v. City of London (2005: US Supreme Court).*

[21] The stamp duty and registration rates in India are relatively higher compared to developed countries. In states such as Uttar Pradesh and Haryana, stamp duty rates are 14.5 and 12.5 per cent of transaction value respectively, see http://www.indiahousing.com/stamp-dity-india.html, accessed 23 December 2019. In contrast, the maximum rate levied in developed markets, for instance, in Singapore or Europe, is in the range of 1–2 per cent, see http://www.indianground.com/legal.aspx, accessed 2 January 2020.

rate, and the solatium of 30 per cent (or even a 100 per cent solatium, as introduced in the RFCTLARR Act of 2013) does not bridge the gap between the market and the registered prices. These practices seem to have grown primarily out of convenience rather than adoption of any scientific approach. In Scheduled Areas (areas with high tribal concentration listed in the constitution for special state protection), the problem is compounded by the fact that the law restricts sale of land by tribals to non-tribals to prevent tribal land alienation. This otherwise progressive measure has the unintended outcome of further depressing the market price of land and quantum of compensation provided to the tribal land oustee. This lack of predictability in the process of determining land value has added to the intrinsically contentious nature of land acquisitions and contributed to the social unrest that inevitably accompanies such proceedings (Porwal and Singh, 2011, 2015).

In India, there are 13 Central Acts, such as National Highway Act, Indian Railways Act and so on, that govern the land acquisition process in India. Of these, the most prominent is the LA Act of 1894 which is the most contested legislation and has been used for acquisition of land for a variety of purposes, including acquisition for private companies by the state. Land is a state subject, but acquisition of land is in the concurrent list of the constitution, where the Centre and state both can legislate on this matter. Some of the salient procedures of the LA Act of 1894 are summarized in Figure 4.1 and in following sections.

Land Market Distortions

A significant reason that explains the preference among many private project developers of industrial and infrastructure projects to acquire land using eminent domain power of the state is the outdated and inaccurate land records in India, which give rise to disputes (over ownership) and litigation. Since projects often require large amounts of land, and landholding in India is typically small and fragmented[22] (Ministry of Finance, 2015), project proponents have to deal with a large number of landowners and, consequently, face substantial risk of protracted litigation. In the case of exercise of eminent domain, however, land vests completely unencumbered in the government, which then hands it over to the acquiring body. This makes acquisition through the state more attractive for project proponents than through the market.

There is another factor which creates distortion in land market transactions, that is, Non-agricultural Use Clearance (NAC). The NAC is normally not granted

[22] Sixty per cent of Indian farmers till less than an acre of land.

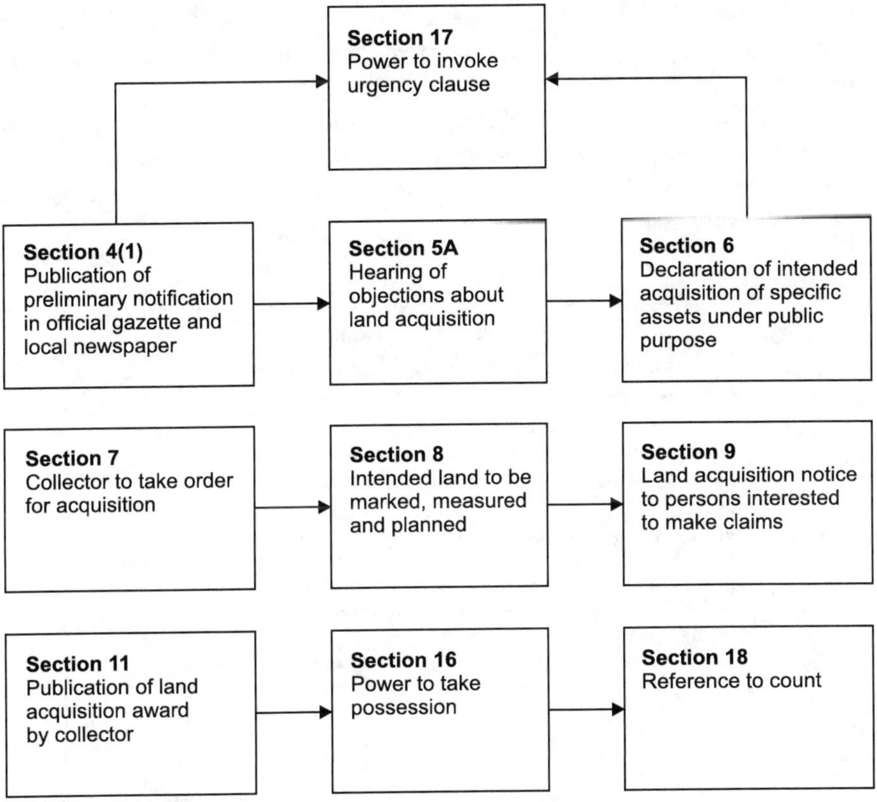

Figure 4.1 Indian land acquisition procedure as per the LA Act of 1894

Source: Author.

to a farmer who wants to continue to use the land for agricultural purposes while looking for a buyer. The NAC is given typically only to the owner who comes up with a concrete proposal for putting the agricultural land to non-agricultural use. Since farmers typically neither have the ability to produce such proposals nor the capacity to pursue alternative uses, they cannot benefit from the value accretion resulting from (potential) non-agricultural uses even when no acquisition is involved. The requirement of the NAC, therefore, means large rents to the purchasers of agricultural land at the cost of agriculturalists who normally cannot even conceive of getting NAC for their lands. In case the land is acquired through market negotiations, it is possible for farmers to bargain some part of the value creation due to anticipated change of use. In case of compulsory acquisition, however, the entire value creation on account of aggregation of landholdings and change in land use pattern accrues to the project proponent – to the buyer from what is legitimately due to the farmers (Morris and Pandey, 2007). This feature of the Indian land market depresses the price of agricultural land relative to their true (potential) values.

The preference of the state-mediated acquisition of land by private corporations over direct land purchase has several advantages. Typical land acquisition practices in India which often lead to social conflicts and unsuccessful land acquisition outcomes are summarized in Figure 4.2.

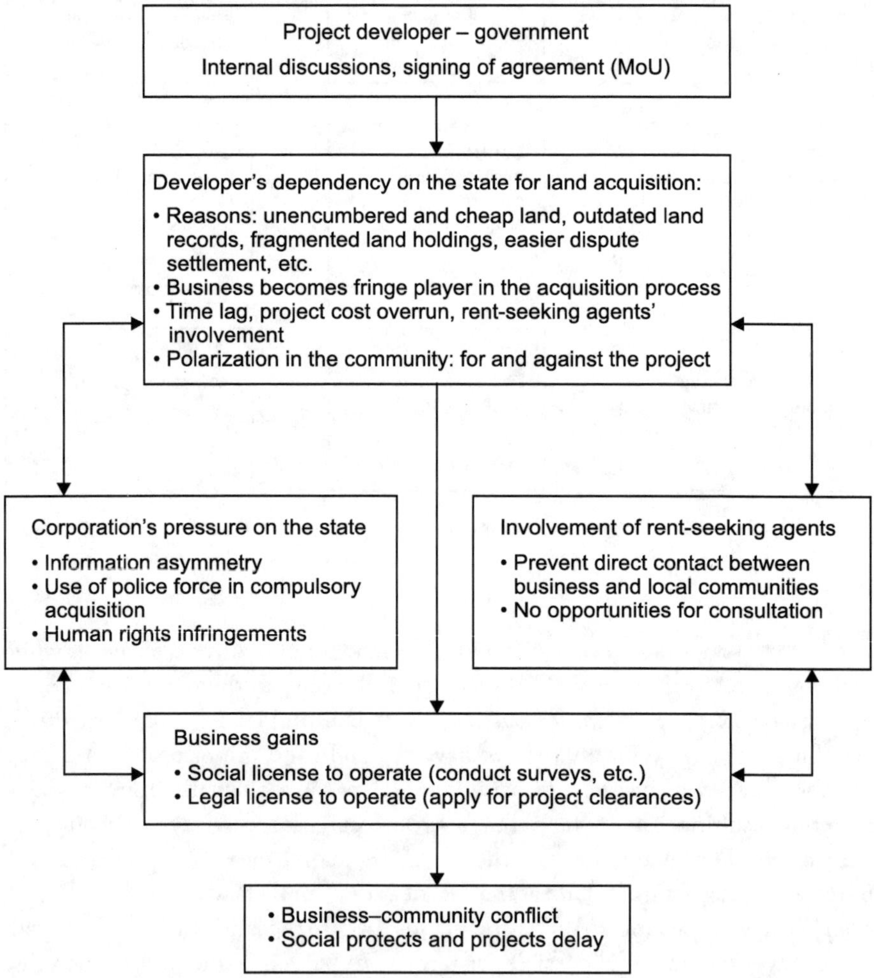

Figure 4.2 Typical land acquisition practices in India

Source: Author.

Land Acquisition: International Practices

The issue of land acquisition and compensation is multifaceted and has been a subject of debate around the world. This section attempts to review land acquisition principles, land acquisition process and its compensation mechanisms in other countries and then study the Indian experience within this context. Around the world, it has been recorded that resettlement action plans (RAPs), which is a step in the land acquisition process, are not supported by economic feasibility analysis capable of examining whether the plans, including the restoration of livelihood as proposed by the project developers, will or will not lead to economic recovery of the project-affected people. Cernea (2008) argues that the projects that forcibly dispossess people of vital productive assets and dismantle their existing economic systems are seldom equipped by the project sponsors with sufficient financial and economic resources to rebuild the livelihoods they dismantle.

Land Acquisition Principles

Across the world, the state is given the power to acquire land for 'public purpose' by invoking the power of 'eminent domain' in lieu of a compensation that may be paid to the landholders. The power of 'eminent domain' and the principle of 'public purpose' are either directly vested in the constitution, for instance, in the USA, China, India and Australia, or is specified in enacted legislation, as is the case in Malaysia, Hong Kong and Singapore. However, the definition of the term 'public purpose' and the rationale for acquiring land varies across countries. Countries such as India, China, France, Japan and Mexico explicitly enumerate projects under which land can be expropriated by the state for public purpose. In India, inclusion of private sector projects under public purpose has been a constant subject of debate (Ramanathan, 1996; Baxi, 1989). In China,[23] land can be appropriated for public purpose for setting up public undertakings, such as national defence, transport, water conservancy, government agencies and so on, while in Mexico,[24] public purpose includes infrastructure development, national security, conservation of history, and projects that preserve ecological balance and natural resources. Other countries such as Brazil, Malaysia, the USA, the United Kindom (UK) and Singapore use a more generic definition of the term 'public purpose', which can therefore be subject to interpretation and potential dispute. In the UK,[25] land can be acquired for 'planning and public purposes if it is suitable

---

[23] Land Acquisition Law, 1988, People's Republic of China.

[24] Expropriation Law, 1936, Mexico.

[25] The UK Town and Country Planning Act of 1990.

for, and required for development'; in Singapore,[26] land can be acquired by the state if it is for 'public benefit or public interest projects'; and in Australia,[27] for 'purposes that the parliament has the power to define by legislation' (Mahalingam and Vyas, 2011).

Land Acquisition Process

The land acquisition process can be broadly categorized into two: one with compulsory acquisition process to forcefully acquire privately owned land and property from landowners with a predetermined compensation package and the other with consultative processes that involve negotiations with stakeholders (IDFC, 2009). The latter process is more applicable to situations where the land acquisition is not done for public purpose and if the land-acquiring agency has more than one option for land. In such scenarios, a negotiation often leads to economically efficient and socially optimal solutions. The earlier case of land acquisition for public purpose with a predetermined compensation distorts the principles of perfect market conditions where there is a single buyer and multiple sellers (unwilling) under the umbrella of eminent domain (Porwal and Singh, 2011). However, even in cases where land acquisition is done for public purpose, countries such as Japan[28] advocate the use of negotiation principle in order to arrive at a compensation acceptable to the stakeholders. Countries such as Singapore and the Philippines combine these two approaches and recommend that land acquiring agencies and developers first negotiate with stakeholders to arrive at a mutually acceptable compensation package that may include monetary as well as non-financial compensation for the property acquired and only if such negotiations fail can the state invoke compulsory acquisition principle based on predetermined formulae as provided in the land acquisition Acts. In India, China, Australia and New Zealand, however, compensation guidelines are prescribed through set formulae, which are enforced on the affected landowners (Mahalingam and Vyas, 2011).

Compensation Methods

The review of literature on international practices regarding land valuation methods can be summarized under three broad principles: value to the owner,

[26] The Singapore Land Acquisition Act of 1996.

[27] Australian Expropriation Law.

[28] Constitution of Japan, Article 49.

just compensation and reasonable compensation. All these principles have their own merits and demerits. The value to the owner principle takes into account socio-economic considerations related to the acquisition of land and aims at compensating landowners for the land value as well as tangible and intangible benefits that are attributed to the land through monetary as well as non-monetary means (Denyer-Green, 1994). This principle is broadly followed in most Commonwealth countries and regions such as Australia (Rost and Collins, 1984) and Hong Kong. For instance, the Commonwealth government's LA Act of 1989 and the New South Wales government's Land Acquisition (Just Terms Compensation) Act of 1991 require compensation to be provided after an assessment of the market value of the land acquired as well as special values attributed to the land, severance payments, consequential financial losses, value loss to other retained land and a solatium (Chan, 2003; Mahalingam and Vyas, 2011).

The just compensation principle aims at providing the landowner with economic parity, primarily through such monetary means that the landowner is at an economically comparable position post land acquisition (Chan, 2003). This is exemplified in the case of *Horn vs Sunderland Corporation* in the UK where the judgment held that a dispossessed person is entitled to compensation 'as far as money can do it, in the same position as if his land had not been taken from him. In other words he gains the right to receive a monetary payment not less than the loss imposed on him in the public interest, but on the other hand, no greater'(Valuation Office Agency, 2000). The Constitution of the USA[29] (fifth amendment) requires 'just compensation' for all takings of private property. On similar grounds, the Constitution of the Philippines[30] requires that payment of just compensation must be made. The Philippines' Republic Act 8974 (2000) provides standards on determining the value of compensation to be paid and aims to 'enable the affected property owners to have sufficient funds to acquire similarly situated lands of approximate areas as those required from them by the government and thereby rehabilitate themselves as early as possible'. Similarly, the Constitutions of Brazil[31] and Cambodia[32] require fair and just compensation.

The reasonable compensation principle envisions the land acquisition process to be a financial transaction where the value of the land alone will be disbursed in the form of monetary compensation without considering any intangible value associated with the land. Countries such as China and states such as British Columbia follow

[29] Constitution of the United States, Amendment V.

[30] Constitution of Philippines Article III.

[31] Constitution of Brazil, Article 153.

[32] Constitution of Cambodia, Article 44.

this principle where landowners should be fully indemnified only for their direct losses. British Columbia's Expropriation Act adopts the concept of market value as the basic measure of compensation and landowners are paid an amount strictly equal to the value of the land. The Japanese constitution, for instance, decrees, 'The criteria of calculation of loss should be socially objective and consideration should not be given to subjective and emotional losses, and any development value or potential value of the property shall not be included in the compensation' (ibid.). However, it has been noticed that dispossessed landowners often suffer huge consequential losses from the sale of the lands that are not compensated for (Chan, 2003).

In general, there are four methods that are used across the world to value land and to arrive at appropriate compensation. These are (a) evaluating the market value of land, (b) evaluating the net value of income from the land, (c) determining original land use value as set by the state and (d) arriving at land values through negotiations (Mahalingam and Vyas, 2011). The Asian Development Bank (2007) defines the fair market value of land as 'the amount that the land might be expected to realize if sold in the open market by a willing seller to a willing buyer'.

Comparable sale deeds in the nearby area over a recent time period are often used to determine fair market value of land. But there are several disadvantages with this method for instance, first, there can be cases where sales data on comparable tracts of land may not be available; second, there are several cases in various developing countries, such as India, where registered value of the sale is kept deliberately low for tax purposes; and, finally, an open, fair land market environment might not be available, thus distorting the value of land. 'Replacement value' method is another land valuation method, which includes not only the cost of acquiring or replicating the property but also all the relevant costs associated with replacement. This method is used in the Philippines and in other countries where legal systems are not robust and land market is not well developed. Where land markets are not well developed, 'net value of income from the land' is used to calculate the value of land. This method has the greatest application in the appraisal of farmland, where value of property is taken to be the value of the expected economic income that could be earned through the ownership of the property. It is used in Tanzania, where the market is assumed to be inefficient (Mahalingam and Vyas, 2011). 'Original land use' method is used in China; the Land Act of China does not permit free transfer of rural land on the basis that there is no active land market; the original use of land is used for compensation purposes with valuation mechanism set by the state (Chan, 2006). Further, in some cases, like Peru, compensation is fixed on the basis of discussion with stakeholders.

As discussed previously, there are various methods of land valuation and these methods have their own limitations that lead to incomplete assessment of land.

Considering some of these factors, some countries also include non-monetary means of compensation and attempt to address the indirect costs of land acquisition. Adding 'solatium' to the compensation amount is the most common method of adding indirect costs to the land acquisition process. McGregor (1988) argues that compensation which is granted as a substitute or solace for what has been lost would seem to comprehend the intangible loss of something that cannot be replaced. This is also referred as 'householder surplus' which reflects the value of ties with the area, friendships, social relations and so on – items which are difficult to value and quantify (Rowan-Robinson, 1990). Bell (1980) points out that great benefits can be achieved by a measure of compensation which provides claimants with a small balance of advantages compared to their expectations, thereby encouraging fewer objections and speedier settlements. Despite these various methods and attempts, the overall international experience (particularly that in India) shows that compensation, even after incorporating intangible costs, is usually unsatisfactory either due to time lag between determining compensation and resettlement or due to failure to adequately account for non-market values such as environmental services, cultural assets, social cohesion, psychological costs and market access (Cernea, 2008).

A review of land acquisition principles, the process and the compensation methods, provides an insight on why land acquisition in India is particularly contentious. India does not have a clearly articulated land acquisition principle, the broad definition of 'public purpose' is an area of potential dispute, and the process does not provide a space for consultation or negotiation, often leading to providing land owners with only 'reasonable compensation'. Despite solatium being incorporated in the compensation to address intangible costs of losing land, the basis for calculating this solatium does not vary with respect to the context within which land is being acquired, and the process of acquisition itself is so lengthy and time consuming that when compensation is paid, market values are higher than the value used to compensate the affected party (Morris and Pandey, 2007; Debnath, 2008). These reasons lead to widespread dissatisfaction among project-affected families (PAFs) and leads to consequent social protests.

Benefit Sharing

Around the world, countries and their specific legislations with respect to compensation have evolved with time in order to be fair and just to the local communities. In some resource-rich countries such as Canada and Australia, there are specific provisions in the legal framework to recognize indigenous land claims and share a part of the profit from resource development activity in that particular region.

Canada

In Canada, resource developers sign legally binding private contracts with First Nation groups called Impact Benefit Agreements (IBAs) to share the benefits from resource development projects. These agreements are used by First Nation groups to influence decision-making in their lands and address concerns about mining impact on their environment, land and their traditional way of life (O'Faircheallaigh and Ginger, 2010). There are two types of agreements: one is legislative and the other is commercial. Legislative agreements are the ones that are between particular aboriginal communities and the federal government of Canada. Commercial ones take place between mining companies and the aborginal groups (O'Faircheallaigh and Ginger, 2010). IBAs are negotiable and are categorized as socio-economic agreements. These can include direct or indirect payments. Direct payments encompass profit-sharing arrangements such as cash or compensation funds. Indirect benefits may include employment, business opportunities, and finance or equity provisions. As far as financial provisions are concerned, sometimes, a fixed annual payment and subsequent payments based on value of minerals are made while sometimes royalty sharing is also considered.

Provisions for contribution of a minimum amount as a base to the trust and some specific percentage contribution from gross revenue from development of new mines is another option that is considered. Agreements also make sure that business opportunities go to the affected sections by encouraging joint ventures between First Nations and others. These agreements are thought to be more beneficial to those communities that have some form of authority over traditional lands.

Australia

In Australia, the revenue sharing mechanisms depend on the applicable Act. Under the Land Rights Act, mining royalties are given to the Australian Business Register (ABR) by the state government. It establishes the ABR, which has the responsibility to receive and disburse royalties to the aboriginal stakeholders. The funds are received in the form of 'mining royalty equivalents', which is the sum of royalties paid to the central and the territory governments by mining companies for activity on aboriginal land (CSE, 2011).

Under the Native Title Act, revenue sharing occurs through agreements between aboriginal communities and mining companies. Agreements are a central feature of the relationship between aboriginal communities and mining companies (O'Faircheallaigh, 2003a). Individual agreements are defined depending on goals pursued by particular indigenous groups.

There are six different types of financial sharing models, which are summarized in the following paragraph.

The first model is a one-time upfront payment to the local community. The second model is a fixed annual payment. In this model, a particular amount is to be paid for some years and a different amount for the remaining years. It is advantageous because a predictable amount will be paid to the community each year and the community does not face an all or nothing situation as in the case of upfront payments. The third model is royalty based on output; thus payments are linked to unit royalty. It can be advantageous because as amount of production increases so does the payout for people. The pitfall is that as production falls, the compensation amount also reduces and even if the prices of minerals are high, the advantage cannot be shared with the community. The fourth model is 'royalty based on value of mineral output'; thus royalty rates are based on production and prices. The fifth model is 'profit after tax'; the said amount is set aside every year. And the sixth model is 'equity participation'. The shares are obtained at a substantial concession or for free for the indigenous groups. For the company, it is beneficial to have an equity share held by aboriginal communities as it increases their stake in making the project a success. In this case, indigenous equity participation is more a cooperation than a negotiation. Combination of different financial models is applied at different stages of the project cycle (O'Faircheallaigh, 2003a).

The review reflects that there are existing practices for compensating affected families beyond just one-time land compensation as practised in India. In fact, the conceptualization of different models and modalities of payments provides the rationale for reducing risks and impoverishment of affected families during post-displacement periods.

While there have been a number of countries that have adopted legislation giving a share of revenues to the state or province, the outcomes have not always been as envisaged. Legislation has not resulted in money actually reaching the provincial level, and where it has gone to the right government level, the capacity to manage these revenues has been in short supply (Luke, 2002). It is imperative, however, to point out that the management of revenue that is distributed and shared is sometimes key to the successful achievement of the policy objectives of distribution. It is in this context that some governments and companies have opted for more targeted approaches through resource foundations and trusts.[33]

[33] A few good examples of partnering foundations in the mining world are the Yanacocha Association, Peru; BHP's Minera Escondida Foundation, Chile; and so on. In Yanacocha mine, Peru, the partners are Aid Four, ITDG, Care International, the Peruvian Department of Health, Community Association leaders and the company foundation, the Yanacocha Association.

5

Resource Development and Compensation Issues

Developments at the state level and the growing interest in resource projects by national and multinational corporations are giving rise to demand for more compensation[1] for dispossessed local communities and to the need for revenue sharing with resource-bearing regions, especially in a federal political system. The lack of clarity about the nature, basis and rationale of compensation and a recognition that issues relating to fair compensation to resource-bearing regions are particularly important in the context of federal democratic polity and have motivated this study.

Legal and Federal Context of Land Acquisition and Resource Development

The right to seek compensation emanates from either principles such as justice, polluter pays, and resettlement and rehabilitation (R&R) policies or from right over the resource itself by absolute ownership, control or usage. Compensation payments need to be supported by legislation or be based on general principles of law such as torts or those developed by judiciary as in the case of compensatory afforestation. Besides their treatment in the constitution and in the laws, the nature of the resource also has an important role in determining any liability that arises for use or depletion of the resource and associated environmental and socio-economic externalities (Divanand Rosencranz, 2002).

[1] The word 'compensation' does not refer here only to payments made by the state to individuals or groups for land acquired but also to the payments made in a direct transaction between the buyer (mine or hydro developer) and the landowner or those with use rights in common property resources. The focus here is the issue of 'fairness' in the land transaction process.

Payment to resource-bearing regions and to people in the region needs to address three primary issues, namely, compensation, corrective (and distributional) justice, and deterrence (Segerson, 2002). The goal of achieving corrective justice is to redress a wrong that of distributional justice is to ensure that proceeds are used to make the project-affected families (PAFs) better off than before the project and to improve the lives of the least well-off; and that of achieving deterrence is to regulate future behaviour.

The exercise of the rights to own, control, use and levy a charge on a resource are all dependent on another right of the government, that is, to legislate on these matters. In India, the proprietary title to the minerals vests in the federal states. However, this ownership is subject to the legislation governing regulation and control of mining enacted by the Indian parliament. With respect to minor minerals, the situation is different as states can make their own rules and regulations (Jetli, 2011; Leelakrishnan, 2008).

Although the union may be empowered by the constitution to take mine and mineral development under its control, the Mining and Mineral Development and Regulation Act does not sufficiently recognize the ownership rights of the states. Despite states being the owners, important matters such as royalty fixation and revision are under the union's control. This control is in place in order to ensure that mineral resources are used in the national interest. While this is reflected in the fact that regulation and control of the major minerals needs to be vested in the centre, an independent body should undertake the control over decisions that relate to revenue augmentation for the states (TERI, 2007, 2008).

A central issue, both from the point of the working of federalism and in terms of the impacts that resource development can have on local people, is the monitoring, regulation and enforcement of laws and rules. It is evident that India has a clear framework for regulating powers and responsibilities in case of resource development and to address environmental (and some social) implications of resource development. Yet poor environmental and social outcomes suggest that there is inadequate oversight by regulatory bodies at various levels of government and poor enforcement of the laws. Evidence of this is unfair payment arrangements for land bought for resource development from the local people and complaints of human rights infringements (Noronha et al., 2009; Singh, 2017).

Multifunctional View of Resources

In order to analyse and discuss the issue of compensation with regard to resource development, Noronha et al. (2009) argue that resource development issues need to be seen in three perspectives: spatial, agency and temporal. A resource project is dependent on spatial context, that is, the region where it is located, as the project is shaped by the exigencies of the location and the community. This context involves local people and their aspirations, nature and its dynamics, the relations between people and nature, and the wider political and civil community. Resource development has an agency perspective as it involves various agents and operates at several levels. As in a federal set-up like India, ownership or user rights of resource are vested in the federating states, while controls such as granting of mining lease, fixation of royalty and so on lie with the centre. These projects, through the externalities they generate, 'create a process of shifting costs on to local communities and regions'. Such externalities create both inter- and intra-generational inequalities in the distribution of pollutions and access to resources, and the economic value they create depends on these inequalities (Martinez-Alier, 1999: 115). And there is a temporal perspective to resource development as these are long-term projects with clear project life cycles and in the context of finite resources, such as minerals, oil and gas, involves inter-generational issues as extraction today implies development opportunity forgone tomorrow.

The complexities for resource development policy, and consequently for compensation issues, arise from the roles that resources perform and the values attached to them. Resources need to be seen not just as natural resources but also as having cultural aspects, not just having material (use) values but also non-use values. Use values refer to both actual (direct and indirect) use and option value; where direct refers to benefits derived from goods and services obtained, indirect are those derived from ecosystem functioning, necessary for production and for living. Option value refers to the potential of using a resource or acquiring information about it. But resources can also have cultural or an existence value, a 'value within a larger economy of signification which crucially shapes their modes of appropriation' (Baviskar, 2003: 5052). They sometimes are also seen as 'resources for collective representations that exceed the concern with immediate material use' (ibid.). The nature of demands made by various stakeholder groups reflects the different meanings and values that are attached to resources. So, resources have multiple values and meanings in context of 'space' and 'place', and their development thus has different meanings and implications for different groups – industry, government and community.[2] In this context, whose interest should get priority, and how, becomes key issues in the compensation debate.

This multifunctionality of resources creates three key policy issues: first, of balancing the interests of the wider constituency with that of the more

[2] Community, of course, is a very broad term and includes several different groups and interests within it. Which community has the greater stake, and who represents them, is another issue that needs to be addressed.

vulnerable, regional groups that often have insufficient information and voice for representation; second, of seeking to understand and include the interests of different stakeholder groups and particularly of the marginalized; and, third, of addressing the aspirations to modernity of *adivasi* groups while providing them with the option of remaining or being able to return to traditional ways of living, given that people have multiple affiliations that are intrinsic to people's lives and that create contradictions between what they want at different points of times (Baviskar, 2003;[3] Noronha et al., 2009).

Thus, the issue of compensation has to be understood by adopting a multifunctional view of resources that involve both material and material values and a multidimensional perspective of resource development that takes into account the spatial, agency and temporal perspectives. Questions of 'who benefits' and 'who loses', 'whose interests are being furthered', and 'who is being marginalized' are key to understanding current disaffections in a number of states that are involved in resource development, infrastructure projects and development of special economic zones (SEZs) and require serious engagement at all levels.

Compensation for What? And for Whom?

The issue of compensation to individuals and resource-bearing regions is complex and, as currently debated, unclear. Is it the amount that currently accrues to the states, or what they are now demanding from resource development, compensation for the use of resources or for the externalities created by the development of resources, or both? Do these demands reflect the concerns of local communities who often have to bear the incremental costs of resource development without receiving a fair share of the benefits? The various aspects of resource development projects and their implications for individuals and for the region provide a multifaceted rationale for compensation. This is explained in Figure 5.1.

Resource Development and Indigenous People

As discussed earlier, resource development projects use common resources and disrupt the ecosystem through operations, very often without paying for them. This may reduce the cost to the developer, but it poses a cost to the local community as

[3] Baviskar depicts the multiple affiliations well: 'The *adivasi* fighting against displacement in the Narmada Valley is simultaneously a tribal, a farmer, a collector of forest produce, a wom[a]n, a mother, a consumer of manufactured goods like fertilizers and saris, a worker on state drought-relief projects…' (2003: 5052).

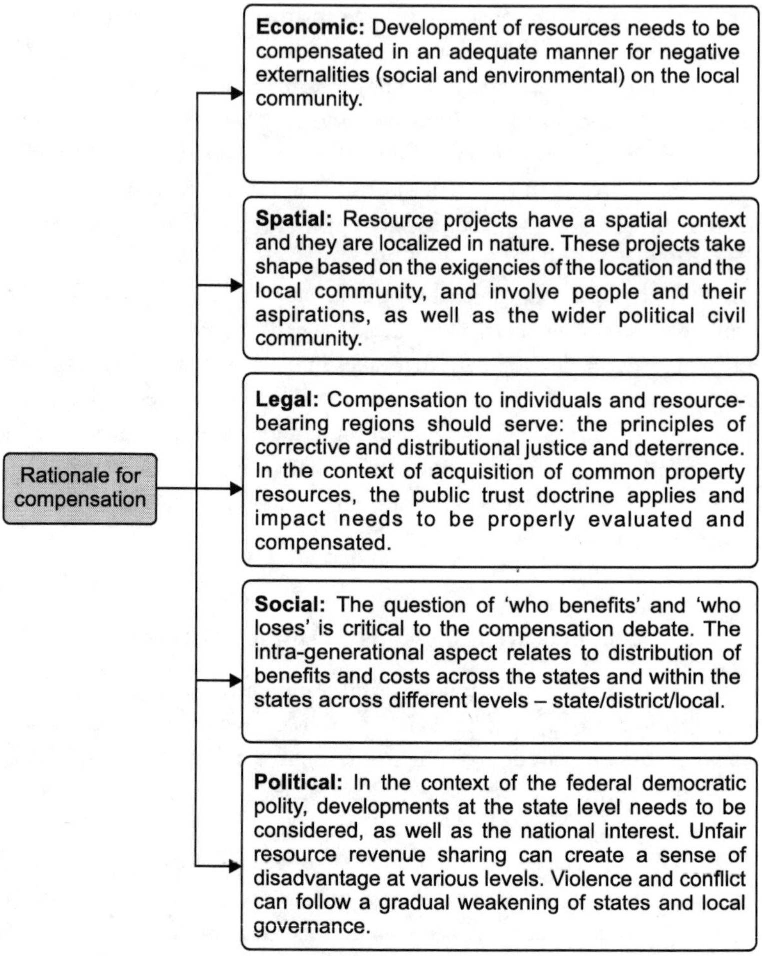

Figure 5.1 Multidimensional rationale for compensation

Source: Author.

they have to bear these costs either because they lose economically (for example, farmers and other forest dependent communities) or through adverse health and reduced well-being (Noronha, 2005). The developer in this case just transfers these costs to the local community. Moreover, not all of the ecosystem disruption costs can be monetized and be amenable to compensation payments. As Turner (1999) points out, an ecosystem has a social value that may not be the same as the aggregate total private economic value of its components.

Tribal and poor peasant women are especially affected through environmental degradation that accompanies development, given their dependency on common grazing lands, fuel and fodder from forests, or cropland for their subsistence needs (Agarwal, 1994). Loss of forests, common property resources and cropland affect their lives and livelihoods in very material ways, often causing a movement into poverty. There is evidence of how their access to water is affected by development activity, for example, mining, either through the pollution of surface water, which they may depend on for their daily needs, or increased depletion of ground water in regions of open-cast mining. All these externalities add considerably to their hardships, prolonging their already long days and travel time, reducing the quality of their nutrition, affecting their health and lowering their income from common property resources (Agarwal, 1992: 337–339).

Existing literature (Sharma, 2002; Xaxa, 1999; Vishwanath, 1997; Agarwal, 1994; Baviskar, 2003; Krishnaswami, 2005) and past experiences reflect that resource policy has either ignored or not engaged centrally with project-affected people, especially in tribal areas, and with the creation of institutions for equitable distribution and sharing of project benefits. The negative externalities associated with resource development suggest that compensation demands by resource-bearing states[4] cannot be seen as just a union–states issue but also involves the substate local level wherein various groups have interests in resource development or their non-development.

Land is a contentious issue, particularly with regard to resource development in areas of tribal populations. The Constitution of India provides specific protection to tribal rights over their customary resources, particularly in Schedule V and Schedule VI areas. The objective of Schedules V and VI of the constitution is to ensure that the *adivasis* remain in possession and enjoyment of the lands in scheduled areas for their economic empowerment, social status and dignity of their person. It is equally argued by the state that mineral resources are wealth of the nation and their exploitation is essential for the development of the nation. The central issue here is that the competing rights of *adivasis* and the state are required to be adjusted without defeating the rights of either.[5] Most geographical areas rich in minerals and other natural resources fall under Schedule V of the constitution.[6] In these areas, the governor is empowered to make regulations and repeal or amend any act of parliament to prohibit or restrict the transfer of land by

[4] http://fincomindia.nic.in/pubsugg/memo_jkhand.pdf; http://fincomindia.nic.in/pubsugg/memo_ori.pdf; http://fincomindia.nic.in/pubsugg/mp_memo.pdf. All three links were accessed on 10 February 2012.

[5] *Samatha vs State of Andhra Pradesh* (1997) 8 SCC 191.

[6] Scheduled Areas in Madhya Pradesh, Jharkhand, Odisha, Andhra Pradesh, Gujarat, Himachal Pradesh, Chhattisgarh, Maharashtra and Rajasthan.

or among members of the Scheduled Tribes in such areas.[7] Schedule V, described in the constitution, is the most comprehensive provision for the protection of the *adivasi* people living in Scheduled Areas against the state and other external forces. Relying on the provisions of Schedule V, the Supreme Court, in the landmark *Samatha* judgment (1997), ruled that government lands, tribal lands and forestlands in Scheduled Areas cannot be leased out to non-tribals or to private companies for mining or industrial operations. Although the facts in this case were specific to the state of Andhra Pradesh, the court categorically ruled that land in Schedule V areas cannot be so transferred.

In the *Hoda Committee Report* (Planning Commission, 2006), which strongly recommends the adoption of the International Council on Mining and Metals principles, the report points to the requirement to go beyond the dependence on local governments and to adopt front-line thinking of offering indigenous communities, direct financial stake in the projects and a share of profits to reflect the ownership aspect (94). However, in this debate, there is a strong argument for having 'no go' areas in some of the resource-bearing regions because there may be areas that are of great cultural and spiritual value to the *adivasi*s (for instance, case of sacred groves of the Dongria tribe in Niyamgiri hills in Odisha) who lived and had rights here prior to the formation of the state. Baviskar (2003) points to the living cultures that are displaced and uprooted through projects and the continuous pressure on them to accommodate use values attached to the resources while giving up the non-use, cultural values. These discussions encourage probing into the multidimensional aspects of land acquisition and resource development.

Mining and Mineral-Rich Districts in India

It is now well recognized across the world that wealth generated by the mining sector comes at a substantial development cost. This has also been exhaustively documented in India. In fact, the major mining districts of India are among its poorest and most polluted (Bhushan, 2008). Considering the negative externalities of the mining sector, new policies and practices are being explored and implemented across the world to ensure that mineral wealth can be converted into sustainable development benefits for local communities. Many mineral-rich countries have enacted legislation in which provisions of benefit sharing with the local communities are explicitly stipulated.

The mining and quarrying sector constituted about 2.26 per cent of gross domestic product (GDP) in India during 2010–2011 (Ministry of Mines, 2011). Coal occupies an important position amongst minerals as about 60 per cent of India's

---

[7] Para 5(2) of Schedule V, Constitution of India.

energy needs are met through coal. In states like Chhattisgarh and Jharkhand, the contribution of minerals to the state domestic product (SDP) is higher than 10 per cent and next only to agriculture and manufacturing. Further, income from royalty from minerals is a significant contributor to revenues in states such as Chhattisgarh, Jharkhand, Odisha and Madhya Pradesh. Royalty was the single most important contributor to non-tax revenue in some of these states. Examining the contribution of various minerals to the royalty revenue in these states, it is seen that coal accounts for 65–90 per cent of the royalty revenue in Chhattisgarh, Jharkhand, Odisha and Madhya Pradesh. Other important minerals in terms of their contribution to royalty in these states are limestone, iron ore, bauxite and chromite.

In India, the geographical distribution of minerals (mainly coal) and metallic mineral reserves is highly uneven. With respect to concentration of mineral deposits, Jharkhand, Odisha, Madhya Pradesh and Chhattisgarh emerge as the top mineral-bearing states (see Table 5.1). About 70 per cent of India's coal, 80 per cent of its hematite iron ore (high-grade ore), 60 per cent of bauxite, 40 per cent of manganese and almost all its chromite are found in these three states (CSE, 2011) with strong overlap of resources with forest dwelling and indigenous populations (see Map 5.1).

The top 50 mining districts, in terms of value of mineral production, are in 13 states. Jharkhand has nine of these districts; Odisha, Madhya Pradesh and Chhattisgarh have six districts each; Andhra Pradesh has five; and Maharashtra has four. The top 50 districts in India, based on value of mineral production, together account for more than 85 per cent of the value of mineral production in the country (CSE, 2011). Another significant fact about these districts is that most of these mineral-rich areas are affected by 'Naxalism' and declared as extremist-affected regions by the Government of India. The appropriation and exploitation of natural resources have frequently been mentioned as a cause of civil wars. Several studies, both from economic (Collier and Hoeffler, 1998, 2004; De Soysa, 2000) and political science (Kaldor, 1999; Klare, 2001) perspectives, suggest that natural resource abundance is an important determinant of the occurrence of internal armed conflict. However, Ross (2004) warns that the empirical linkage between natural resources and civil war is fragile and proposes that the resource–conflict relationship should be differentiated with respect to both the type of natural resources and the kind of civil conflict.

In the context of resource development, land emerges as an important and highly volatile issue at many points during the life cycle of a project. Corporations need to secure access to land and community consent, and communities need to be assured that land rights are properly recognized, that free and informed consent is obtained and that appropriate compensation policy is in place where land is lost or affected (Dutt, Krishnan and Ahmad, 2012). Past experience demonstrates that

Table 5.1 Mineral-rich states and value of mineral production

State	*District*	*Value of minerals (crore) 2010–2011*	*Population 2011 (lakh)*	*Mine lease area (as of 31 March 2008) (hectare)*	*Population affected*	*Literacy rate (%)*	*SC/ST population (%)*	*Area under forest (percentage of total area)*
Madhya Pradesh	Chhindwara	1,776	20.9	5,359	18,970	63.0	46.3	38.4
	Shahdol	1,729	10.6	3,291	11,322	58.5	51.8	27.4
	Balaghat	600	17.0	2,282	8,396	68.8	29.5	54.1
	Betul	395	15.8	1,203	3,777	60.9	50.9	35.6
	Umaria	294	6.4	464	1,466	56.9	50.9	49.9
	Sidhi	3,392	11.3	9,563	44,375	55.0	41.9	39.0
	Overall	8,187	82.0	22,162	88,306	61.6	44.0	40.5
Chattisgarh	Korba	9,121	12.1	13,907	46,966	63.0	51.5	50.8
	Dantewada	3,961	5.3	2,742	3,230	36.5	81.9	64.4
	Sarguja	1,081	23.6	61.98	17,893	51.5	59.4	45.6
	Koriya	778	6.6	1,100	2,425	61.3	52.6	62.3
	Raigarh	494	14.9	991	4,533	64.3	49.6	36.2
	Durg	366	33.4	3,860	30,234	69.7	25.2	9.0
	Overall	15,801	96.0	28,798	105,282	61.1	45.7	44.3
Jharkhand	Dhanbad	3,760	26.8	6,362	163,387	65.3	24.4	6.8
	Hazaribagh	1,895	17.3	15,075	120,601	59.4	26.8	34.2
	Singbhum	1,195	15.0	16,596	69,371	49.5	58.2	38.7
	Chatra	1,083	10.4	10,321	56,766	50.9	35.8	47.8
	Godda	1,041	13.1	3,909	48,628	47.4	32.2	18.8

	Bokaro	953	20.6	7,032	100,698	63.4	25.6	29.0
	Ranchi	541	29.1	5,828	64,108	66.9	47.0	24.7
	Palamau	250	19.4	1,576	12,009	54.8	44.4	40.7
	Deogarh	202	14.9	518	6,238	54.7	24.8	6.8
	Overall	10,921	166.7	67,218	641,806	58.8	35.5	31.2
Odisha	Keonjhar	7,370	18.0	28,724	124,661	59.3	56.1	38.9
	Angul	3,049	12.7	13,700	54,526	69.9	28.9	41.9
	Sundergarh	2,705	20.8	14,604	62,504	65.3	58.8	41.8
	Jharsuguda	1,324	5.8	6,491	35,570	70.0	48.4	14.4
	Jajpur	1,149	18.3	4,195	52,862	71.3	30.8	8.8
	Korapur	191	13.8	6,565	20,483	42.1	62.7	19.1
	Overall	15,788	89.4	74,279	350,607	62.7	48.2	31.9

Sources: CSE (2011), Office of the Registrar General and Census Commissioner (2011) and Singh (2015: fieldwork data from 2013 to 2015).

Note: 1 lakh = 0.1 million and 1 crore = 10 million.

Map 5.1 Mineral-rich states of India

Sources: Adapted by author from CSE (2011) and www.d-maps.com/, accessed 10 February 2012.

Note: Map not to scale and may not represent authentic international borders.

people in project areas contribute to a project through the land that they give up and that the project would not be possible without access to this land. And yet, payments made to the project-affected people are only for the damage caused or for the loss incurred; they are not necessarily benefitted. Communities or individual beneficiaries in projects and the loss of opportunity for the affected people in benefitting from enhanced land values as a result of resource development are not recognized. Even when land rights of local people are clear, these resources tend to be valued more cheaply in a deal as negotiations depend on the distribution of information, power and influence, and these are typically asymmetrical. Women are especially affected when productive assets, such as arable land, are lost to mining because of their greater dependence on agriculture, as men migrate to mining or other non-farm jobs. Compensation payments by project authorities for this land are one-time payments, which tend to go to the males of the households and which are often used for immediate consumption needs rather than investment purposes (Noronha, 2005).

New Economic Policy, Social Protests and Policy Change

As discussed earlier, in Indian economy, the year 1991 is referred to as the economic reform period but the actual implication of the new economic policy has been witnessed during 2005–2020. This duration has witnessed active participation of private and foreign capital in large infrastructure projects, mining, thermal power generation and roads, which were earlier under state operation. The major political parties (Congress and Bharatiya Janata Party [BJP]) in India have openly welcomed foreign capital in diverse sectors and even the Communist Party of India (Marxist) (CPI[M]) came to embrace the principles of liberalization. The Communist Party of India (CPI) has continued to speak out against some aspects of the national reform agendas proposed by the United Progressive Alliance (UPA) government (between 2004 and 2014). But in its West Bengal heartland, its attempt to attract private capital in Singur and Nandigram revealed its embracement of liberalization, which was countered by the opposition (Trinamool Congress) and civil societies in the state (Corbridge, 2009).

In the 1990s, the pace of private investment was slow but it accelerated soon after the 2000s, and also there was change in the centre–state relations and many of India's states were able to improve their bargaining position vis-à-vis the centre. Rob Jenkins (1999) has argued that the reform process has empowered states to behave as 'competition States' instead of competing with one another to draw down funds from New Delhi; states such as Maharashtra, Karnataka, Tamil Nadu or West Bengal now fight with one another to host foreign direct investments. In Jenkins' view, the real momentum of economic reform in India lies with the states. A process of 'Provincial Darwinism' has taken hold, he argues, that compels states to compete with one another for foreign capital that will reduce their fiscal deficits and dependence on the centre. Forceful land acquisition and eviction of peasants is one such instrument to attract private capital. The sanction and approval of hundreds of SEZs during 2005–2008 was another significant policy move in this direction (IDFC, 2009).

Farmer and civil society protests in Singur and Nandigram against state-mediated land acquisition for private corporations brought the land acquisition issue to the fore at the national level. However, West Bengal was not the only state where public protests arose during this period due to land acquisition projects. Simultaneously, there were protests against land acquisition throughout the country, for instance, Tata Steel project in Kalinganagar, Odisha; POSCO (*Hindu*, 2013) and Vedanta (*Statesman*, 2015) in Odisha; Jindal project in Raigarh, Chhattisgarh; Arcelor Mittal Steel project in Jharkhand; Reliance SEZ in Navi Mumbai; and so on, due to land acquisition and environmental clearance issues (IDFC, 2009). The role of civil society has been critical in the process of halting projects and bringing the social and environmental issues centre stage. Civil society intervention has been much organized and strengthened compared to the earlier period. However, the contribution of the Narmada Bachao Andolan (NBA) in the 1980s has been significant in highlighting the importance of R&R policies. The sustained struggle of NBA in the 1980s spread awareness about land acquisition and its socio-economic and cultural implications and impacted the central and state governments along with public sector undertakings (PSUs) to conceptualize the R&R policies (Baviskar, 1995).

Popular protests have, in the recent past, been frequently politicized by complex interplay of vested interests. But these protests have awakened the project-affected persons to assert their right to question the land acquisition and compensation process and participate in the future stream of gains from the envisaged development, as a supplier of a prime factor of production, namely land. There are several instances where companies have displayed sensitivity to this sentiment while appreciating the business wisdom of approaching the landowners directly instead of seeking shelter behind the new Right to Fair Compensation and Transparency in Land Acquisition and Resettlement and Rehabilitation (RFCTLARR) Act. They have offered a fair price or an acceptable package to successfully conclude compensation negotiations and proceed with their projects, for example, the Raheja Group in Haryana; Reliance in Navi Mumbai, Maharashtra; and, on a smaller scale, JCT Steel (a Jindal Group venture) in Salboni, West Bengal (IDFC, 2009). Successful land acquisition for state capital Amravati (*Indian Express*, 2015) has been recently in news for its benefit-sharing provisions and stake for farmers in future development of the region.

Policy Change

The Government of India has been deliberating on a national R&R policy since 1994, and the policy has undergone several rounds of revision in 1997, 2003 and 2007. During this period, emphasis was laid on making the land acquisition process fair, with adequate compensation, comprehensive R&R benefits, tribal development plan, farmers' consent, importance of social impact assessment and so on.

The first policy on R&R of post-Independence India (Draft National Policy for Resettlement and Rehabilitation of Persons Displaced as a Consequence of Acquisition of Land, 1994) was drafted by the Ministry of Rural Development (Land Resources Department). Following the initiative of the Ministry of Rural Development, it put moral obligations on other ministries to draft their respective R&R policies to address the problems of involuntary displacement, such as draft national Policy for Resettlement and Rehabilitation of Persons Affected by Reservoir Projects of 1994 by the Ministry of Water Resources, Resettlement and Rehabilitation Policy of 1993 by National Thermal Power Corporation, Resettlement and Rehabilitation Policy by Coal India Limited and so on.

Despite its social imperatives, the National Rehabilitation and Resettlement Plan was found inadequate to protect the rights of the displaced people. It did not clearly identify the actual figures while providing for the consent of people required, amount of compensation to be paid, and identification of directly and indirectly project-affected people. It could only initiate superficial changes in the existing law without translating them into real safeguards against displacement (Kujur, 2005: 138–151; Asian Indigenous & Tribal Peoples Network, 2006).

The landmark RFCTLARR Act of 2013 corrected the historical injustice embedded in the LA Act of 1894 and completed the unfinished task of filling the gaps left by earlier R&R policies. The new law clearly testifies to the balancing act of the UPA government by incorporating concrete provisions in law. First, to check the rigours of forcible acquisition, the requirement of the consent of 80 per cent of affected families in case of private sector projects and 70 per cent in case of PPP projects was made mandatory. The figures amount to a large majority of affected families and in a way legitimizes land acquisition through popular majority will. The second most marked feature of the Act was the identification of rural occupational groups under social impact assessment. These were artisans, labourers, sharecroppers, tenant farmers, fishermen and small traders. This is in contrast with the earlier plans that confined the identification to farmers or agricultural labourers. The compensation revisions adequately incurred the loss borne by the affected families. The new compensation figures amounted to four times the market rate of the land in rural areas and two times that in urban centres. This is in stark contrast with the compensation being arbitrarily decided by the government under the LA Act of 1894. Finally, the Act placed the onus of accountability on the head of the department (RFCTLARR, 2013). However, the rationality of multiplying the circle rate by four or two times has not been defined, nor whether this achieves the objective of discovering the correct market value of land. The RFCTLARR Act of 2013 is a marked improvement upon the earlier policies for land use. The law clearly strikes to achieve a balance between the industrialization and infrastructural drive of the government and legitimate compensation for the displaced people.

This chapter demonstrates some of the salient aspects of the land acquisition and resource development debate and the complexities in determination of compensation payments. The Indian experience reflects that, so far, the existing provisions for determination of compensation have not been adequate, and this has been repeatedly challenged in the court of law. Also, with regard to resource development, the multidimensional aspects of compensation have not been taken into account while designing the compensation package. The Singrauli case selected for the study substantiates this argument – how the individuals and the resource-rich region have been neglected in this growth process in the name of 'public purpose' or 'national interest'.

Policy Shift towards Benefit Sharing: MMDR Act of 2015

Mineral-rich states, for instance, Madhya Pradesh, Jharkhand and Odisha, have been in discussion with the Central Finance Commission, and there has been a long-standing demand that the centre should propose a 'fairer' revenue-sharing mechanism to compensate for the social and environmental externalities that these regions encounter. Civil society and advocacy groups in India such as Samatha, Centre for Science and Environment (CSE), and The Energy and Resources Institute (TERI) have had similar opinions, and they also represented these concerns at several forums. During the UPA regime, between 2006 and 2010, there have been series of deliberations at the Ministry of Mines to draft a new Mines and Minerals (Development and Regulation) Bill (MMDR Bill) to replace the MMDR Act of 1957. In 2010, the Group of Ministers (GoM) gave recommendations on various issues, including benefit sharing, and suggested an amount equivalent to the royalty paid during that financial year for major minerals – like coal and lignite – an amount equal to 26 per cent of the profit after tax. This proposition was unanimously opposed by the industrial groups (including Coal India Limited) arguing on the premise that such propositions will make the projects financially unviable.

In 2011, the MMDR Bill detailed the provisions of sharing mining benefits through a District Mineral Foundation (DMF) under Section 9B, but the bill lapsed in February 2014. Under the BJP-ruled government in January 2015, the MMDR amendment ordinance was introduced, which revised several provisions of the 2011 Bill, including the cut-down amount in the share of money that mining leaseholders will pay to the DMF, that is, not exceeding one-third of the royalty paid for respective minerals. In 2015, the Indian parliament passed the MMDR Act, and the centre specified that mining companies will pay 10 per cent of the royalty paid to the state government to the DMF for the mining lease granted on or after 12 January 2015 and declared a cut-off date and 30 per cent of the royalty for the lease granted before the cut-off date. Simultaneously, the Government of India also introduced a Pradhan Mantri Khanij Kshetra Kalyan Yojna (PMKKKY) in September 2015 and aligned it to the DMF guiding fund utilization. PMKKKY clearly indicates the categories of development projects in high priority as well as low priority areas and instructs the utilization of funds in a specified manner to benefit the people in mining-affected areas. However, the case study of Singrauli indicates that at the ground level, DMF is experiencing several challenges in terms of its actual objectives. The case study of Singrauli has been discussed in Chapter 8.

In two financial years (2016–2017 and 2017–2018), approximately ₹58 billion has been collected under DMF trusts in various mining districts. However, the potential corpus is even higher as certain states are still in the process of establishing DMFs. Undoubtedly, the fund will be a boon for some of India's poorest and most underdeveloped districts, many of which are in the country's top mining states. In India's top three mining states – Odisha, Jharkhand and Chhattisgarh – nearly 40 per cent of the people live below the poverty line. Many districts in these states, also identified as backward districts by the NITI Aayog (NITI stands for National Institution for Transforming India), fare very poorly in terms of human development indicators such as nutrition and health, mortality rate, access to clean water, sanitation, education and so on. These three states alone account for close to 70 per cent of the total money deposited in DMFs so far. Coal mining districts, such as Korba, Angul and Dhanbad, have the most significant shares of DMF funds, followed by some of the major iron ore mining districts such as Kendujhar, West Singbhum and Dantewada.

Besides fund inflows to DMF trusts, two determining factors related to DMF implementation are the institutional arrangements of DMFs and the planning and allocations for DMF funds. On both these fronts, the progress in most districts is still at the inception stages. In case of the institutional set-up, while most districts have identified the DMF body members of the governing council and managing committees – the administration is dominated by government officials with poor representation of people. DMFs are functioning without a fixed administrative set-up, such as an office for planning and coordination, relying on intermittent meetings of the DMF body. However, the encouraging part is that some key mining districts and states do recognize the need for this and are working on it; at the time of the report, 20 districts were in the process of implementing this.

Another important issue is ensuring accountability of the institution. For DMFs, this entails registration of the trust under the appropriate law and authorities. But the approach towards this has been mixed so far, largely due to lack of clarity on the appropriate registration mechanism.

Part II
Case Study

6

Singrauli

A 'Space' of Dependence

Resource Development and Regional Economy

The 'space' of Singrauli is 'blessed' with abundant natural resources, and the extraction of coal started during the colonial period. The capitalist class was familiar with these geographical strategic advantages and the potential benefits that could be derived from this region. From a political and economy point of view, it will be relevant to analyse the course of resource development in this region post-Independence and how the state–market nexus plays out in resource development projects. Historical discourse reflects how, during the post-Independence period, much before liberalization or introduction of a new economic policy in India, the state–market operated, economic powers influenced state policies and the path of resource development (Bardhan, 1997), and the 'public purpose' clause in the Land Acquisition (LA) Act of 1894 has been misused for serving 'private' interests. The chapter also demonstrates how certain resource-rich spaces, for instance, Singrauli, become a 'space of dependence' to serve public or national interest by largely neglecting regional costs and local development. Moreover, it is the people in such regions who bear such 'costs' (social and environmental) and subsidize the cost of resource development.

Political Economy of Singrauli: Initial Transition

During the late 1950s, Chaudhary Charan Singh – a renowned Indian political leader – for the very first time raised his concerns over the relationship between the state government of Uttar Pradesh (UP) and the Birlas (a known Indian corporation close to Gandhi) regarding the potential benefits and use of generated hydroelectric power from the Rihand Dam and the issue of prioritizing industry over agriculture, considering the status of Indian farmers and needs of the society at that time. It was Charles Betelheim who, in the early 1960s, suggested that in India, the central government was largely under the control of a national capitalist class, while the states were dominated by landed interests. In 1962, while inaugurating the Rihand Dam, Jawaharlal Nehru, in his speech, said, 'Singrauli will one day become Switzerland of India.' Thousands of people from the Singrauli region gathered to welcome Nehru, with the ray of hope that millions of families who lost their lands and livelihoods for the dam and reservoir will one day benefit as it was a project in 'public interest' and that the upcoming thermal power and mining projects in Singrauli will lead to regional development and transform their lives.

In my interview[1] with Paul Brass, he recalled his personal discussions with Charan Singh in the 1960s, 'that the issues between him and Dr. Sampurnanand [then Chief Minister of U.P.] on these arrangements reflect fundamental differences in their respective assessments of the needs of the country, whether its salvation lay in improving agricultural practices and increasing production or in industrial development'. Charan Singh opens his analysis of the issues concerning the Birlas by remarking that 'the Chief Minister has a somewhat soft corner for big industrialists'. For a long period, Charan Singh and others opposed Sampurnanand in his continuance as chief minister alleging that he was favouring the Birlas on 'the matter of the rate at which electric power from the Rihand River project is being made available to the Birlas'. In a letter to the chief minister in April 1959, 46 Congressmen had objected to the proposed arrangement with the Birlas and called for a discussion on the issue, which Sampurnanand ignored. Charan Singh was bluntly opposing the favouritism shown to big industrialists and the construction of big dams, in the Singrauli case, especially to what he considered the misuse of its electricity production to serve the needs of a private aluminium factory – which immediately absorbed one-third of the entire output of the Rihand Dam when it began to produce – a supply that Charan Singh, of course, thought should be made available to the farmers instead. Indeed, alone in the government, though he was the revenue minister at the time, he opposed supplying 'any energy at all to the Aluminium Factory'.[2]

Document analysis of a dossier prepared by Charan Singh and an interview with Paul Brass indicate that there were different views within the government for the diversion of electricity to the Birlas' aluminium factory. The correspondence made by Charan Singh further noted,

> As for the second example [of the chief minister's fondness for big industrialists]: on February 9 [1959] the Chief Minister wanted the Cabinet to commit itself to

---

[1] Interview, Paul Brass, March 2010 and 2012, Singrauli, during his visit to Singrauli.

[2] Note for the Council of Ministers concerning the 'All[o]cation of Rihand Power to Aluminium Factory, from Ram Sahay, Secretary, Electricity Department (Vidyut Vibhag), dated 11 March 1959'.

> supplying more than 50,000 kilowat[t]s of electrical energy from the Rihand Dam to Messer Birla for running an aluminium plant of 20,000-ton capacity merely on the basis of a verbal reference. The item had not been included in the agenda; no note on the subject had been circulated. I held the portfolio of power, but had not been consulted and was completely in the dark. Allocation of electric energy to the Birlas from the Rihand Power Project is an important matter.... The project is now expected to produce 103,000 kilowatts of energy.... With the commitments already made to Madhya Pradesh, the Railways, the Churk Factory and the Soda Ash Factory of the Sahu Jains at Varanasi there were hardly 50,000 k.ws available. This entire balance of about 50 per cent was sought to be allocated to the Birlas. People in eastern and central districts of the State have been fed on promises of plenty, when the Rihand materialized, for the last twelve years or so.... However, before the energy could actually be produced, we have so disposed things that not a single unit will be available for public use or for small enterprises. (Brass, 2012: 37)

Charan Singh's statement on this and related matters continues at length. He challenges the arguments in favour of the factory – that it will provide employment to many persons – noting that it would provide employment for no more than 5,000 persons. He argues further that it is misleading to make the argument, which was part of the justification for the award of so much power to the Birlas, that, otherwise, it would go 'unutilized'. Charan Singh, of course, ridicules this argument because of its total neglect of the needs of the cultivators for electric power, not to mention the needs even of 'big cities like Allahabad, Lucknow and Kanpur', all situated within the potential range of the Rihand Dam project. He goes on further about the favouritism shown to the Birlas on the matter of rates (Brass, 2012).

> Government has undertaken to sell energy to the Birlas at the rate of Rs. 150 per k.w. per year and, in justification, the Chief Minister has pleaded that, in as much as electricity is used as raw material in the manufacture of aluminium, Birlas wanted cheap power. That there will be no loss to the public exchequer inasmuch as the cost works out at Rs. 148 per k.w. and we will be getting Rs.150 from the Birlas.... Now, taxation of the public with a view to putting up long-term projects largely for the benefit of one big industrialist or two on a No Profit-No Loss basis can never be accepted as sound public policy. We ourselves are taking huge loans, sometimes, at more than 4 per cent and realize 5.5 per cent from the cultivators for takavi loans, which we advance to them. (Ibid.: 37–38)

Charan Singh then goes on to make his own calculations of the financial outcome of such favouritism to the Birlas, concluding that the result would be 'a permanent loss of Rs. 13.75 lakh per year' and that, according to other calculations ha has made, the Birlas would be getting a virtual 'subsidy of Rs. 39.60 lakhs a year' by one calculation and as much as 'Rs. 52.25 lakhs' by another calculation (ibid.: 39).

Charan Singh comes then once again to the issue of the needs of industrial development weighed against those of the cultivators. 'Aluminium', he says, 'may be important but in no case as important as agriculture.'[3] Moreover, if subsidies are to be granted to any enterprise, they ought to be provided 'to the cultivators instead of the industrial magnates'. When confronted with this argument during a no-confidence motion in the legislature, the chief minister replied 'that, if necessary, we will reduce the tube-well rates so as to bring them in line with the rates of the aluminium factory'. Charan Singh gave short shrift to this idea in his statement.

> This means that the Birlas have to be helped at any cost, for it is not the rate of Birlas, which can be increased. If the tube-well rates are to be reduced, they should be reduced on merits. But in as much as the Chief Minister intends to reduce the rate because the rates to the Birlas are lower, the State Government is likely to suffer further loss of lakhs and crores, of rupees for the sake of the Birlas. (Brass, 2012: 40–41)

Charan Singh's statement continues relentlessly, exposing in further details the inequities involved in relation to the needs of the cultivators and the state exchequer, the extraordinary extent to which the government had gone to satisfy the Birlas, including a provision in the agreement that would allow them on short notice to increase the amount of power reserved for them 'up to a total of 110,000 k.ws' (ibid.: 43).

Nothing, however, could stop the UP government from going forward with the agreement with the Birlas, which was signed and sealed on 29 October 1959[4], nor, though he never prevailed, did Charan Singh ever stop condemning the agreement or seeking to find ways of altering it. Thus, in 1965, when he was home hinister in the government of Sucheta Kripalani, he reviewed the matter again in a brief note in which he noted, among other features of the agreement, that 'we allowed perhaps 50 per cent of the energy to this big firm of industrialists with the result that, looking to our other commitments which had already been made, little or no energy was left for consumption by the public'. Further, he calculated that the 'total loss' to the exchequer would ultimately come to 'about twenty crores'.[5]

---

[3] In fact, Charan Singh was against the whole idea of allowing an aluminium factory at Rihand at all, arguing correctly – it seems to me – that the enormous requirements for both water and power that are involved in aluminium production far outweigh any advantages for a developing country short of power for other needs.

[4] Articles of agreement was signed on 29 October 1959 by Ram Sahay, Secretary to Govt, Power Department, and K. M. Srivastava on behalf of the Hindustan Aluminium Corporation Ltd. The corporation was thereafter generally referred to in government documents as HINDALCO.

[5] Note of CCS to MM (Sucheta Kripalani), 22 September 1965.

Analysis of the documents reflects the association between state representatives and the capitalist class in the earlier decades of the planning process. The discourse over construction of the Rihand Dam and its initial objective under public purpose and the actual realization of benefits by the Birlas clearly demonstrates the state–capital nexus and how policies are framed in private interests. In studying the discourse on Singrauli, a relationship can be drawn between the initial developments (in the 1960s) and the recent development (2008) of reorganization of space or redrawing of geographical boundaries of the Singrauli region for the private-driven motives. The state has always travelled that extra mile in facilitating private investments. There are a few things that have remained constant during this 'development' discourse since the 1960s the people of Singrauli have been bearing this significant 'cost' for development in national interest and neither the people nor the region have benefitted from the resource development projects. The state-mediated transfer of land at cheap rates and several tax/industrial benefits have fuelled the growth of private corporations with limited benefits in public interest.

Land Acquisition and Displacement Experience, 1960–2015

In discussions of 'involuntary' displacement caused due to the setting up of megaprojects and their traumatic impact on the affected people, the Singrauli region stands out in its intensity of land/homestead acquisitions, diversion of forestland for industrial use and displacement spread over five decades. As the Singrauli region is difficult to approach by road or train, its inaccessibility and geographical remoteness has been one of the factors for not drawing many civil society groups to take up the cause of the affected people. In the 1980s, there was some dissent against the mass displacement of people, mainly from a few civil society groups from Delhi, the leading one being Lokayan, under the leadership of (late) Smithu Kothari. It formed an activist group in Singrauli, known as the Singrauli Jan Lok Hit Samiti, which mainly drew attention of policymakers, non-governmental organizations (NGOs), academics and even the World Bank to the plight of people displaced in the region on a massive scale due to various megaprojects.

Extensive literature (Kothari, 1988, 1996; Reddy, 1994; Sharma, 2003, 2009; Dana, 2003; Cernea, 1999a, 2000a, 2002; Mathur, 2011; Porwal and Singh, 2011; Sharma and Singh, 2009) on the issues related to involuntary displacement has largely recorded the adverse socio-economic impacts on the affected people. The earlier phase of displacement (until the 1970s) was marked by meagre compensations towards the losses and minimal understanding of resettlement and rehabilitation (R&R) of the affected people. However, people surrendered their lands and homesteads under the notion that a few have to suffer for the general public cause. Nevertheless, in the recent phase, there is more awareness and consciousness about rights, and there is a significant change at the policy level.

Singrauli Land Acquisition Phases

In order to discuss the emerging situation in the Singrauli region, it is important to go back to the historical experiences of people in this region who have faced repeated displacement and acquisition of their properties for various megaprojects for over five decades. Their experiences have taken place over three phases: the setting up of the Govind Ballabh Pant Sagar (GBPS) reservoir and the Rihand Dam by displacing people from 146 villages, including acquisition of their lands for the purpose (1960–1970); the setting up of various mega thermal power projects (since the 1980s), followed by coal mining from nine coal mines and, in the process, acquiring lands of 20,504 title-holders (several of them facing displacement for the second time); and finally, thc most recent phase of land acquisition that started very recently, 2008 onwards, where five more super thermal power projects and five coal-mining projects, all in the private sector, are in the process of being set up and have resulted in further acquisition of 15,000 acres of land and displacement of around 10,000 families in the region (Singh, 2015: fieldwork data, 2015; see Table 6.1).

The First Phase: Rihand and Displacement, the 1960s

Construction of the Rihand Dam and the GBPS reservoir was the first 'development project' in the Singrauli region aimed at dcvcloping this backward region. The construction started in 1954 and it was inaugurated by Nehru in 1962. The reservoir covers an area of 457.65 square kilometres, of which 343.95

Table 6.1 Singruali land acquisition phases

Land acquisition period	*Nature of project*	*Developer*	*Institution*	*Number of villages affected (approx.)*
First Phase, 1960–1970	Dam and reservoir	UPSEB	State government	146
Second Phase, 1980–1990	Thermal power plants and coal mining	NTPC and NCL	Central government (PSUs)	81
Third Phase, 2008–2012	Thermal power plants and coal mining	Reliance, Essar, Hindalco, Jay Pee, Mahan, etc.	Private sector	35

Source: Singh (2015: fieldwork data, district administration, June 2015).

square kilometres are in Dudhi *tehsil* of Sonebhadra district of UP and 113.70 square kilometres are in Singrauli district of MP. The water storage capacity of the reservoir (between 235.60 and 267.52 metres) is 79.3 million metric tons. It has the potential of generating 105,000 kilowatts of power at 100 per cent load factor. But at 50–60 per cent load factor, the hydel project could generate a maximum of 250,000 kilowatts of electricity at the water level of 237.52 metres (Planning Commission, 1962) and supply 200 megawatts of electricity to eastern UP. This project has served the needs of local industries and provided employment opportunities, leading to a large influx of population from neighbouring states. Such development has also resulted in resource exploitation, environmental degradation, soil erosion and displacement of approximately 146 villages in the Singrauli region (Lokayan, 1985).

In 1958, government issued the land acquisition notice to vacate 146 villages, but neither the local administration nor the local people took it seriously for about two years (ibid.). In 1960, suddenly, evacuation notices were issued and an announcement was made by loudspeaker to vacate the villages that would come under submergence. Officials were not entrusted with the task of devoting adequate time in the villages. Moreover, proper psychological or social help was not extended to the oustees who became ecological refugees on their own land. People thought thinking that it was similar to the notice of 1958, but the situation suddenly turned and water from the *bandh* (reservoir) was released in a short spell of time and created havoc. People were not able to even carry their valuables and their cattle with them.[6] There was considerable loss of life and property, and there is no record of where thousands of families have finally moved.

Compensation

Analysis of records[7] from the revenue offices and field interviews reflects that government fixed the compensation rate at 30 times higher than the *lagan*[8] of the land. The compensation rate was fixed such that the landowners and the landless displaced families would be provided 5 and 3 acres of land respectively but without *patta* (land registration deed). At that time, the population in the region was not very high and the government owned large tracts of deforested land, so land for land was a relatively feasible option for the government. In the absence of a

[6] Interview, PAP Gm first phase.

[7] The first phase records were collected from revenue offices, and land notices were collected from the PAPs.

[8] *Lagan* was a system of revenue collection in British India, which was based on the agricultural produce of a particular piece of land.

rehabilitation policy, people accepted the meagre amount of compensation which was not adequate even to construct a new house. Field interviews suggest that even to this day, more than 60 per cent of the Rihand oustess do not have *patta*, and they express lack of resources and awareness as reasons for non-registration of these lands in their name. And in cases[9] where these parcels of land are getting acquired for private sector projects in recent years (third phase), they are deprived of any compensation for it, as the government considers it as revenue land. However, there is no proper record available in the government department about the status of the displaced families. Field interviews and group discussions on the first phase of the project-affected persons (PAPs) suggest that around 60 per cent of the Rihand oustees got resettled by themselves along the shore of the Rihand reservoir (northern stretch) only to be displaced again during the setting up of the super thermal power projects by the National Thermal Power Corporation Limited (NTPC), 20 per cent of the oustees moved to the adjoining districts of Sarguja and Mandla in search of arable and forestland, and there is no record of the remaining 20 per cent of the oustees (Jan Lok Hit Samiti, n.d.; Kothari, 1988). Thus, it was difficult to trace these families and their settlements in Singrauli. From good farmers, many of them have been turned into contract labourers. This situation prevails for the oustees and displaced people who have lost everything in the name of so-called development. Displacement has taken place in manifold forms. Many of the families have faced multiple displacements: twice and thrice. According to Hardikar (n.d.), over 0.2 million people have been displaced due to the dam/reservoir, mining, and thermal power projects in Singrauli. He quotes Dana, a US attorney with the Centre for International Law, who has closely monitored developments in Singrauli, especially the role of the World Bank. 'The story of the suffering of the villagers in Singrauli is shocking and should lead to a comprehensive review of people whose lives have been destroyed in the name of development' (ibid.). In contrast, in recent years (in the last 10 years or so), due to spirited protests by affected people and civil society groups, like the National Alliance for People's Movement (NAPM), the situation has changed considerably and no project, whether in the public or private sector, can escape its responsibilities towards the affected people (Sharma and Singh, 2009). In order to analyse the actual socio-economic situation of these displaced families, a detailed field survey was conducted in the region.

[9] Interview, (PAP OBCm first phase) Nahar (88), case of 12 acres of land in Sidhikhurd village which was acquired by the MP government for the Reliance project; no compensation was paid for the parcels of land that were allotted to him under the Rihand project.

The Second Phase of Development and Displacement, the 1980s

The abundance of water in the GBPS reservoir and a long stretch of open coalfields – spread over 2,200 square kilometres – were favourable for setting up super thermal power projects in the region. It turned out to be a curse, however, for the people who had not even recovered from the earlier trauma of losing lands and homesteads for the dam and reservoir project. NTPC proposed several super thermal power projects in the Singrauli region (between 1977 and 1990) and the state governments of Madhya Pradesh (MP) and UP acquired land under the LA Act of 1894 for 'public purpose' to set up the Singrauli Super Thermal Power Project (SSTPP) followed by the Vindhyachal Super Thermal Power Project (VSTPP) and the Rihand Super Thermal Power Project (RSTPP). Also, the Uttar Pradesh State Electricity Board (UPSEB) set up its own plant at Anpara (part of the Singrauli region). These projects, in turn, initiated the coal mining projects in nine open coal mines, owned by the NCL (Northern Coalfields Limited).

The land acquired by state governments on behalf of NTPC in the Singrauli region fell into one of the following land tenure categories: private, government, forest, revenue forest and submergence lands. In all the three projects, state governments had acquired the land much before the thermal power plants were constructed. In Vindhyachal, as a result, some land that was acquired in the mid 1980s was not required until 2010 for project purposes. In PAPs' opinion,[10] it was unfair to hold the land for more than 30 years on the previously acquired land rate and not allow PAPs to benefit from the enhanced land rate. For the Stage 4-ash dyke development (part of VSTPP), NTPC acquired 500 acres of land at a significantly high rate[11] in 2013. This justifies the intention of project developers to acquire more land than actual requirement, which could be used for future expansion of projects at low costs. However, it denies the opportunity for the landowners to benefit from the hike in land prices.

One significant entitlement issue with regard to land acquisition in the Singrauli region was the legal status of PAPs who had cultivated the forestlands that were acquired for the projects. As discussed earlier, the LA Act of 1894 only recognized legal title-holders to be entitled for compensation and, hence, occupants on forest and government lands were excluded from receiving compensation. A local NGO, Banwasi Sewa Ashram, filed a writ petition in the Supreme Court on behalf of affected PAPs claiming that they should be entitled to receive compensation. The

---

[10] Interview, PAP Gm second phase.

[11] According to the revenue department, in 2013, NTPC acquired 500 acres of land at ₹2 million per hectare, which is significantly high as compared to the 1980 rate, that is, ₹32,000 per hectare.

Supreme Court in 1992 decided that forestland cultivators who lost land for the project should be considered as landowners and be adequately compensated and rehabilitated. The Court also directed NTPC to employ the displaced people, subject to the availability of employment at the thermal power stations, and also to create self-employment opportunities for their benefit so that they could improve their standard of living. The landmark judgment[12] clearly shows the constitutional rights of an oustee to not only obtain compensation but also receive the benefits of development from the projects that displace them.

Between 1980 and 1990, the three NTPC projects led to the acquisition of 14,133 acres of land, displacing 6,388 families (see Table 6.2). Several families were facing displacement for the second time. The detailed break-up of families/landowners affected under the thermal power and mining projects is given in Table 6.3. The nine coal mining projects by NCL led to the further acquisition of approximately 35,000 acres of land and displacement of around 6,175 families (NCL files). The concerned state governments decided the rates of compensation using the methodology provided in the LA Act for the acquired land and other payments associated with the land (house, well, trees, land development and so on). The compensation rate per acre of land in the Singrauli Thermal Power Project (the oldest one) area ranged from ₹4,500 to ₹6,000. In Rihand and Vindhyachal project areas, the rates varied from ₹7,700 to ₹13,000 per acre for agricultural land and ₹1,000 to ₹20,000 for a homestead area depending on the size and type of construction (Revenue Department, Singrauli). In addition, solatium and interest on compensation (from the day of acquisition until the day of payment) were also paid to the 'property losers'.[13]

Employment

As evident from the data (see Table 6.4), only the coal mines performed better in offering total employment to the affected people, primarily because of the availability of unskilled and semi-skilled jobs. However, as far as offering regular jobs was concerned, the thermal power projects were able to accommodate only 10 per cent of the total oustees. Thus, out of some 11,500 oustees under all the mega power projects, only about 1,050 got regular jobs in those projects. Repeatedly, the PAPs represented their case to the World Bank, and the GHK/MRM Singrauli study was one of the several efforts on the part of the World Bank to improve the conditions of the land oustees. The idea of developing the whole region, along with PAPs, did not take off due to the lack of cooperation by the UP and MP

[12] *Banwasi Sewa Ashram vs State of UP*, AIR 1992 SC 920.
[13] NTPC reports and interview, R&R officer, NTPC.

Table 6.2 Land acquired for NTPC projects (in acre)

Project name	*Private*	*Government*	*Forest*	*Submergence*	*Total*
Singrauli	2,313	2,440	—	—	4,753
Vindhyachal	4,136	721	—	1,281	6,178
Rihand	832	513	1,089	768	3,202
Total	7,281	3,674	1,089	2,049	14,133

Source: NTPC files.

state governments. A few programmes were finally initiated by the respective power projects' managements for the oustees, such as offering loans, giving labour contracts to cooperatives of the oustees, providing opportunities for skill upgradation and environmental improvement in resettlement colonies. However, all these fell short of creating a sustainable source of livelihood for a majority of PAPs. The syndrome of 'regular jobs in the project and nothing less' gripped the PAPs in the Singrauli area, as elsewhere. That is, those PAPs who did not get regular jobs in these projects continued agitation for years. The hope of a regular job in these projects prevented them from searching for other means of livelihood.[14]

People protests and civil society interventions compelled the World Bank to constitute an Independent Monitoring Panel (IMP) to investigate the Singrauli projects and directed NTPC to prepare a more comprehensive and pragmatic 'rehabilitation action plan' for the affected people. It also commissioned the previously discussed study (GHK/MRM International, 1994; see Table 6.4) for preparing a detailed development plan not only for the affected people but for the region as a whole (then under the jurisdiction of Special Area Development Authority), including 8 towns and over 100 villages. The idea was that only a two-pronged strategy of developing the region and the affected people would make it a sustainable approach.[15] As discussed earlier, the GHK/MRM Singruali study

Table 6.3 Number of PAPs

Project name	*Total*
Singrauli	1,755
Vindhyachal	3,311
Rihand	1,322
Total	6,388

Source: NTPC files.

[14] Interview, R. N. Sharma, Tata Institute of Social Sciences (TISS), Mumbai.

[15] Interview, World Bank official and Singrauli social cctivist.

Table 6.4 Details of employment opportunities provided to the PAPs

Project	*Total number of land oustees*	*Permanent employment*	*Contract labour*	*Shops allotted*	*Total employment*
NCL	6,175	3,360	—*	—*	3,360
SSTPP	1,457	400	527	29	947
VSTPP	7,014	244	658	21	923
RSTPP	1,689	125	350	22	497
UPSEB (Anpara)	1,307	233	300	7	540
UPSEB (Obra)	229	161	—*	—*	161
MGR	2,633	—**	—**	—**	–
Total	13,865	4,523 (34)	1,831 (13)	74 (1)	6,428 (48)

Source: GHK/MRM International (1994).

Notes: * No provision to offer contract labour jobs or allot shops to oustees.

** Invariably these oustees are not entitled to jobs due to loss of a small amount of land.

Figures in parentheses indicate percentages.

brought out the status of jobs (regular or contractual) offered by various projects (up to 1993) to the PAPs.

Compensation Bias in R&R

Disbursement of one-time compensation under the provisions of the LA Act of 1894 was perceived as the most convenient option for the developers as part of fulfilment of their responsibility, as R&R is a slow and continuous process that requires sustained efforts over a period of time. NTPC paid inadequate attention to the PAPs' livelihood rehabilitation, although it was a key component of NTPC's R&R policy. Instead, it focused on compensation rates and various compensation packages to satisfy the World Bank as well as the PAPs.[16] Until 1995, it did not have a 'Resettlement and Rehabilitation Unit' in its Delhi corporate office or an R&R cell in each thermal power project. Thus, for more than 25 years, it did not consider resettlement to be an important component of project planning and management, although some resettlement guidelines were prepared as early as 1980. NTPC's engineering bias in project planning and management was also one of the reasons behind its failure to understand the social and cultural issues in the R&R planning process.

In 1995, NTPC for the first time appointed sociologists to each project (on the advice of the World Bank) to assist the implementation of the 1995 revised

16 Interview, ex-NTPC employees, Vindhyachal and Rihand.

Rehabilitation Action Plan. The sociologists were casual employees of the NTPC with fixed low wages. In each project, the post of senior manager/manager of the R&R cell is still reserved for an engineer. Although R&R managers possess good knowledge of social structure and organization, their lack of training in sociological and anthropological disciplines makes them poor social scientists.[17] This is quite conspicuous in the manner they handle R&R issues and in their attitudes towards the PAPs. NTPC's field staff feel that the PAPs should be grateful to them for their hard work and commitment to helping them. Senior managers at the corporate and project offices believe that NTPC has done more than it should have to compensate the PAPs. The field staff members at Vindhyachal and Rihand, for instance, display a sense of hurt and hopelessness over the attitudes of the PAPs towards the NTPC personnel. They tried to avoid confrontations with the PAPs and accusations from NGOs and the World Bank.[18]

NGOs and rural activists also contributed to the 'compensation' bias in the resettlement process. Many of them believed that high compensation would help the PAPs to improve their living standard and did 'fight' for higher compensation rates. As a result, on the one hand, they hardly show any interest in income rehabilitation strategies or in helping the PAPs to develop such strategies. For instance, they could have helped in identifying suitable land to purchase and suggested some investment programmes. On the other hand, 'adversarial relationships' the local and international NGOs maintain with project personnel often revolve around compensation rates as found in the petition submitted by a social activist[19] to the World Bank Inspection Panel on behalf of the PAPs.[20]

Compensation, Income Restoration and Poverty Issues

Resettlement policies, in general, emphasize the need for at least restoring the pre-displacement income and living standards of the PAPs (World Bank, 2001). Although resettlement agencies often take this policy to mean the payment of 'reasonable' compensation for the acquired property, in recent years, however, governments as well as some resettlement agencies have recognized the need for restoration of pre-displacement income levels of the PAPs. In most cases, on the one hand, this recognition is directly related to the loan covenants as international donors emphasize income restoration as part of resettlement. On the other hand,

[17] Interview, Prof. R. N. Sharma, TISS, Mumbai.

[18] Interview, R&R officers, NTPC.

[19] Madhu Kohli, an independent lawyer, submitted a petition to the World Bank regarding the inadequacy of compensation and rehabilitation of Singrauli's PAFs.

[20] Interview, R&R manager of NTPC.

project managers agree to include income restoration as a part of compensation packages mainly to avoid resistance from the PAPs as well as NGOs and activists. The agreement between NTPC and IMP on enhanced compensation for Singrauli project-affected families (PAFs) illustrates the practice (World Bank, 2001). Moreover, courts and human rights commissions also direct the projects to compensate the PAPs and also to provide them with employment.

After 1993, economic rehabilitation of the PAPs became a 'developmental' issue in the Singrauli region under the new R&R policy of NTPC. The policy prescribes that the PAPs are entitled to R&R packages in addition to compensation, at least to restore their livelihoods. However, in practice, on the one hand, the project personnel believe that the large amount of money given as 'compensation' is sufficient for the PAPs to restart their life at a higher income level than what they had in the pre-displacement phase. On the other hand, the PAPs still think[21] that they are entitled to some 'lump sum' money from NTPC because they have been displaced. Their negotiations with NTPC and their resistance to surrendering land were mainly to get a better compensation package for their lost lands, houses, employment and sociocultural 'disturbances' caused by the projects. These divergent views reconfirm the prevailing belief that compensation is central to income restoration.

The confusion over 'compensation' and 'rehabilitation' arises from the practice of using land ownership as the basis for calculating an economic rehabilitation package (see Table 6.5). The entire rehabilitation policy revolves around land ownership and how to compensate for the acquired land. For instance, NTPC's 1999 Resettlement Action Plans for Stage 2 resettlers consider a landless labourer as an owner of 'less than two acre of land' (see Tables 6.5 and 6.6). In other words, according to the plan, a landless labourer and a landowner who owns less than 2 acres are entitled to the same package. Although in an agrarian society land is the fundamental source of livelihood, this policy tends to emphasize the importance of compensating 'land losses' whether actually owned or not as per revenue records.

Resettlement agencies often find it difficult to provide the PAPs with new livelihoods. For instance, NTPC pointed out its inability to employ[22] all PAPs owing to the non-availability of such work opportunities in large numbers at the thermal power plants. Moreover, state governments of MP and UP could not find suitable land to implement a 'land based' rehabilitation programme. Thus, NTPC was compelled to provide higher cash compensation which covers not only the value of the acquired property but also compensates for its inability to provide or

[21] Interviews, PAP Gm, PAP OBCm and PAP SCm second phase.
[22] Interview, general manager, Human Resource, NTPC, Singrauli.

Table 6.5 Rehabilitation package for Stage 2 PAPs

Land acquired	*Basic grant*	*Solatium (15 %)*	*Registration @ ₹6,000 per acre*	*Land development @ ₹10,000 per acre*
<2 acres	140,000	21,000	12,000	20,000

Source: NTPC files.

find secure income opportunities either through 'land based' strategies or through 'plant based' strategies.

The heavy emphasis on compensation had a negative impact on income restoration and improvement strategies. On the one hand, large amounts of cash as compensation encourage PAPs to live on compensation without actively searching for land to purchase or starting non-farm enterprises for their livelihood. The policy of compensation enhancement has created the impression among the PAPs that they could expect more compensation from NTPC. On the other hand, NTPC has developed a sense of complacency because it granted a large cash sum to each PAP. The minimum award of ₹140,000 would provide a landless labourer in Stage 2 group, according to the resettlement personnel, with adequate means to become a landowner. NTPC field officers pointed out that a landless PAP with his/her compensation money could buy about 6 acres of good-quality land. The field officers know of many landless labourers who have improved their incomes substantially by investing their compensation money in land. However, the irony of both thought processes is that they overlook the high risks PAPs encounter in building up a secure income level in the post-displacement phase and the responsibility of the resettlement agency to plan viable income strategies for the benefit of PAPs.

In this context, it is pertinent to ask how useful a comparison between the pre- and post-displacement income levels of PAPs to judge the success or failure of a resettlement project is. A significant characteristic of the PAP households in the Singrauli region prior to land acquisition was below poverty level subsistence. For example, in Rihand, 41 per cent of PAPs were landless and another 38 per

Table 6.6 Landholding pattern among Rihand PAPs before displacement

Landholding size	*Number of PAPs*	*Percentage*
Landless	465	41
<1 acre	424	38
1–2 acres	131	12
2–5 acres	79	7
>5 acres	18	2
Total	1,117	100

Source: NTPC files.

cent were almost landless (see Table 6.6).[23] If a 2-acre landholding is taken as the minimum size of landholding to produce a subsistence level income, 91 per cent of PAPs then subsisted below the poverty line. A similar pattern of income level was noted in Vindhyachal where 50 per cent of the PAPs were labourers, while another 32 per cent owned less than 2 acres of land. Related to this is the poor quality of land they cultivated as owners and sharecroppers. At the time of land acquisition, an average owner-cultivator could earn a net income of about ₹8,000 in a year from an acre of land if two seasons were cultivated. The most common source of income in this region was hired labour. In the 1980s, an agricultural labourer's average annual income was ₹3,000. In 1999, it was ₹6,000 (at ₹30 a day for 200 days in a year).[24]

The compensation package offered to PAPs far exceeds the replacement value of such holdings or the average income from hired labour. The package included the minimum grant of ₹140,000 paid for any PAP whether he owned land or not. This grant was meant for those who owned less than 2 acres of land and for the landless. Compensation was paid up to 5 acres of land acquired at the basic rate of ₹70,000 per acre. In addition, a PAP was entitled to receive 15 per cent solatium. If he bought land with the grant, then he was entitled to get ₹10,000 per acre to develop the land (NTPC). If a 2-acre compensation was taken as the norm, a landless labour got 30 times his annual income, while a small landowner got 22 times his annual income as compensation. As mentioned earlier, using the basic grant, a PAP could have bought about 5 acres of irrigated land at about ₹12,000 per acre. Thus, if the income levels of PAPs in their pre-displacement phase are taken as the basis for preparing post-displacement income restoration strategies, NTPC could argue that it has not only restored but also provided a sound base for improving their incomes. But in reality, this has not happened in the Singrauli region.

One reason for this failure is the ambiguity in the R&R policy with regard to the core concepts of 'income restoration' and 'income improvement'. The definitions of the two concepts do not specify a clear baseline against which post-displacement actions or strategies could be formulated. This is particularly the case in rural economies where household income cannot be estimated easily due to diversified livelihoods. Social networks, communal subsistence ethics and access to common property resources constitute a substantial part of a household income. The Operation Evaluation Department of the World Bank has summarized some of the ambiguities of the definitions:

---

[23] Socio-economic Survey Report, NTPC.

[24] Focus group discussion (FGD) with second phase PAPs at Navjeevan Vihar, NTPC Resettlement Colony, Singrauli.

> What does 'income restoration' and 'income improvement' mean if the regional economy is deteriorating? When should improvements be expected in remote valleys? Clearer specification of objectives, alternatives, and the time horizon is required for planning, monitoring and evaluation purposes. (McMahon, 1998a, 1998b: 9)

The field experiences and discussions suggest that PAPs tend to use the one-time compensation and rehabilitation allowances for their immediate subsistence during the transition period without making productive investments in land or other livelihood generating activities. In the Singrauli region, for example, PAPs who had received enhanced compensation towards income restoration expected NTPC to provide them with land and employment as well. PAPs pointed out that they want a land-based package with large amounts of money as compensation. If it is possible, they want employment at the plants as unskilled labourers in the coal processing, housekeeping and cleaning activities. Many of them ignored their search for new lands because they did not want to lose the opportunity of getting employment at the power plants. Currently, NTPC Vindhycahal in the Singrauli region permanently employs around 245 PAPs. PAPs prefer NTPC employment to any other rehabilitation package. They pointed out that a regular income from the 'Company' would ensure their children's education, better living standards and job security. Another reason is the dependency syndrome that PAPs experience during the displacement and resettlement phase. Once uprooted from their lands, PAPs tend to develop a strong dependency on the resettlement agency. From their point of view, the resettlement agency has taken control of their lives, property and economic resources. Displacement has severed their family and community networks, social contracts and economic interdependencies.

At the time of acquisition, it was primarily an agrarian society and the only skill they possessed was farming and allied activities. Hence, in the absence of arable land, compensation appears to be the only lifeline for most of the PAPs. One of the PAPs said, 'You cannot expect us to be entrepreneurs overnight and be innovative and enterprising.' These local PAPs became more vulnerable when they had to compete with outsiders who swamped the project sites to grab new business and economic opportunities. The resettlement officials were quick to brand the PAPs as 'lazy', 'illiterate' and 'backward', and the outsiders who arrived to take over new opportunities as 'skilled', 'risk taking' and enterprising. NTPC officials tend to support the latter because they have capital and are willing to get through hardships to survive and make profits.[25] On the other hand, the PAPs often lack the necessary business skills to start small businesses. For example,

[25] Interview, NTPC official, Delhi.

several PAPs rented out to outsiders the shop spaces they had received as part of their compensation package.

Social Protests and World Bank Intervention

During the late 1980s, a few civil society organizations, for instance, Lokayan, under the leadership of Smithu Kothari, Madhu Kohli (an independent lawyer), Upendra Pandey (a local PAP) and others, drew the attention of the World Bank and NTPC to the unfair compensation and dissatisfaction of the PAPs concerning the rehabilitation programme. NTPC, on the recommendation of the World Bank[26] and following its own R&R policy, classified the PAPs in the Singrauli region into two groups: Stage 1 resettlers (those who were resettled before 1993) and Stage 2 resettlers (those who were to be resettled). The PAPs (particularly Stage 1 resettlers) challenged this classification as it was ambiguous and faulty, and this was the main cause of delay in the project and clashes between NTPC and the PAPs that characterized the resettlement process in the Singrauli region. When land was acquired and compensation was paid, there were no two groups[27] of displaced people. All of them (Stages 1 and 2 resettlers) were compensated for their lost property and given land plots at the resettlement colonies to rebuild their houses. About 70 per cent of them moved out of their land at this stage. They are the Stage 1 resettlers. Others remained on their land with the permission of NTPC. NTPC permitted them to stay because it did not immediately need all the acquired land for construction works. Stage 2 resettlers had the additional privilege of cultivating the land for which they had already received compensation. NTPC, according to its R&R policy, carried out retrofit socio-economic surveys in 1993 in order to ascertain the socio-economic conditions of Stage 1 resettlers. Based on the survey findings,[28] the NTPC formulated Remedial Action Plans (ReAPs) for their benefit. The plans consisted of plant-based employment and self-employment schemes (SESs). The plant-based employment strategy did not take off as expected because the power stations did not have sufficient number of vacancies to absorb unskilled workers. But self-employment schemes expanded rapidly since 1995. The establishment of R&R cells at each project and an R&R unit at the NTPC corporate centre in New Delhi contributed to this speeding up of SESs (NTPC Reports).

[26] Interview, World Bank official, Delhi.
[27] Interview, PAP Gm second phase (Stage 1 PAP NTPC).
[28] Interview, R&R officer, NTPC, Delhi.

As mentioned earlier, no additional land was needed to expand the Vindhyachal and Rihand projects as sufficient land had already been acquired and compensated for. However, under the loan agreement, Stage 2 PAPs were to be provided with an attractive cash rehabilitation package to buy new lands. Although this package was a rehabilitation allowance, the NTPC, state administration, many NGOs and PAPs considered it as an enhanced compensation payment.

The shifting of Stage 2 PAPs from the Rihand and Vindhyachal ash pond areas under the 1995 resettlement action plans (RAPs) continued for over a year without much delay. This progress was, however, affected by a case filed by Stage 2 PAPs of the Vindhyachal project at the Jabalpur High Court challenging the adequacy of their compensation package. At that time, 70 per cent of the PAPs who had already left the area and self-settled in faraway places returned to their former lands anticipating that the high court would enhance their compensation as well. The high court, in April 1996, decided that the 1995 package was adequate and fair and ordered the PAPs to shift from the area within a prescribed time period. The PAPs challenged the high court order in the Supreme Court. The Supreme Court dismissed the appeal in early 1997. Subsequent to the Supreme Court judgment, NTPC attempted to coordinate its R&R activities with the district administration in order to remove Stage 2 PAPs from 'its' land. NTPC set up camps to pay the PAPs their compensation. At the same time, it moved bulldozers into the ash pond area to construct and expand ash ponds.

The PAPs, however, with the support of local activists and NGOs, continued to resist relocation. A few activists[29] submitted a petition on behalf of 33 PAPs of Rihand to the World Bank Inspection Panel in April 1997 requesting it to investigate some irregular resettlement actions of NTPC and omissions of the World Bank, which were contrary to the bank's policies and procedures. The inspection panel found that 'many of the displaced people suffered as a result of an alleged failure by the Bank to comply with Operational Directives 4.30' (World Bank, 1997: 13). The panel refrained from commenting on NTPC's resettlement performance. However, the panel requested NTPC and the World Bank to investigate the resettlement programme in order to find ways of improving its performance according to the project loan covenants. In response to the inspection panel's request for a full investigation, NTPC in consultation with the World Bank, in November 1997, appointed a three-member IMP to systematically and regularly review and advise on the implementation of R&R programmes in the Singrauli region. In addition, NTPC appointed a consultant (Xavier Institute of Development Action and Studies) to conduct social impact assessment in

[29] Interview, Singrauli social activists, Udvasit Mazdoor Kisan Samiti, Singrauli.

the Singrauli region. Based on the findings of the impact assessment surveys[30] in 1999, NTPC revised the 1995 ReAPs and RAPs. It reopened the issue of compensation. It reformulated the compensation cum rehabilitation package guidelines, formulae, amounts and the manner of payment. IMP, beyond its terms of reference, negotiated with NTPC and enhanced the compensation cum rehabilitation package for Stage 2 PAPs. But it did not negotiate a rehabilitation package for Stage 1 PAPs, although most of them hardly had any rehabilitation support. One main reason for this was that IMP considered them as 'resettled' who moved out from their lands upon receipt of compensation and land plots to build houses.

Singrauli Second Phase Sum Up

The current legal procedures pertaining to land acquisition also contribute to the 'compensation bias' in resettlement projects. According to the law, the state administration calculates and pays compensation to the property owners who lost land to the project. In this process, there is no direct interaction between PAPs and project developers, although the latter provides the compensation funds. From the state administrator's point of view, the payment of compensation was the end of the displacement and resettlement. Perhaps one reason behind this perception could be that the LA Act of 1894 does not specify rehabilitation needs of the PAPs. Compensation, both legally and socially, has two main functions to fulfil. One is to recognize the private property rights of the citizens. This includes use rights over common property resources such as forests and meadows. Second is rehabilitation – to restore the pre-displacement incomes and living standards of the PAPs. However, in practice, the distinction between these two tends to get blurred. In other words, all support to the PAPs are usually grouped together under the general term 'compensation' and delivered. This accentuates the primacy of compensation payment and diminishes the responsibility of the state and the project developers to rehabilitate the PAPs.

This exercise has highlighted several inconsistencies between the resettlement policy and practice. Although resettlement policies generally pay attention to compensation, relocation and income restoration, in practice, however, compensation takes primacy over the other two in resettlement programmes. This heavy compensation bias sometimes averts opportunities for PAP's social, economic and cultural rehabilitation. As discussed in the experiences of the second phase of displacement in the Singrauli region, compensation packages were adequate to

[30] Interview, GM (R&R), NTPC, Delhi.

restore the pre-displacement income levels of the PAPs or even to improve them if invested in carefully planned income generating programmes. But unfortunately, such programmes do not receive serious attention of the governments, project managers, NGOs and PAPs as all of them are preoccupied with compensation rates and payments. Resettlement agencies tend to think that large compensation packages would redeem them from the responsibility of restoring and improving the well-being of the PAPs. For example, in the Singrauli region, NTPC and IMP as well as NGOs and rural activists so far have focused on compensation; they have not shown serious interest in developing appropriate investment and employment programmes for the benefit of the PAPs. On the other hand, the PAPs for many good reasons depend on the compensation to survive, at least during the initial stage of resettlement, thereby losing the opportunities of investing the money in productive schemes. Also, there has been no assistance in providing financial literacy awareness from the developer or the district administration to productively utilize the compensation. The lack of entrepreneurial skills, difficulties in finding suitable land to purchase, as well as households' characteristics, such as indebtedness, need of large sums of money for weddings, and so on, may exhaust such funds before they are prudently invested. They also tend to think that they can get more compensation for their property. The compensation bias in resettlement programmes not only increases the PAPs' dependency on external agencies but also undermines the urgent need for formulating income restoration strategies for the benefit of the resettlers.

The Third Phase: Private Capital and Redrawing of Geographical Boundaries

The third phase of land acquisition refers to the period after 2008, that is, since the creation of the district. As discussed earlier, Singrauli has always been an important 'space' for the central and state governments due to its resource abundance and geographically strategic location for thermal power generation and coal mining activities. Singrauli, presently contributing more than 13 per cent to the total thermal power generation in the country, provide electricity to some of the major states and union territories: Maharashtra, Punjab, Haryana, Himachal Pradesh, Uttaranchal, Gujarat, Jammu and Kashmir, Delhi, Goa, Daman and Diu, Dadra and Nagar Haveli, and Madhya Pradesh (singrauli.nic.in, ntpc.co.in). It is expected that by 2017, Singrauli itself will supply 35,000 megawatts of electrical power to the grid. Singrauli has a major contribution in revenue generation of the state as well as central governments in the form of royalty, cess and taxes (see Table 7.2). However, approximately 50 per cent of the villages in the region are still not electrified (State Planning Commission, 2012) and half of the region's population still lives below the poverty line (State Planning Commission, 2010).

For the people of Singrauli, there seems to be no end to the displacement they suffer. In fact, the third phase of setting up of mega thermal power and coal-mining projects emerged in 2006, when the state government organized an industrial meet to attract private capital to the Singrauli region. Table 6.7 presents basic information on new projects, which are under different stages of construction. The data shows the proposed addition of over 13,000 megawatts of thermal power generation through the private sector companies in coming years. This is in addition to the execution of the second phase power generation projects, at the existing sites, by NTPC. The new thermal power projects would require over 10,000 acres of private lands and would affect over 5,000 families in Singrauli district (Singh, 2015: fieldwork data, 2015). These are captive thermal power projects with dedicated coal mines in the area, for which the process of land acquisition has already started, and in most cases, the land has already been handed over to the developers. The mining sites are primarily in the forest areas which are inhabited mainly by tribal families who have been staying in these forests for decades, with or without formal titles to their properties. The issue of land acquisition and displacement tends to become more complex in such circumstances. Thus, the Singrauli region has once again turned into a battlefield between the land oustees and project developers, this time mainly private corporations. In 2008, the geographical boundaries of Singrauli were redrawn and a geographical space of around 5,500 square kilometres (out of which 2,200 square kilometres were demarcated for coal mining) was carved out of Sidhi district to provide it the status of an independent district. It clearly demonstrates that the reason behind developing the separate administrative unit of Singrauli was to facilitate the entry of private capital into this region and provide better administrative support to the corporations.

In this 'third' phase of displacement in the region, a significant change is visible. The affected people are no longer 'taken for granted' either by the projects' managements or the government. On the contrary, their entitlements and R&R have become crucial not only for mitigating the adverse impact of these projects on their lives but also for the very success of these projects.Civil society groups and the affected people make this possible through sustained agitation across the country. Those business groups who ignore this changing environment are, in fact, struggling to see their projects take shape. The overall impact of such movements is that the central and state governments have come out with comprehensive R&R policies for mitigating the ill effects of such displacements. Several business groups in the private sector are, in fact, offering generous compensation (and rehabilitation) packages to the oustees, so that the implementation of their projects can proceed

Table 6.7 Thermal power and coal mining projects in Singruali, third phase

Name of the project	*Nature of project*	*Quantum of land acquired (government land + private land)*	*Number of displaced families (or to be displaced)*
Sasan Ultra Mega Power Project (Reliance ADAG)	4,000 MW thermal power plant	3,883 acres	1,079
Mahan Super Thermal Power Project (ESSAR Global)	2,000 MW thermal power plant	1,822 acres	916
Jaypee Power Ventures Ltd Nigri (Jaypee Group)	1,320 MW thermal power plant	855 acres	250
Chitrangi Power Pvt. Ltd. (Reliance ADAG)	4,000 MW thermal power plant	3,000 acres	1,000
Mahan Aluminium and Captive Thermal Power Plant (Hindalco)	900 MW 3.59 lakh tons/annum production	3,517 acres	1,617
Madhya Pradesh Jaypee Minerals (Jaypee Group)	Mining	305 acres	—
Amelia Coal Blocks (Sainik Mines)	Mining	—	—
Reliance Coal Ltd (Amlori Coal Block)	Mining	3,500 acres	1,700

Source: Singh (2015: fieldwork data, 2013).

smoothly. Despite this, however, they are not sure of achieving their objectives.

Considering the experiences of the earlier decades, a Rihand oustee explains, 'Meagre compensations were paid, say Rs. 150 for a "pucca" well or Rs. 5 for a guava tree in the Singrauli area.' In the 1990s itself NTPC and NCL were finding it extremely difficult to acquire lands for the 'merry-go-round' (rail track for carrying coal to plants). The affected PAPs insisted on market-based compensation for lands and a regular job in the project. One can imagine the prevailing situation today in Singrauli where the new thermal power projects are virtually competing with each other to 'win the heart' of the PAPs by offering them generous R&R packages. But how many of these promises are actually delivered and how far they transform the lives of the PAFs still remains a critical question.

In the earlier phases, the affected people (hundreds of them, repeatedly), as a result of the acquisition of their lands and/or homesteads, suffered untold miseries due to a lack of adequate R&R programmes and conflicts between various projects and the people. In fact, there was a major agitation by the people against 'involuntary' displacement due to the mega industrial/infrastructure projects in the Singrauli region. Such agitations have now culminated in a civil society movement all across the country because of such megaprojects emerging all over India, more so under the present paradigm of a market driven economy. This has brought about a distinct awareness among the people against such projects where the sovereign right of the state to acquire properties of citizens for setting up projects in 'public interest' is being challenged by the people and civil society groups. The earlier two phases of displacement in the Singrauli region tell a story of misery and hardships, including the disruption of sources of sustenance for a majority of the affected people. Those few families (around 4,523 against the total displaced families of about 14,000) who got regular jobs, in the 1980s and the 1990s, in the mega thermal power and mining projects, were the lucky ones as against the majority who suffered for decades due to the loss of their lands, the main source of their sustenance.[31]

The recent (third phase) displacement of around 5,000 families who are in process of losing their lands or homesteads for the thermal power projects – to be joined by those families to be affected under the new coal mining projects – comes under a changing legislative environment, where the affected people are 'empowered' through a fairly comprehensive national R&R policy and protests by civil society groups resulting in better bargaining for sources of livelihood. Industrial groups are offering favourable packages, in relation to what has been offered earlier (towards land compensation and R&R), so that their projects do not fizzle out, as is happening in several cases in other parts of the country. However, the 2002 R&R policy of MP raises certain contentious issues about 'entitlements' and the very definition of 'displaced' person/people under various projects. The experience of 'involuntary' displacement in the Singrauli region in the last five decades or so and its consequences for the affected people bring out relevant lessons for future policymaking and for the rights of the affected people. Chapter 7 discusses the socio-economic impact of land acquisition on the project-affected families of the third phase of land acquisition.

[31] FGD, Navjeevan Vihar, R&R colony, NTPC, Singrauli.

7

Singrauli

A 'Development' Dilemma

This chapter provides an overview of the impact of resource development on the regional economy of Singrauli and how it has become a 'space of dependence' (Cox, 1984), serving 'national interest' since 1960. Singrauli, popularly known as the 'energy capital of India', hosts more than 10 per cent of the total installed thermal power capacity of India, presently providing thermal power to 16 states and union territories, and is a geographically isolated and socio-economically backward region of Madhya Pradesh (MP) (NITI Aayog, 2019). In 2008, the space of Singrauli was carved out of Sidhi district and declared to be an independent district. It continues to be considered South Asia's biggest industrial area. Literature suggests that ever since 1840, when coal was discovered in Singrauli, the area's development has revolved around exploiting this mineral resource.[1] The Singrauli region hosts some of the oldest thermal power stations and operational coal mines in India, set up by the National Thermal Power Corporation (NTPC) and Northern Coalfields Ltd (NCL).

From 1960 to 2010, Singrauli has suffered from a spiral of development-induced displacement and systematic acquisition of agricultural and forest land, first for the Rihand Dam and the Govind Ballabh Pant Sagar (GBPS) reservoir in the 1960s and subsequently for opencast coal mines and coal-fired power plants in the 1980s. The recent phase of land acquisition started in 2008 after the formation of the district, primarily by private sector corporations. The Singrauli region has a long story of displacement and deprivation, of neglect and underdevelopment. Loss of livelihood and displacement has become a recurring feature for the people of Singrauli due to dams, thermal power and coal mining projects (Sharma and Singh, 2009). During 2006–2016, the state government of MP received a large number of proposals by private companies to establish resource-based industries in Singrauli. In fact, it is the only district in the region that has received more

1 http://www.blacksmithinstitute.org/projects/display/147.

than ₹1,000 billion in private investment[2], despite the large-scale dissatisfaction with the land acquisition laws. Communities are again in the process of being displaced with private players setting up four coal mining projects and five super thermal power projects in the area. The landscape of the region has undergone a huge transformation with the sprouting of hills (coal overburden) and series of chimneys of thermal power plants all across the region. It was just two generations earlier that small landholders were tending their parcels of agricultural land and the area's original tribal inhabitants (primitive tribes) were essentially dependent upon the forests. The social and demographic profile of the area has undergone a significant transformation with massive industrial changes to the landscape (Kothari, 1996).[3] It is estimated that 0.2–0.3 million people had been displaced in Singrauli, some of them for 'three to four times in the last 50 years' (Lokayan, 1985). The people displaced by the various thermal power and mining projects have been forced into resettlement colonies or have moved away in search of increasingly scarce arable land.

Energy Capital of India and Beneficiary States

As discussed earlier, the Singrauli region hosts more than 10 per cent of the total installed thermal capacity of the country and presently supplies power to around 16 states and union territories: Maharashtra, Punjab, Haryana, Himachal Pradesh, Uttaranchal, Gujarat, Jammu and Kashmir, Delhi, Goa, Daman and Diu, Dadra and Nagar Haveli, Uttar Pradesh (UP), and MP (see Map 7.1). The paradox of resource development and thermal power generation in Singrauli is that half of its own villages were un-electrified until 2018. Considering the fact that about 90 per cent of the population is still engaged in agriculture, no efforts have been made to irrigate the agricultural lands and increase the agricultural productivity of the region.

As discussed earlier, coal mining activities and generation of thermal power involve large-scale acquisition of forest and agricultural lands, displacement of families, loss of livelihoods and environmental degradation. And many of the costs

[2] www.singrauli.nic.in.

[3] In a listing of those projects that lead to the largest source(s) of displacement and destruction of habitat, Smitu Kothari (1996: 1276) lists at the top hydroelectric and irrigation projects, mines (particularly opencast mines), super thermal and nuclear power plants and industrial complexes. By these criteria, the Rihand–Singrauli area has been home to all of the most environmentally degrading and people-displacing projects, excluding so far only nuclear power plants. Singrauli also has the distinction of having the largest opencast coal mine in Asia (1477).

(social and environmental) are not accounted for in the cost of production in the process of resource development. And it is the people of the Singrauli region who have subsidized the cost of production of thermal power, which is used by the beneficiaries of other states. In Chapter 8, some of the gaps have been identified in the existing policy framework, which need to be accounted for and compensated by project developers. The past experience of resource development in Singrauli highlights the fact that in the name of 'development' and public purpose, the 'regional costs' have been largely ignored over the past decades.

It is the tendency of capital to create its spaces of dependence for its profit motives, which create a geographical fulcrum of unevenness. The Singrauli region is a classic example of resource exploitation and uneven patterns of development. From a typical resource curse argument, the resource abundance in Singrauli became a curse for the local populace, as even after five decades of resource development, more than half of the population still lives below poverty line in a degrading environment (CSE, 2011).

The Singrauli region, with more than 50 per cent of the population below poverty line, is still inhabited by some of the primitive tribes of the nation such as the Baigas and Gonds along with other tribal groups. However, the enactment of the Mines and Minerals (Development and Regulation) Act (MMDR Act) and establishment of the District Mineral Foundation (DMF) fund will enable the availability of funds at the local level, which can be utilized for the welfare of the local people and also for the improvement of the degrading environment. Undoubtedly, the region needs special focus in terms of resource allocation and localized development.

Social Development Profile

Singrauli[4] is the 50th district of MP, and it was carved out of Sidhi district in 2008 and was declared an independent district.[5] The region is geographically isolated[6] and relatively disconnected from major urban centres. Singrauli has three *tehsils*,

[4] Historically, the area in the eastern part of the state of MP and the adjoining southern part of Sonebhadra district in the state of UP was collectively known as Singrauli. But, according to state administrative boundaries, the present district of Singrauli lies in the state of MP.

[5] Singrauli district has been carved out from the erstwhile district of Sidhi vide Notification no. F-1-1-2007-vii-sec.-6 dt 15.05.2008.

[6] The region is geographically isolated, and the place was considered so treacherous that it was used by the kings of Rewa State (who ruled the area until 1947) as an open-air prison for detaining errant civilians and officers.

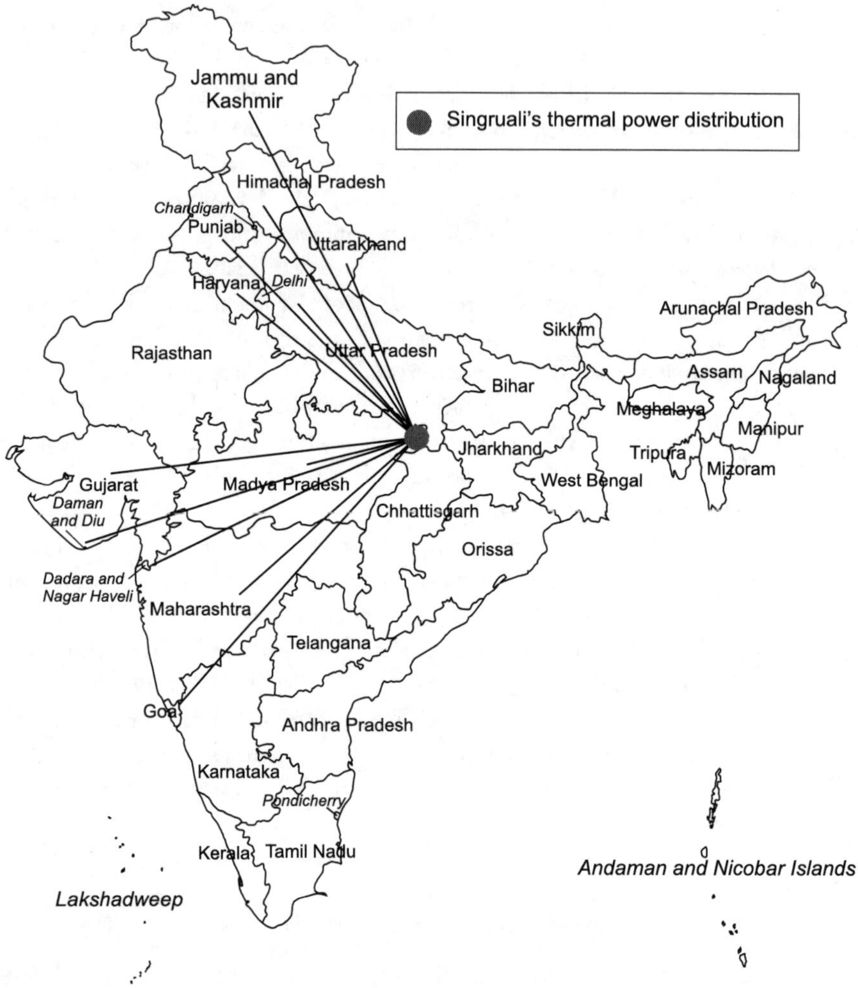

Map 7.1 Beneficiary states

Source: Adapted by author from www.d-maps.com.

Note: Map not to scale and may not represent authentic international borders.

namely Singrauli, Deosar and Chitrangi, and it has three development blocks by the same names. In 2018, the NITI (National Institution for Transforming India) Aayog under 'aspirational district program' declared Singrauli as the '3rd Most Backward District' of the country. The NITI Aayog report highlights that even after six decades of continuous and massive industrial activities, the 'people' and the 'region' have not benefitted from the development process. According to the 2011 Census, the district has a population of about 1.1 million with a growth rate of 28 per cent (mainly because of influx of working population due to industrial

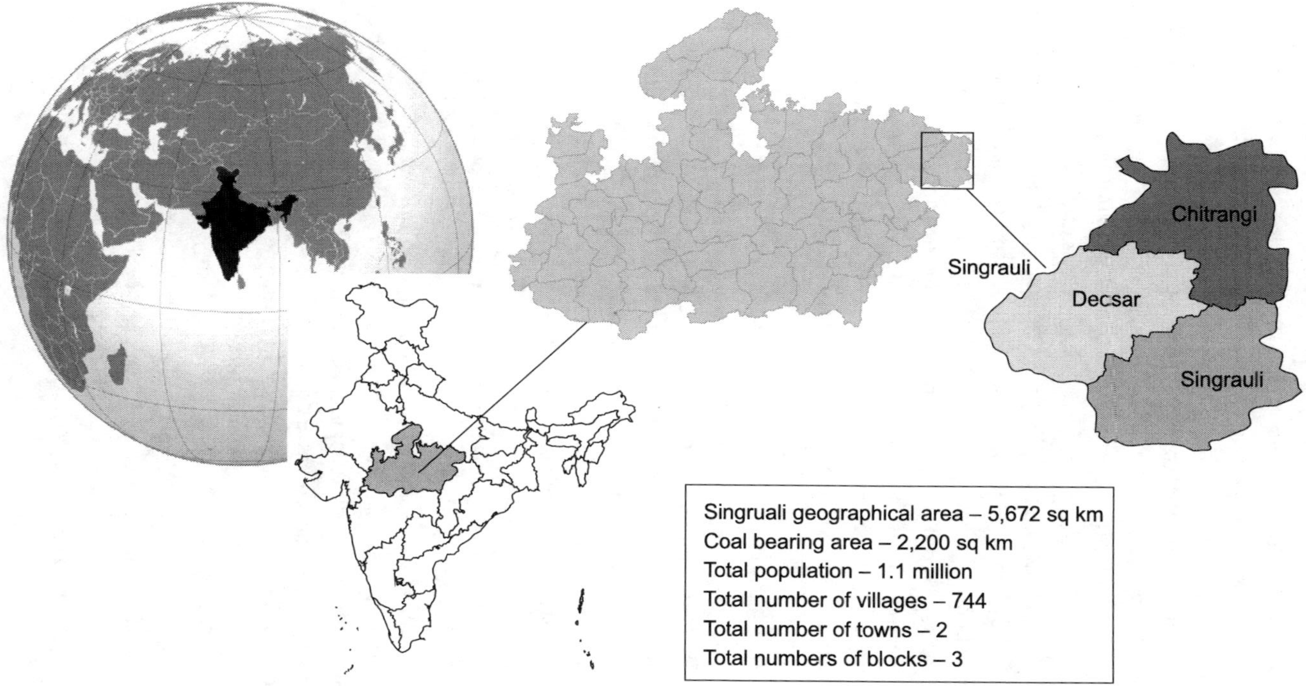

Map 7.2 Singruali district map

Sources: Adapted by author from NCL files and www.d-maps.com.

Note: Map not to scale and may not represent authentic international borders.

projects). The district of Singrauli has an administrative area of 5,675 square kilommetres with 2,200 square kilometres earmarked for coal mining activities (see Map 7.2).[7] The geographical area of Singrauli and the earmarked coal-bearing zone signify that a large industrial activity is concentrated in a small region with a large rural population. As per the recent statistics (Census 2011), 80.75 per cent population of Singrauli resides in the rural area and 19.25 per cent lives in the urban area. The data indicates that rural landscape dominates the Singrauli region, with limited urban centres, informal settlements and company townships. The Singrauli region, due to multiple displacement, also lost a large number of its indigenous populations (Gonds, Kols, Agatias, Panikas and Baigas among others) and the Scheduled Caste (SC) population who are considered socially and economically backward communities as per the Constitution of India.

Madhya Pradesh is one of the largest and backward states of India with a vast population living below the poverty line. Within the state, there are significant regional inequalities, with extremely high poverty levels in tribal districts, and for Scheduled Tribes (STs) and SCs the poverty levels stand at 59 and 43 per cents respectively (State Planning Commission, 2010). The state's low Human Development Index (HDI) generally reflects the lack of educational attainment, poor health welfare and a lower standard of well-being, which is exacerbated in the predominantly SC/ST districts with the lowest HDI. Sidhi and Singrauli are included in the Integrated Action Plan districts, considering their level of poverty and backwardness. The state also has one of the largest tribal populations in the country with 18 districts being predominantly tribal districts. The share of the ST and SC populations is 20.27 per cent and 15.17 per cent respectively.

In the district, about 56.45 per cent of the households are below poverty line, which is much higher than the national average of 28.6 per cent and also higher than that of the state, 37.43 per cent (State Planning Commission, 2010). The high incidence of poverty in the district can be explained by the fact that though the major economic activity of the district is agriculture, due to the undulating terrain, lack of irrigation facilities, dependence on rain-fed agriculture and dependence on traditional methods of farming, agricultural productivity is low. A vast majority of the population either depends upon subsistence agriculture or non-timber forest products (NTFPs) or they migrate to neighbouring districts and towns for casual labour work. The region is relatively backward with 60 per cent literacy rate and sex ratio of 920 female per 1,000 males (see Table 7.1). The literacy rate of the district is poor in comparison with the national and state averages. The education sector has seriously suffered because of the lack of proper infrastructure

[7] Geographical area and coal-bearing area data have been collected from the NCL head office in Singrauli.

Table 7.1 Singrauli district profile

District	*Area (sq. km)*	*Population (million)*	*Growth rate (%)*	*Urban population (%)*	*Rural population (%)*	*Sex ratio*	*Below poverty line HH (%)*	*Infant mortality rate/1,000*	*Literacy rate (%)*	*Life expectancy*	*SC (%)*	*ST (%)*
Singruali	5,675	1.18	28	19.25	80.75	916	56.5	110	60	58	12.8	32.6
MP	308,000	70	20	27.6	72.4	931	37.5	54	69	58	15.2	20.3

Source: Census 2011.

Note: HH stands for household.

required for the local community. Primary and middle schools get enough funds for buildings and other infrastructure under central government schemes, for instance, Sarva Siksha Abhiyan (SSA). The experience of running the District Primary Education Programme shows that infrastructure plays an important role in enrolment, attendance, retention, transition and, most importantly, in imparting quality education. Since SSA funds are used for providing facilities to primary and middle schools only, there is a serious need to create infrastructure for secondary and higher secondary schools (State Planning Commission, 2010).

The status of basic health facilities for the people is aptly reflected in the infant mortality rate (IMR) and maternal mortality rate (MMR) of the district. The number of community health centres, primary health centres, sub health centres (SHCs) and Anganwadis in the district is satisfactory but in the absence of basic infrastructure, people are deprived of the basic health facilities required. Most of the SHCs and Anganwadis are functioning from rented premises. The rented premises do not have adequate space for the equipment, thus compromising on hygiene and better healthcare facilities. The health indicators of the district are far below the national and state averages. The IMR is 110 (per 1,000) and the average age of the people in the district is 58 years. Singrauli is one of the hundred districts of Empowered Action Group states of India where IMR is very high and belongs to the top 25 administrative divisions with respect to MMR (Brahmapurkar, 2019).

The biggest irony of the Singrauli region is that 578 out of 1,024 villages are un-electrified[8] (State Planning Commission, 2010). There is also low consumption of electricity because of the low percentage of households being electrified due to the lack of proper infrastructure required to sustain greater number of connections, and also because the villages are sparsely located. Since most of the villages are located in dense forests, electrification is a tedious job. Due to the unavailability

[8] The data on un-electrified villages is before the formation of Singrauli district, when Singrauli was part of the Sidhi district.

of proper infrastructure for electricity in villages, farmers are not able to use water pumps for agriculture and thus face difficulty in irrigating their land. Despite the fact that the population is heavily dependent on agriculture, not much priority is given to supplying power and water to the farmers; rather the focus has been on acquiring the agricultural land.

State Government View

In the state government's view, Singrauli is fast emerging as the power hub of India, especially for electricity and coal and therefore, locally, it is also called Urjanchal (a Hindi word which means land of energy). The chief minister of the state has the dream of developing Singrauli into another Singapore (Halarnkar, 2011). In the district magistrate's[9] (DM) view,

> thc Singrauli district is the ultimate destination for the private players to set up power plants and coal mining projects, due to its strategic location and professional approach of the district administration. The district administration has developed an effective mechanism for speedy land acquisition process and time bound delivery of land for project development. In fact it is one of the rare districts of India which has facilitated such speedy acquisition of land.

However, it has been observed that within the district administration, different DMs have adopted different approaches towards land acquisition and rehabilitation issues. In an earlier DM's[10] view,

> it is the responsibility of the State to properly compensate the PAF's and address the grievances of the people, the private developers exerts enormous pressure through State government senior officials and political leaders, on the district administration to speedily transfer land to the project developers, but land acquisition is a complex issue which requires adequate time to facilitate the process.

The approach of the Government of Madhya Pradesh (GoMP) is evident from the industrial meet in Khajuraho, where the state opened its arms for private investments with the promise of providing a conducive 'investment climate' with better administrative support for setting up projects at the district level (Tripathi, 2007).

---

[9] Interview, Singrauli, district magistrate 2 (2010–2012).

[10] Interview, Singrauli district magistrate 1 (2008–2009); he was transferred within one year of his posting due to political reasons; he was earlier involved with the land acquisition process for the Narmada Valley Project as subdivisional magistrate and was exposed to the complexities of land acquisition.

Coal Mining in Singrauli

In Singrauli, NCL is spread over a vast area, generating about 20 per cent[11] of the total coal production in the country. There are 11 opencast mines of NCL, which supply coal to 9 power projects spread in and around Singrauli, both in MP and UP. In the last one decade, the GoMP has received massive private investments to develop six thermal power and five opencast coal mining projects in Singrauli. The land acquisition process for most of these projects is over, and the land has been transferred to private developers. The state government claims that Singrauli, with its natural resources and enabling environment, has become a most suitable destination for private investment.

As discussed in Chapter 3, considering the growing energy need of the country, India's coal production is going to increase by 2–3 times by 2030 (TERI, 2012). This indicates that the major coal reserves in Singrauli, Jharkhand and Chhattisgarh will be exploited in the coming decade. The Singrauli coalfields are spread across 2,202 square kilometres, and this mineral rich region can be divided into two basins, that is, the Moher sub-basin (312 square kilometres) and the Singrauli Main basin (1,890 square kilometres). A significant part of the Moher sub-basin lies in the Singrauli district of MP and a small part lies in the Sonebhadra district of UP. The Singrauli Main basin lies in the western part of the coalfield and is largely unexplored. The present coal mining activities and future blocks are concentrated in the Moher sub-basin (NCL, Singrauli).

The exploration carried out by the Central Mine Planning and Design Institute and the Geological Survey of India has proved abundant resource of power-grade coal in the area. This abundant coal along with easy water source from the GBPS reservoir makes this region geographically strategic for high capacity pithead thermal power plants. The coal extraction by NCL has made it possible to produce about 10,515 megawatts of electricity from pithead power plants of NTPC, Uttar Pradesh Rajya Vidyut Utpadan Nigam Ltd and Renupower division of Hindalco Industries. The ultimate capacity of power generation of these power plants is 13,295 megawatts, and NCL is fully prepared to meet the increased demand[12] of coal for the purpose. In addition, NCL is also supplying coal from Singrauli to power plants of Rajasthan Rajya Vidyut Utpadan Nigam Ltd, Delhi Vidyut Board and Haryana State Electricity Board.

During 2010–2011, coal production of NCL was 66.253 million tons. NCL has 10 working opencast coal projects, which produced 70.021 million tons of

---

[11] Geographical area and coal-bearing area data have been collected from the NCL head office in Singrauli.

[12] Interview, executive director, NCL, Singrauli.

coal during 2012–2013. The production targets are increasing every year, as there is huge demand for upcoming thermal power plants in the region. Undoubtedly, the overburden will compound the existing environmental degradation and the adverse health impacts on the local people.

Resource Revenue Generation

Northern Coalfields Limited

The state of MP is blessed with natural resources and is among the top eight states of the country and around 30 per cent of the geographical area is under forest cover. During 2010–2011, the state contributed 26.7 per cent of the total coal production[13] of the country. In the state of MP, more than 90 per cent of the coal production comes from the Singrauli region (see Table 7.3). The coal mining projects of NCL, which is a public sector undertaking (PSU) and a Maharatna company operating in the Singrauli region, are profitable projects, and the data collected for over last five years indicates that Singrauli has been contributing significant revenue in the form of royalty and various other taxes to the state and central governments. Undoubtedly, the mining projects contribute in a significant way to India's gross domestic product (GDP) (Chapter 3). During 2010–2011, the state of MP contributed 5 per cent to the total mineral production (excluding oil and gas) value of the country. However, the regional information gathered through field interviews suggests that there has been no significant change in the regional development despite these industrial projects.

Singrauli is among the top 50 mining districts[14] of India in terms of value of mineral production. During 2010–2011, the Singrauli district produced minerals worth ₹33.92 billion and generated significant revenue for the state and central governments (see Table 7.2). During 2011–2012, the state earned ₹31.15 billion[15] as royalty from minerals from Singrauli district. The district has a mine lease area of 9,563 hectares and approximately a population of 45,000 is expected to be affected due to coal mining.[16]

Figures 7.1 and 7.2 reflect that the amount of royalty and tax deposited by NCL has been growing in the subsequent years after the formation of the district due

---

[13] MP Planning Commission Report, 2014.

[14] CSE (2011).

[15] MP Planning Commission Report, 2014.

[16] Field study and analysis of district records suggest that the displacement figure is often under-reported by the government and many of the non-title holders are not accounted in the total displacement figure.

Table 7.2 Payment to central and state exchequer made by NCL (in ₹ crore)

Particulars	*2008–2009*	*2009–2010*	*2010–2011*	*2011–2012*	*2012–2013*
Royalty	645.17	676.2	578.54	609.99	854.99
Central and state sales tax	103.69	112.99	108.16	164.38	180.6
Clean energy cess	0	0	132.38	181.16	177.59
Excise duty	0	0	31.57	176.97	281.28
Sales tax on works and scraps	2.03	2.27	1.98	3.02	3.78
Entry tax	5.19	6.62	7.17	5.24	6.4
Service tax	0	0	1.4	1.32	4.09
Stowing excise duty	48.76	51.08	46.51	44.87	49.63
SSADA cess	0	0	0	0	0
Property tax	0.07	0	3.27	0.68	1.76
Forest fee/transit fee	36.8	16.88	12.2	11.63	26.22
Professional tax	2.21	2.35	2.39	2.29	2.33
MPGATSVA	0	0	0	1,152.86	288.35
Total (in crore)	843.92	868.39	925.57	2,354.41	1,877.02
Total (2008–2013)			6,869.31		

Source: NCL (2013).

Notes: 1 crore = 10 million. MPGATSVA stands for Madhya Pradesh Gramin Avsanrachna Tatha Sadak Vikas Adhiniyam.

to the increase in the demand for coal. And it is expected that in the next decade, coal production will be doubled to feed the new projects and, hence, revenue generation will also increase significantly.[17]

Table 7.3 Coal production and annual profit, 2008–2013

Name of the project	*Coal production (million tons)*	*Annual profit (₹ crore)*
Amlori	30.87	710.47
Dudhichua	61.04	2,926.17
Jayant	68.68	3,827.65
Jhingurda	9.82	45.13
Khadia	20.82	764.42
Nigahi	60.43	2,682.55
Block B	18.97	2,208.06
Total	270.63	13,164.45

Source: NCL (2013).

[17] Interview, executive director, NCL, Singrauli.

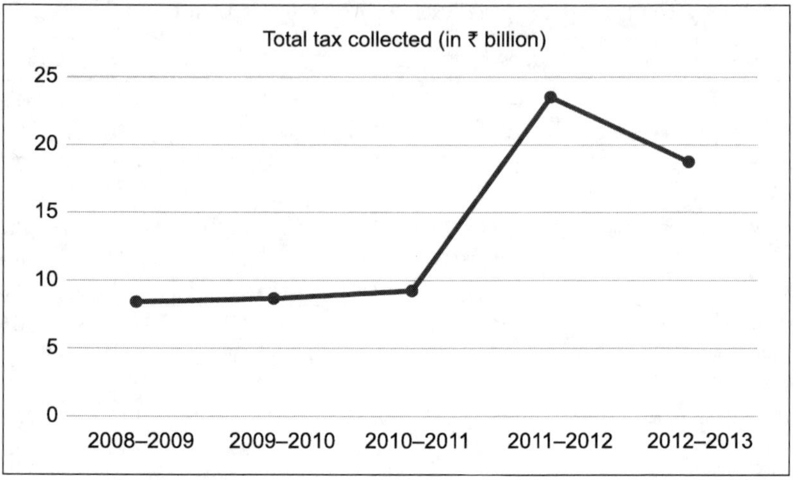

Figure 7.1 Royalty and tax collection, 2008–2013
Source: Singh (2015: fieldwork data of 2013).

Social and Regional Benefits

Considering the fact that these projects generate so much profit every year, even the corporate social responsibility (CSR) initiatives of NCL are not much appreciated by the local villagers. They are ad hoc, not well organized and do not incorporate the local needs of the community. These activities are taken up more on a casual basis and its presentation in the annual reports of the company is demonstrated in an exaggerated way. The people complain that at most instances, issues related to labour union and local needs are heard only when they come out for public demonstration and halt the coal production.[18] NCL had the policy of granting employment on land acreage basis, that is, on acquisition of 2 acres of land one employment is offered to the family members. However, some of the interviews[19] of the youths reflect the company's irrational approach of cancelling their job application in case of inheritance or land transfer among family members after the cut-off date, and there were 92 such youths who were technically entitled for employment. One of the respondents said, 'We keep running to the NCL and district offices with the job application but no authority is willing to look into this matter, they simply say that it's tedious task to filter between genuine vs non-genuine applications.'

[18] Focus group discussion (FGD), Nigahi village, Singrauli.

[19] Interviews, PAP Gm and PAP OBCm, Phase II Nigahi Village NCL, Singrauli.

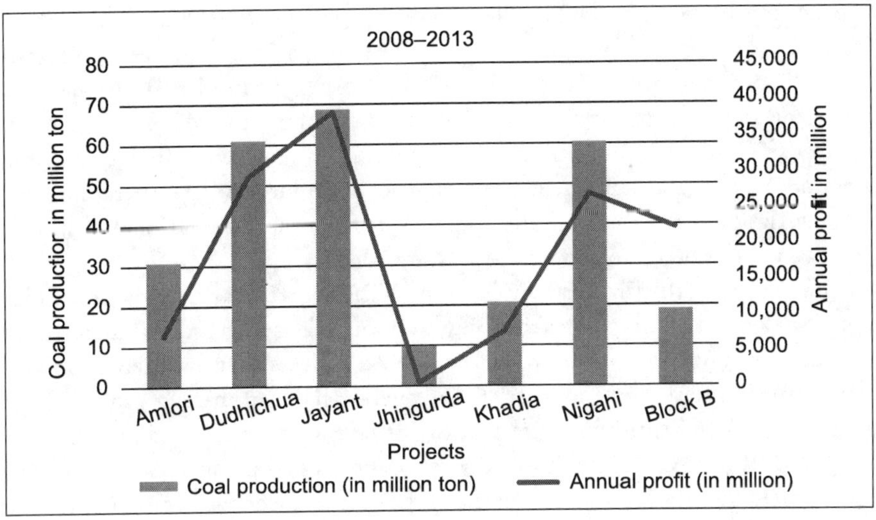

Figure 7.2 Coal production and annual profit
Source: Singh (2015: fieldwork data of 2013).

The reason for such problems is primarily because for some of the NCL projects, preliminary notification of land acquisition was issued in 1982, but for a long period land was not acquired (as it was not immediately required for mining). Due to such long delay, the land title owners crossed their employable age and the younger members of the family were denied of this employment opportunity. There are numerous such problems that exist in and around project villages, and the affected families have to continuously struggle for their basic entitlements. It raises a serious question about the objective of 'public purpose' under which this very land was acquired and the immediate 'public' who sacrificed their lands and livelihoods and have to struggle for their basic rights.

MMDR Act of 2015 and Financial Implications on Singrauli

The government's proposal to replace the MMDR Act with the MMDR Bill 2011 to include a specific provision for sharing 26 per cent of the net profits with local communities is an important step ahead in building an inclusive growth model. This proposal is also in line with the best practices being followed around the world. The principles are not new and many mineral-rich countries have been following them for years without impacting the actual profitability of mining companies. The fund will be deposited annually to the DMF, an amount equal to 26 per cent of profit after tax (PAT) or a sum equivalent to the royalty paid during the year, whichever is higher. The DMF will then distribute monetary benefits directly or indirectly to the affected people. However, there are many ambiguities with regard to identification of beneficiaries, who will administer the fund, utilization of the funds and so on. Also, with the recent amendment under the MMDR Bill 2014, the clause of 26 per cent of profit sharing has been replaced with a 'reasonable amount' or 'annual development fee' being set aside for mining benefit sharing. The legislation is evolving, and there is pressure from the business lobby that such provisions will make projects financially unviable.

To understand the financial implications of the benefit sharing provision under the MMDR Bill, mining data from Singrauli was analysed in order to understand the revenue flow at the district level. Table 7.4 reflects that between 2008 and 2013 (after formation of the district) the operational coal mining projects have generated ₹131,650 million as net profit. Considering the proposed provisions of the MMDR Bill, ₹34,229 million (26 per cent of net profit) would have come to the DMF in the last five years under the profit sharing mechanism (see Figure 7.3).

This indicates that on an annual basis, the district would have received ₹6,845 million for its regional development. During the survey, the information on annual district budget allocation was also studied and it was noticed that approximately ₹8,000 million is presently allocated to the district by the state government (Singh, 2015: fieldwork data, 2013). If we study the mining benefit share in relation to the district budget, it clearly indicates its significance. The data on resource revenue generation, annual district budgetary allocation and social development profile substantiate the argument that Singrauli has been strategically used as a 'space of

Table 7.4 Operational mining projects and revenue generation in Singrauli between 2008 and 2013

Name of project	*Mine lease area (ha)*	*Total land acquired private/ govt/forest (ha)*	*Project-affected family (no.)*	*Employment (permanent positions) (no.)*	*Coal production (MT)*	*Value of mineral/ sale value (₹ million)*	*Annual profit/net profit (₹ million)*	*Amount to district mineral fund (₹ million)**
Amlohri	2,383	2,383	226	1,471.8	30.87	30,853.4	7,104.7	1,847.2
Dudhichua	1,752	1,752	353	2,368	61.04	75,261	29,261.7	7,608
Jayant	2,480	2,480	668	2,534.8	68.69	72,435.5	38,276.5	9,951.9
Jhingurda	1,200	1,200	57	921.4	9.83	9,065.5	451.3	117.3
Khadia, UP	1,640	1,640	494	1,428.2	20.82	24,463.3	7,644.2	1,987.5
Nigahi	3,036	2,650	1,178	2,468	60.44	70,748.9	26,825.5	6,974.6
Block-B	1,339	1,339	482	325.4	18.98	30,973.4	22,086.0	5,742.4
Total	13,830	13,444	3,458	11,518	271	31,3801	13,1650	34,229

Source: Singh (2015: fieldwork data of 2013, NCL/Revenue Department, Singruali).

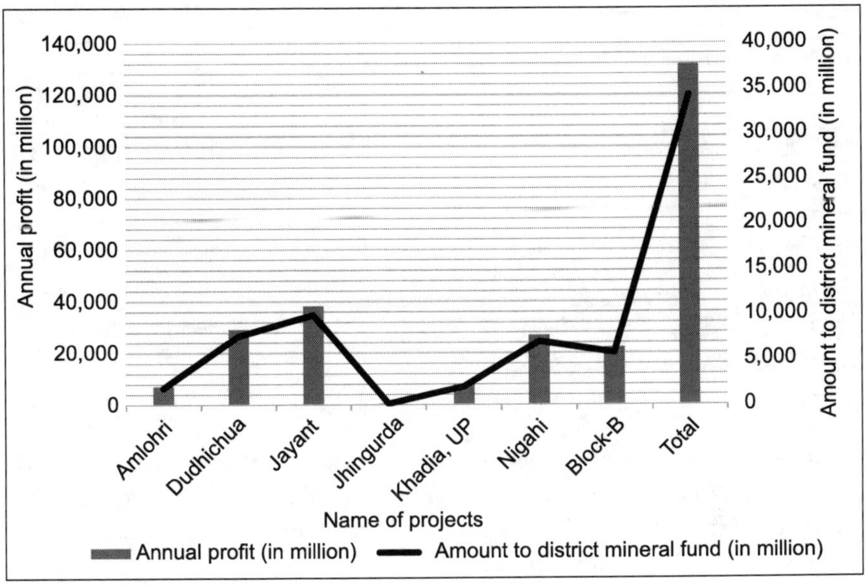

Figure 7.3 Revenue generation and profit sharing for mining projects in Singrauli

Source: Singh (2015: fieldwork data of 2013).

dependence' and kept deprived in the name of 'public purpose'. The findings of this research indicate the need for policy reforms if resource development projects have to be in national interest.

Table 7.5 provides a detailed break-up of mineral funds received in the Singrauli DMF between 2015 and 2020. The funds are calculated and deposited as per the guidelines of Section 9B of the MMDR Act of 2015, that is, a DMF will receive 10 per cent of the total royalty the mining corporations are depositing to the central and state governments. Madhya Pradesh has also created an exceptional provision of a state mineral fund under the State DMF Rules, which will receive a percentage of the DMF accruals from various districts. Under this scheme, for accruals amounting from ₹5 million to ₹250 million, 25 per cent of the DMF fund will be transferred to the state mineral fund. For accruals above ₹250 million, 50 per cent of the DMF fund will be transferred. This state fund has been placed under the aegis of the state finance department (CSE, 2017). From public policy viewpoint, there are two questions that emerge from this approach: First, if the DMF objective was to develop a dedicated financial revenue stream to correct the historical injustice and mitigate the adverse impacts of mining then why is 50 per cent of the DMF fund being taken back by the MP state government? Second, how efficiently even the fund of ₹10,280 million (see Table 7.5) has been utilized

Table 7.5 Singrauli District Mineral Fund collection, 2015–2020 (₹ crore)

Year	*DMF Trust-received fund*	*District mineral fund*	*State mineral fund*	*Administrative expense*	*High priority expenditure*	*Low priority expenditure*
2015–2016	4.97	4.97	0	0.15	2.89	1.93
2016–2017	698.84	356.92	341.92	10.71	207.73	138.48
2017–2018	348.18	181.59	166.59	5.45	105.69	70.46
2018–2019	414.39	214.69	199.69	6.44	124.95	83.3
2019–2020	525.62	270.31	255.31	8.11	157.32	104.88
Total	1,992	1,028.48	963.51	30.85	598.58	399.05

Source: District Administration, March 2020.

in the last five years and what has been done to strengthen the local institutions in terms of allocation of skilled manpower, local participation and decision-making? The global experience suggests that mere allocation of resource revenue does not necessarily benefit the local people.

NTPC

NTPC is another profitable PSU in the Singrauli region, which has three of the oldest thermal power stations in the region: NTPC-Singrauli (2,000 megawatts), NTPC-Vidhyachal (4,260 megawatts) and NTPC-Rihand (3,000 megawatts). Coal is supplied to these thermal power stations by the nearby coal mines operated by NCL, and water is sourced from the Rihand reservoir. Collectively, these thermal power plants generate around 10,000 megawatts of electricity and supply power to 16 states and union territories of India (NTPC). For NTPC, Singrauli remains a strategically important region due to its existing stations and future potential of thermal power generation. The current expansion of existing NTPC thermal power stations in Singrauli indicates the growth potential and financial return for NTPC. The interviews of NTPC officials reflect that they take pride in associating with NTPC in nation-building and are also concerned about the society they operate in. But, from the community viewpoint, the CSR projects undertaken by the NTPC fall short of their expectations.

Table 7.6 highlights the financial statement of NTPC over the last five years and, considering the provisions of the recent CSR law, NTPC was required to spend ₹2,520 million in 2013 on social development projects. As per the provisions of the Companies Act of 2013 (Section 135), companies are required to spend 2 per cent of PAT on CSR projects in their areas of operations. As Singrauli

Table 7.6 Financial statement (₹ million)

Financial year	*Profit after tax (PAT)*	*Profit before tax*	*Tax net*
2012–2013	126,190	165,780	39,590
2011–2012	92,230	123,260	31,020
2010–2011	91,020	120,490	29,470
2009–2010	87,280	108,850	21,570
2008–2009	82,010	93,590	11,580

Source: NTPC Annual Report 2014.

hosts the three of the oldest and largest NTPC power plants, a significant CSR budget is allocated for the region. However, CSR practices in the region have been unplanned, uncoordinated and ad hoc. Mostly, CSR events are organized on the request of the local political leaders in their specific constituencies and the CSR fund is diverted to many unproductive activities. The response of the local inhabitants[20] reflects that the CSR projects have not benefitted the local populace and have failed to address the immediate needs of the population. Few events, for example, blood donation camps or sports events are organized when senior NTPC officials from Delhi visit NTPC stations in Singrauli. According to an NTPC manager (prefers to remain anonymous), a large sum of the CSR budget (in the range of hundreds of millions) is accumulated at the corporate level, which was unspent in the previous years. The manager further indicates a high level of bureaucracy and lack of capacity and interest within NTPC for CSR projects.

Considering the financial statement and profit of NTPC, if 2 per cent of PAT had been judiciously spent on CSR projects, many basic social and economic issues of the local community could have been addressed. The basic requirement is the motive and capacity of the NTPC staff to adequately plan and execute the CSR budget. The NTPC view is that there is no community ownership for these projects and barely no cooperation from the community. An independent observation is that NTPC lacks social scientists or staff with social academic training. And even for CSR or R&R activities, the job is delegated to the engineers. It would be generic to comment that engineers cannot perform socially oriented jobs but to understand the complexities of the society and develop rapport with the community, one needs training in social sciences or social work. For instance, to conduct a needs assessment exercise, one should be able to understand the social reality and other significant facts which are not apparently visible.

[20] FGD at NTPC Rehabilitation Colony.

Singrauli Revenue Contributions

As discussed earlier, in 2008, the Singrauli region was carved out of Sidhi district and was given the status of an independent district (Nagaraj and Motiram, 2017). Since the formation of the district, royalty and tax collection from mining activities has been gradually increasing in the subsequent years (see Figure 7.4). There is a series of proposed projects in Singrauli and in the forthcoming years, the revenue generated in the form of royalty and tax will increase exponentially. In the next five years, the Government of India plans to double coal production from the Singrauli region (CII, 2014). The district administration has the role of tax collection and the state government allocates the annual district budget.

Conclusion

India has the world's fifth-largest coal reserves and a few cleaner fossil fuels, such as natural gas. The government is also determined to spread the benefits of economic development more widely among its population, one-third of whom still have no access to electricity (State Planning Commission, 2010). In 2014, Indian coal production from both private- and state-owned mines was 620 million tons, of which 85 per cent of coal was derived from opencast mines, and an additional 400 million tons were imported. Total coal production from the Singrauli coalfields in 2014 was 87 million tons and it is planned to double in the next five years (Coal India, 2014). The coal ministry's target is to double the coal production and reduce reliance on imports. In August 2014, the Supreme Court cancelled more than 200 mining licenses awarded

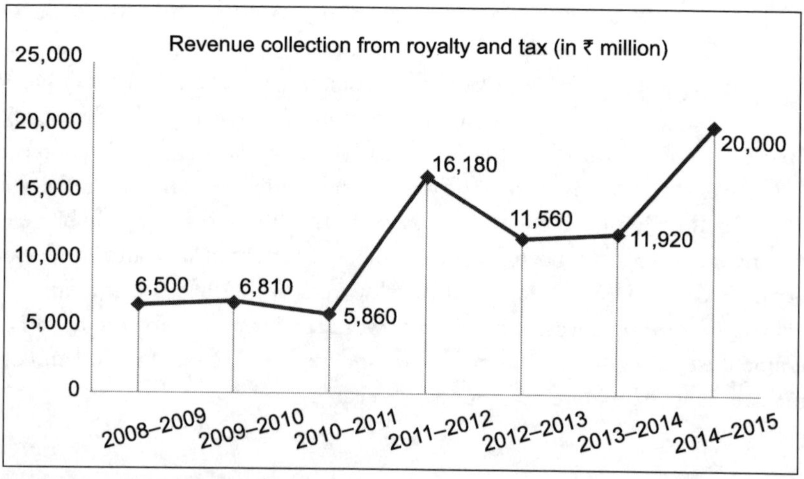

Figure 7.4 Total revenue generated by minerals, 2008–2014

Source: Singh (2015: fieldwork data from 2013 to 2014, Singrauli district office).

by the government before 2010 due to inadequacy in the allocation process, which led to the cancellation of numerous planned projects. The Bharatiya Janata Party (BJP) government in 2015 has given environmental clearance to 41 new mining projects, which indicates the urgency and need for power generation.

The BJP government has introduced a new scheme under which coal blocks are auctioned to the highest bidder. It creates huge incentives for the state governments to foster new mines and generate revenue for the state. However, many of the richest, untapped coal reserves lie in heavily forested areas, some near Singrauli in MP, but mainly in Chhattisgarh and Jharkand in central India. Those whose land will be subject to 'acquisition' are some of India's poorest inhabitants, many of them *adivasis* – members of indigenous tribes.

The development and displacement discourse of Singrauli, spread over the past five decades, reflects that the local community and the region have not benefitted from the resource development process. The so-called energy capital of India – Singrauli – is also an isolated backward space. Apart from thermal power plants and mines, the region has few towns (two), poverty-stricken villages and islands of well-planned prosperous corporate colonies with all the basic civic amenities. In a federal democratic polity, it is crucial to understand the regional interest and the need to be attentive to local concerns if resource development projects are to truly be in national interest. It is important to internalize that there are layers of 'public' in the bracket of 'public purpose': one who loses his/her land and livelihood because of such projects and the other who is an actual beneficiary residing 1,000 kilometres away. There is need for a 'just' development approach which can stabilize this 'geographical fulcrum of unevenness'.

Diversion of Forest and Allocation of Coal

As the mining and thermal power expansion in Singrauli continues, almost all the coal blocks that are being allocated for mining are located in forest areas. About 5,872.18 hectares of forestland from the Singrauli region has been officially diverted for non-forest use since the initiation of the Forest Conservation Act in 1980 (DFO, Singrauli). It includes 5,760.55 hectares of forest and 111.60 hectares of revenue forestland. However, it does not include the several instances of encroachment on forestland that may have occurred as a result of the existing and proposed industrial operations.

Field data gathered from the divisional forest office record that 3,229.06 hectares of forest is awaiting approval for diversion for the third phase of projects in Singrauli (Greenpeace, 2011). The allocation of coal blocks and diversion of forest need to be understood in these contexts.

> The setting up of coalmines and thermal power stations is linked to the establishment of ancillary activities. The project developers do not disclose this entirely at the time of approval. Further, in many instances the construction of a thermal power plant makes later mining approval a fait accompli. The negotiations over the 'no-go' areas between the Ministry of Coal and Ministry of Environment and Forests (MoEF) have also determined how these coal blocks are being traded and forests clearances sought. While the Ministry of Coal has allocated the coal blocks, approvals must be sought from the MoEF if forestland needs to be used for mining purposes. (Greenpeace, 2011)

When the 'go, no-go' list for coal mining in the country was first released in March 2010, several forest blocks of Singrauli coalfields across the states of UP and MP were categorized as 'no-go' zones. This included forest areas such as Mahan, Chhatrasal, Amelia and Dongri Tal II as coalfields not to be mined (UNDP, 2011). The conversation around 'go' and 'no-go' zones was initiated by the Ministry of Coal and the Ministry of Environment and Forests (MoEF) to identify which blocks in India's existing nine coalfields could be allowed to be mined and which would remain untouched for use as strategic energy reserves in future. The latter had to satisfy the limited forest density criteria of more than 10 per cent.

According to Greenpeace (2011) and the Right to Information reports, file notes indicate that the first 'go, no-go' list specified 222 coal blocks in the central and eastern coalfields to be withheld from granting coal mining approvals. By a year later, negotiations had led to a different scenario: the number of 'no go' coal blocks had come down to 153. On 1 March 2011, the then Minister for Environment and Forests, Jairam Ramesh, submitted in the Rajya Sabha that Mahan's forest would be let out to Essar and Hindalco companies and possession of Chhatrasal would go to Reliance's Sasan power plant operations. Dongri Tal II and Amelia had been allocated to Jaypee. Each of these area allocations is towards feeding the coal requirements of thermal power plants belonging to the same corporations in the Singrauli region.

The politics over allocation of coal blocks clearly reflects the strength of capital in influencing policies and paving the way for institutionalizing private investments. The coal allocation scam, popularly tagged by media as the 'Coalgate' scam, was one of the significant scams under the United Progressive Alliance (UPA) regime regarding allocation of coal blocks to public and private corporations by the Government of India during 2004–2009. The Comptroller and Auditor General of India (CAG) report of March 2014 accused the Government of India of making inefficient allocation of coal blocks to corporations (CAG, 2014). As discussed earlier, some of the disputed coal blocks also fall within the Singrauli region. But Singrauli's future is etched with the ambitions of several private and public sector mining and thermal power operations, many of which are already under construction or in the process of negotiation.

Community Forest Rights in Singrauli

There are two specific cases with regard to community forest rights (CFR) issues in the Singrauli coalfield region which need to be highlighted in the study. According to Greenpeace (2011), there were 91 CFR claims by tribal communities and traditional forest-dwelling communities (DFO, Singrauli) in the Mahan coal block area (a joint venture of Esaar and Hindalco). However, it is important to understand that many of these claims are related to the developmental activities which forest-dwelling communities are entitled to as per Section 3(2) of the Forest Rights Act (FRA) of 2006 and not under Section 3(1) of the CFR. It was noticed that a large number of forest-dwelling communities in Singrauli were not adequately aware of their rights under the FRA, and it was only after community mobilization by the Greenpeace team that the local forest-dwelling communities started voicing their concerns for forest land acquisition.

The allocation and approval given to this project have been at the centre of negotiations between the MoEF and the Empowered Group of Ministers which was set up to look into coal block allocation and other related environment regulatory issues. It is important to note that Essar and Hindalco's power plants – which will use the coal – are already under construction in the area, and the companies have put forth this *fait accompli* argument to seek the forestland diversion of 1,182 hectares. The two corporations have already acquired land for thermal power stations and paid compensation to the PAFs. The developers argue that an investment of ₹36 billion has already gone into the existing plants; it is claimed that the Mahan coal block linkage is urgently required if the plants are to start producing power (Kohli, 2012).

The other case in point is related to the communities affected by the allocation of the Moher and Amlori coal blocks which have been given as coal linkage for Reliance's Sasan thermal power project. The villages impacted by this diversion come within the Singrauli municipal area, even though they largely have forest dependent livelihoods. But, unfortunately, since they fall within the urban jurisdiction, their rights and livelihood engagements are not recognized for compensation.

As noted in the Report of the National Committee on the Forest Rights Act (UNDP, 2011), there are many areas where customary rights of villages (both individual and community) are in areas that are now within municipal city limits. Several such sites are still used by nomadic or seasonally migrant pastoral (and other) communities. The report notes that such communities have no way of making their claims, since the relevant institutions under FRA do not exist in towns/cities, but a way must be found for such claims to be possible. According to the Ministry of Tribal Affairs, in its circular dated 4 March 2010 clarifying this issue, rights cannot be claimed or given in urban areas, since subdivisional level committees and district level committees cannot be formed. This, however, amounts to continuing the historical injustice such communities have faced, rather than coming up with a more creative resolution to this. Singrauli district has a unique blend of urban and rural landscapes. The provisions and recommendation under the Special Area Development Authority (SADA) to include over a hundred villages under special area development as urban territory had left many of the areas on record as urban; however, the landscape, habitation and people's livelihood, all exhibit rural characteristics. In fact, much of the private land under the Moher coal mining project falls under the urban circle rate (municipal wards), which needs to be compensated as per the municipal rate, which is much higher than the rural circle rate. But these issues are completely ignored during the land acquisition process as this will incur high land costs to private developers.

But, even as we discuss the interpretations related to the central legislation and subsequent clarifications, implications are already being felt in coal blocks set aside for power plants. Take, for instance, the story of Jeetlal Baiga, a former resident of the Moher forests within the municipality limits of Waidhan, Singrauli district, which have now been cut down since the forestland has been diverted for a captive coal mine for the Reliance Ultra Mega Power Project.

Jeetlal was living along with his family in the Moher forest and was later displaced by the mine and has now been shifted to a rehabilitation hut on the outskirts of Amlori village. Though Jeetlal has been living in the Moher forest for generations, he did not get any rights under the FRA. The then collector, P. Narahari, said that he was helpless in this case because FRA does not provide rights to people living in 'urban forests'; Moher was one such forest. There are around 80–90 families in Amlori *basti* (all Baiga *adivasis*) whose forest rights have not been recognized because of this issue. This has cost them their livelihood, as the Moher forests have now been diverted for mining, and these tribal families did not get anything in lieu of this diversion.

Jeetlal says:

> When I was living in the forest I used to make plates with leaves from the forest and collect medicinal plants which I used to sell to earn my livelihood; since they have shifted me here, I have no means to earn my livelihood. They gave me 50 kg rice and some money as compensation which is all finished now.

So, even with the legislations in place, there are incidences where significant numbers of people are left out from the compensation process due to administrative inefficiency. Singrauli is a typical case where the rural–urban dilemma further complicates the issues; however, considering the characteristics of Singrauli, it can hardly be called urban. SADA, while preparing the regional development plan for Singraili, did some exercise on paper; however, that plan was never executed on the ground due to several deadlock.

8

Administering Singrauli

Governance and Institutions

This chapter documents the role of the state government, financial institutions, public sector undertakings (PSUs) and private developers in facilitating resource development projects in the Singrauli region. It explores the objective behind the creation of the Special Area Development Authority (SADA) in the 1980s, the challenges faced by the institution, and how the institution has evolved in the course of time. This research attempts to document the responses of respective stakeholders concerning the development of institutions in Singrauli. It also records the researcher's own experiences and associations with the district. It is important to note that the discourse on SADA has not been documented adequately, and there is sparse literature on the subject. Relevant documents related to this aspect were collected and analysed and concerned officials were interviewed to gather different perspectives on the successes and failures of SADA. This chapter highlights the reasons behind the reorganization of space or redrawing of geographical boundaries of the mineral-rich space of Singrauli and the creation of this new district. This chapter documents the existing compensation mechanisms and stakeholders' views with regard to resource development and centre–state relations with regard to land acquisition and resource development issues. Local community perceptions of the administration, mining benefits sharing and potential institutional framework for regional development were captured.

Administrative Region: Singrauli

Prior to the formation of the district, the Singrauli region was referred to as a large area (heavily forested) spread across the states of Madhya Pradesh (MP) and Uttar Pradesh (UP). Earlier, the region straddled the states of UP and MP and encompassed a part of Sidhi district of MP and Sonebhadra district of UP. The Sidhi and Sonebhadra districts have traditionally been considered backward districts (NITI Aayog, 2019) and, in particular, the area of Rihand in UP and Waidhan in MP were heavily forested, inhabited mainly by tribals and subsistence farmers and largely isolated from modern Indian society. Infrastructure was sparse, and subsistence agriculture and forest gathering were the predominant sources of livelihood in the region (Lokayan, 1985).

The discovery of coal, coupled with the creation of the Govind Ballabh Pant Sagar (GBPS) reservoir, or the Rihand lake, drastically altered the situation in the region. Hindalco (company owned by the Birlas) established a large alumina smelter and aluminium plant, and Northern Coalfields Ltd (NCL) developed opencast coal mining in the region. The rapid development of Singrauli placed considerable demands[1] on the prevailing administrative set-up to manage and direct the 'development' of the region. Some of the demands included coping with the aspirations of displaced families forced off their traditional land and livelihood, providing shelter and service needs of the local population and for the large number of migrants attracted by the new industrial activity, and dealing with negative externalities (environmental pollution) arising from mining operations and increasing industrial pollution.

The availability of coal, although of low grade (coal with high fly ash component), which could be easily extracted by opencast mining, and water from the Rihand lake led to the decision to establish a series of thermal power plants in both the UP and MP sides of the region. Thermal power generation in the Singrauli region is of strategic national importance, and the region is almost certainly destined to become one of the largest producers of coal-based thermal power in the world. Drastic economic and social changes in the Singrauli region were not, however, reflected in appropriate and parallel changes in the way it was managed. The administrative or institutional arrangements in both Sidhi and Sonebhadra remained under their respective divisions based on the district, block and *tehsil* as the administrative units headed by a district magistrate (DM) at the district headquarters, which is the core of local administration and includes representatives of all departments of the state government. These include both regulatory and developmental functions and responsibilities.[2]

In districts such as Sidhi and Sonebhadra, where agriculture provided the main occupation for more than 90 per cent of the population, the district administration was particularly not equipped to handle the transition and the complexities which arose from rapid industrialization and the consequent urbanization, changes in land use pattern, and increased demands for infrastructure and services (Lokayan, 1985). At the third tier, the local panchayats, with weak or non-existent technical

[1] Interview, Professor R. N. Sharma (TISS).

[2] Ibid.

and financial resource base, were incapable of offering any response to the pressures posed by the rapid industrialization of the region.

In Singrauli, government, at all levels, is involved in the 'development' of the region. The central government is involved primarily through the activities of NCL, which mines coal, and the National Thermal Power Corporation (NTPC), which generates power. Further participation by the central government is restricted to minor activities of the Ministry of Rural Development, Ministry of Urban Development and Ministry of Environment and Forests, which are undertaking national projects in the region. State government involvement is focused on their own economic activities, on those of the various line agencies undertaking small infrastructure or other development programmes in the region, and on the activities of MP and UP SADAs.

Decisions related to the location of resource-specific projects and capital-intensive industries are taken at the national and state levels. The local administration becomes involved only when asked to facilitate land acquisition, provide infrastructure support (power, water, communication and supporting services) and perhaps housing. These are beyond the capacity of the district administration. There appear to be weak coordination between departments of the central government that make the decision to locate massive commercial investments in a particular region and the local government agencies that are required to expand their own activities in order to provide the required infrastructure and service support for the proposed investment. Therefore, provision of infrastructure, especially that relating to activities other than the purely industrial, always lags behind demand.[3]

Special Area Development Authorities (SADAs)

The state governments of MP and UP partially anticipated the 1993 Constitutional Amendment Act[4] when they established SADAs in the Singrauli region. These were set up in response to the urban or industrial impact of the Rihand lake, power and industrial development and *inter alia* to deal with the interface between urban and rural development. The two SADAs were formed under the Madhya Pradesh Town and Country Planning Act of 1975, under notification number 645-XXXII-85, of 8 February 1985, and the Uttar Pradesh SADA Ordinance

[3] Interview, DM 1, Singrauli.

[4] The 73rd and 74th Amendment Acts of the Constitution of India, in 1993, led to the division of powers and functions to local self-governments (panchayats at village level and municipalities and municipal corporations in towns and large cities).

1985 and UP SADAs Act 1986 respectively.[5] SADAs were conceptualized as urban entities acting as municipal corporations, administered by a chief executive reporting to a board. The review of the documents (letters, reports and so on in the NTPC library; EDF, 1995; GHK/MRM International, 1994b) and interviews[6] suggests that the principal functions of SADA include (a) land use planning and development control, (b) infrastructure and service development, (c) rehabilitation and resettlement of oustees, (d) municipal management, (e) land acquisition, development, and disposal and (f) assessing and collecting taxes and fees. While the Singrauli SADA from the MP region undertook all of these functions until 1998, the UP SADA, known as the Shaktinagar SADA (SSADA), only undertook functions (a) and (e) and has yet to implement any actions under function (f).

Singrauli SADA (MP) and Rural–Urban Dilemma

SADAs were directly controlled by the state governments and they theoretically acted as urban development authorities with the powers of municipal corporations. The Singrauli region, however, can hardly be considered 'urban'; it still comprises scattered pockets of semi-urban, formal and informal townships in a rural area. The project developers, that is, NCL, NTPC, UPSEB and private corporations, administer their formal townships autonomously. However, SADAs faced several difficulties in executing their roles primarily because of limited revenue generating sources and lack of local support, due partly to: the exemption of local, state and central governments from property tax, which removes a large potential source of revenue for the region; their inability to raise property or holding taxes from NCL and NTPC (due to those being central government undertakings); the limited urban area and, hence, limited property tax base; and their being not accountable to the inhabitants of the SADA area. Moreover, because the MP SADA was given development functions, the 133 villages that fall within its jurisdiction no longer qualify for centrally funded rural assistance programmes. Although urban programmes are available, these are concentrated in the larger urban centres and have not reached out to the more rural parts of the area (EDF, 1995).[7]

It also appears that SADAs are to a degree neglected by the states, which consider large-scale mitigation measures for the problems of the Singrauli region to be primarily the responsibility of the central government, which financed and

---

[5] Documents, letters, reports and so on in the NTPC library.

[6] Interviews, SADA ex-officials and commissioner, Nagar Nigam, Singrauli.

[7] Interview, SADA ex-officials.

owns the majority of the industrial development in the area.[8] A World Bank report[9] notes, 'The State Government of UP considers the problem of the Singrauli area to be a Central Government concern.' There is a marked difference between the levels of activity and commitment of the two SADAs, perhaps reflecting the differing attitudes of the respective state governments. One indication of the difference is their varying levels of responsibility and ability to utilize funds. The World Bank financed the Uttar Pradesh Urban Development Project (Loan 2797-IN), which included an element for the Shaktinagar area of the region, with a loan of ₹30 million. This opportunity to upgrade social and physical infrastructure for local communities, however, was not taken up by the UP government.[10]

Singrauli's SADA activities have included the rehabilitation of oustees from the VSTTP (NTPC) projects. It involved resettlement and rehabilitation (R&R) of approximately 2,300 families from 20 project villages. Review of the documents suggests that the MP SADA performed some of its developmental functions during this period (see Table 8.1). However, NTPC claims that the Navjeevan Vihar Township (which is NTPC's R&R colony) is only one-third completed, whilst most of the funds entrusted to SADA for its development have been disbursed during that period. Analysis of the letters (correspondence between NTPC and SADA) and the GHK report indicates that shortage of funds bedevils SADA's activity; programmes amounting to ₹86.4 million were prepared for 1993–1994 but forecast income was not expected to exceed ₹56.4 million. Of this, only ₹27.9 million was the actual revenue, the balance of ₹28.5 million being loans, grants and subsidies. Revenues do not match expenditure and are based on subventions; financial self-reliance of these institutions seems a long way off (GHK/MRM International, 1994b). The Singrauli SADA was dissolved in 1995 and the Singrauli Nagar Nigam came into existence under the MP Municipalities Act of 1956. Presently, the municipal corporation covers an area of 280 square kilometres comprising 65 villages (Directorate of Census Operations, 2011).

Despite inadequate coordination and weak institutional governance, substantial economic progress in the context of resource development has been made in the region. Several power stations have been built; NTPC is an important and profitable national utility and NCL is the most productive opencast coal subsidiary of Coal India Limited (CIL). In the last one decade, the region has received huge private sector investments, which have led to the creation of an independent district to facilitate this private capital into the region. This reflects economic progress in absolute terms, yet the benefits of this economic progress and the associated

---

[8] Interview, R. S. Sharma, Tata Institute of Social Sciences (TISS), Mumbai.

[9] World Bank Inspection Panel Report on Singrauli; interview, World Bank officials.

[10] Interview, World Bank official.

Table 8.1 Development activities undertaken by SADA until September 1992

Activities	*Numbers*
Construction of primary and middle schools	46
Villages electrified	30
Shops construction	44
Residential plots allotments	500
House allotments	1,000

Source: Author.

development in the region have been felt more by people outside the region (through provision of cheap power to some of the major states of India) than by those within, the relatively few inside the region being those benefitting as employees of NCL, NTPC or the private industries, even though most of the skilled professionals are from outside Singrauli and only some of the unskilled jobs have been offered to the local populace of Singrauli. These capital-intensive industries employ relatively few, and many of these employees are skilled technicians and professionals who have to be brought into the region from outside. Employment opportunities for the indigenous people of the region have been limited and mostly in menial service roles. Major industries can be characterized as having attracted migrant skilled labour into the region whilst displacing the indigenous unskilled labour.

Institutional Weakness of the SADAs

While the MP SADA and SSADA are dissimilar, there are a number of problems common to both which have seriously compromised their effectiveness. People affected by the upheaval have had little say in the management of the change that has taken place in the region. There is lack of local representation, since all SADA members are appointed by the state government rather than elected by local residents. Local political leaders V. P. Singh and Ram Ashok Sharma of the Congress party said, 'SADA has primarily been an administrative body and we were never invited to discuss local issues as it is done for Municipal and Panchayat bodies; political representations must be there, otherwise the real issues would never get highlighted.'

Review of letters[11] and reports indicates that the financial planning was inadequate and there was lack of strategic management. There was severe lack of financial resources and an underdeveloped and porous revenue base (property

[11] A dossier was prepared of all the correspondence between NTPC, the state and the central governments, and the World Bank during this period, and NTPC files were reviewed to draw an understanding of the opinion of the concerned stakeholders.

tax arrears appear to be significant). There was lack of technical and skilled staff; the SADAs have either the divisional commissioner or the district collector as a part-time chairman, and there was lack of professional officers capable of discharging various functions vested in and required of the SADAs. The SADAs do not have at their disposal an interdisciplinary planning team that has the capability of preparing a prospective regional structure and development plan, the implementation of which could go a long way towards ensuring that industrial and urban activity is appropriately located and sustainably managed within the region. There was lack of support from the states; senior state representatives often express the belief that many concerns in the region should fall within the remit of the central government due to the significant presence of public sector corporations.[12] The SADAs were unable to tax, influence or control the activities of NCL, NTPC and large private sector enterprises. A crucial concern is the lack of financial resources available to the SADAs. Despite enormous capital investments and cash flows from the sale of coal, electricity, aluminium, carbon chemicals, and so on, there was no effective tax base to underpin the necessary existing institution.

The district administration has its budget approved by the state and allotted and devolved to the district's various heads of departments. The district administration does not have taxation powers and cannot raise additional resources. The local government, that is, a municipality or a development authority, does have taxation powers, including tax on property, service charges, receipts from the sale of immovable property and betterment levies. However, so far as service charges and property taxes are concerned, very little is received by the local bodies due to evasion by the centrally owned, politically powerful heavy industries combined with a certain lack of commitment; inadequate evaluation and collection capabilities have prevented the resource base of the development authorities from achieving any significant size. Furthermore, because the state government holds the land, even this resource is largely denied to the development authorities.

In all probability, the states hope that the central government will assist them by diverting resources to the region and by pursuading public sector agencies and private interests to contribute more to the costs of development in the region. The interview of DM reflects that

> the regional needs of Singrauli are very different, it is primarily a rural set up, all the industries in the region irrespective whether it is a Public undertaking or Private, must be taxed at a local level may be a 'development cess', which could be directly utilized for the regional development. The normal routine budget of the

[12] Interview, ex-commissioner, Sidhi.

> district would not be capable of handling these massive transformations in this region. And this is not matter of charity or CSR, it should be seen as their legal right. If locals are bearing these hardships since last so many decades why they should not be benefit from this.[13]

Ineffective and Inefficient Institutions

The structure of government in the region appears to be inadequate and inappropriate to cope with the development which has already taken place and which is proposed. The region straddling the borders of two states with differing legislation, development priorities and programmes makes the situation worse. It appears that the establishment of SADAs covering part of the region led to the withdrawal of the activities of many central and state government programmes. The SADAs, however, appear to be unable to fill the gap left by the 'withdrawal' of other agencies. Traditionally, the smaller municipalities or municipal councils report to the DM, with the larger municipal corporations reporting directly to the state government. Municipal corporations reporting in the latter manner are known as incorporated municipalities. The relationship which has developed between the smaller municipalities and the DMs varies from state to state, but in general it is probably fair to say that DMs responsible for large districts, typically 10,000 square kilometres in MP and 5,000 square kilometres in UP, will have leanings towards the rural areas. This is understandable, but does little to help urban areas, which, because of their broad range of interacting activities, have not been easily understood by the 'rural' oriented administration. District administration working in tribal remote areas where communications are poor can hardly be expected to understand the abrupt urbanization process; when urban impacts are parachuted into areas of this kind, the effect can be dramatic. Despite SADAs, the traditional institutions have not been capable of responding to the externally induced 'development' in the region, nor had they the resources to do so, nor have they been able to cope with the disruption caused, particularly at the rural–urban interface (EDF, 1995).[14]

To summarize the experiences of earlier decades, the region was previously a traditional, geographically isolated and backward area. The administrative set-up was neither designed to cope with nor was it capable of coping with the dramatic changes that occurred after the 1960s, when significant mining and industrial operations were established. Administrative capabilities still lag behind those needed to positively respond to the prevailing and expected economic and social structural changes in the Singrauli region. The present

---

[13] Interview, DM 1, ex-commissioner, SADA.

[14] Ibid.

research reflects that even till today, the development in the Singrauli region has been largely unplanned and uncoordinated and has frequently been socially and environmentally 'unjust' or inappropriate. The region is characterized by inadequate and ineffective governance, which has played a major part in the problematic and uneven development that plagues the region. Strengthening the regional administrative framework is vital if the problems created through past growth in the region are to be mitigated and if future development is to be carried out based on the principles of sound and efficient economic and land use planning and environmental sustainability. Despite the formation of the two SADAs, to strengthen regional development control and planning capabilities, the overall institutional framework remained weak, with poor resource mobilization, and the management of the region's growth was fractured and uncoordinated. Almost all the agencies of the state were underfunded and lacked resources to cope with the issues and dynamic changes that occurred during 1990s.[15]

Space Reorganization and Formation of Singrauli District

During 2000 and 2005, the government of MP, with the objective of creating a 'better investment climate', conducted several rounds of industrial meets in its state capital, Bhopal, by offering industrial tax rebates and other benefits to attract private investments to the state. Simultaneous to this process, during 2005–2006, the Government of India proposed to set up ultra mega power projects (UMPPs) to accelerate the generation of thermal power in the country. A public sector company, Power Finance Corporation Ltd, first formulated these UMPPs, with a special purpose vehicle created for each UMPP that obtains most regulatory clearances and consents, and then transfers these to the successful bidder based on the lowest levelled tariff. Reliance Power received three of these UMPPs,[16] one each in MP, Jharkhand and Andhra Pradesh. As a result, by 2006, the government of MP received ₹1,400 billion of private investments[17] for developing thermal power and coal mining projects in the Singrauli region. The redrawing of the geographical boundaries of Singrauli and the setting up of a new district is clearly linked to the need for capital. The decision was taken in order to facilitate private investment in the Singrauli region and to provide better administrative support to facilitate land acquisition and land transfer to the private corporations. It also demonstrates a form

[15] Interview, NTPC officials, ex-SADA officials, Singrauli.

[16] UMPPs: These are large thermal power projects with the average investment in the range of ₹200 billion and thermal power generation capacity of around 4,000 megawatts.

[17] See https://singrauli.nic.in/en/, accessed on 7 February 2020.

of 'crony capitalism' where the role of the state has been reduced to performing managerial functions for capitalists. However, this special attention for Singrauli was never felt by the state earlier, to electrify its very own villages or to focus on poverty alleviation, socio-economic and cultural issues of the local inhabitants, and environmental concerns of the region.

It is also important to discuss the resource development activities in the Sonebhadra district of UP and why the neighbouring state government did not feel the need for such space reorganization. As discussed earlier, a significant part of the Moher sub-basin lies in the Singrauli district of MP and a small part lies in the Sonebhadra district of UP. The Singrauli main basin lies in the western part of the coalfield and is largely unexplored. The present private sector investments (2008 onwards) in thermal power generation and coal mining activities for the future blocks are concentrated in the Moher sub-basin. It clearly indicates the concentration of private investments in Singrauli and the need for better administrative support for facilitating these investments. The coal blocks in Sonebhadra district have already been allocated to NCL units in the 1990s by the central government, and they are engaged in the mining of coal for the last three decades, and at present there, there are no coal blocks available for allocation to private industries in that region.

To understand the objective behind the creation of this district, further investigation was done and district and revenue officials were interviewed. In one of the interviews, the *tehsildar*[18] in charge of Singrauli land acquisition explained,

> The land acquisition is a tedious and exhaustive process which requires day to day communication and interactions with the project developers regarding their land requirement from civil work point of view, land and family survey, relocation of families, etc. and it is not that only revenue department gets involved in this process but sometimes police department has to intervene to control the law and order situations, as land acquisition work often lead to public protest and violence. Previously the earlier district headquarter was in Sidhi, which is 130 km away from Singrauli and the connecting road is in terrible condition, it takes 3.5 hours to reach there, in fact the road condition is so bad that even if you are not suffering from backache problem you will develop one if you travel on that road for few months. It would have been extremely difficult to administer the land acquisition work from Sidhi district head quarter. The initial procedure for land acquisition such as preliminary notification for land acquisition under Section 4 of the L.A. act 1894, for some of these private projects such as Reliance-Sasan, was done in August 2006 from Sidhi office only but later on the government decided that it should be done from Singrauli itself and hence a district status was provided to the region.

[18] Interview, *tehsildar*, Singrauli.

The interviews of the revenue and other district officials suggest that facilitating the third phase of private investments into the Singrauli region and land acquisition could be definitely one of the significant reasons behind the redrawing of the district boundary. However, it is important to note that the previous land acquisitions for Phase I and II projects (state and central government projects) were administered from the earlier district headquarters of Sidhi. It is only for the third phase of acquisition that this need was felt by the state government.

Blurred Lines of Administration: 'Who' Is 'Who'?

On 22 May 2008, the district of Singrauli was officially created and the DM office was set up at the tourism department guesthouse in Waidhan, which is now the district headquarters. The private corporations that made investments in the district simultaneously set up their own regional offices in Singrauli (with their corporate head offices in Mumbai and Delhi). The private corporations set up the DM office by providing all the necessary logistic support such as furniture, stationery, 50 desktop computers, laptops, 35 vehicles for government officials, human resources (25 computer operators, 10 retired revenue officials, 10 executives, and casual employees were hired on the payroll of the companies), land acquisition survey team and so on. Undoubtedly, the existing local infrastructure in Singrauli was not adequate to perform the enormous task of acquiring land for the private corporations. The interview of a general manager of a private company recorded,

> We have just created the working environment for the district administration so that they can comfortably work and perform their duties. However, as per the law we have also deposited the land acquisition service charge (i.e. 10 per cent of the land acquisition award which is charged for executing the land acquisition task) to the government. And these logistics support are just to create a working environment for them.

To expedite the process of land acquisition, the corporations provided all the necessary support to the government, rather sometimes encroaching upon and taking over the duties of the district administration. For instance, the land and asset survey under Section 6 of the LA Act is to be conducted by the revenue officials of the district but, in most of the cases, it was conducted by the hired survey team of the private corporations, and data was entered and compiled by the private offices and sent to the DM office for endorsement. One of the DMs said,

> We are working on mutually agreeable timelines with the project developers, and the district administration has adopted professional approach in time bound delivery of land to the projects. The developers come with their project timelines

> deliverable that they have agreed with the financial institutions, and they are under continuous pressure from the Banks that have provided them with loan for the projects. The delay in land acquisition and the project cost overrun is one of the major concern for most of the stalled projects in India, which is creating unfavorable investment climate in the country, so it is critical for the State to ensure favorable conditions so that these financial irregularities do not affect the development in the country.[19]

The interview clearly suggests that these officials were posted with clear instructions from the state government to facilitate the time-bound delivery of land to the project developers. One of the revenue officials said,

> These company officials create a lot of pressure on us through the state government, everybody is involved in this process from the Chief Minister's Office to the junior revenue staff (patwari) of the district. Land acquisition is a humongous task it requires time and resources, the companies are providing all the resources but they are not giving us time. We do not want to be unfair with the people, ultimately it's the company who has to pay for all the losses under acquisition, but in the process of quickly finishing the tasks we make some mistakes. We are under lot of pressure ... sir....

It was observed that there was a high level of interference by industrialists (project developers) in the functioning of the district administration. The officers were under tremendous pressure to expedite the land acquisition tasks and DMs were frequently transferred in case they failed to deliver according to the project developers' timelines. However, it was also noticed that the first DM of Singrauli, who took charge in 2008, perhaps because of his past experience of handling land acquisition projects, was sensitive enough to revise the compensation package and develop a comprehensive rehabilitation plan for the affected families. But he was transferred within nine months of his posting and a new DM was posted with a clear mandate for time-bound land acquisition.

In recent years, it has been noticed that communities are demanding fair compensation for their loss of lands and livelihoods and greater share in project benefits. In the past decades, the state government was able to acquire large tracts of agricultural and forestlands with the outdated LA Act of 1894 by providing bare minimum compensation. There was discontent regarding compensation at two levels: between individuals and the project developers and also between the state and the central governments. However, the situation is now changing and the central government is deliberating on both land and mining laws to come up with fair and just compensation principles.

---

[19] Interview, DM 2.

Centre–State Relations

In the context of this study, analysing the way federalism plays out in the natural resource sector is very critical at this juncture of the evolution of the Indian political system, given its commitment to a more decentralized system of governance. In no sector is such an engagement more urgent than in the context of natural resource development, given the sharing of administrative and fiscal powers, along with growing responsibilities at the local level. A central issue, both from the point of the working federalism and in terms of the impacts that the resource development can have on local people and the region, is the monitoring, regulation, and enforcement of laws and rules in place.

Both the centre and state collect revenue through different taxes and levies imposed on mineral development under different legislations. States collects revenue through royalty, dead rent, cess, sales tax, environmental protection fees, prospecting and mining lease fees and so on. The centre collects revenue in the form of excise duty, forest conservation charges, corporate taxes and so on. There is discontent between the states and the centre, and the government is trying to resolve these issues; in fact, the Mines and Minerals (Development and Regulation) (MMDR) Bill is an initiative in that direction.[20] The interview of a senior district official[21] highlights that the quantum of revenue generated by Singrauli is significant, but the region does not receive a development budget in relation to the profit it generates for the state and central governments. There is no programme from the central government to compensate for the losses faced by the region due to mining activities.

The present analysis suggests that the key issue that is voiced by states[22] is about augmenting the revenues from the sources of wealth that the states have in order to promote development. At the local level, however, the local communities' concerns with resource development revolve around the impact it has on their lives and livelihoods and the need to address externalities when they arise as well as to increase the sharing of benefits of resource development with them. At Singrauli, public consultation meetings[23] in and around mining villages reflect a clear sense of dissatisfaction with the mining operations and their benefits. The local community is demanding a clear stake in the revenue stream of these projects

[20] Interview, additional secretary, Ministry of Coal, Delhi.

[21] Interview, commissioner, Sidhi.

[22] See Memorandum by the Mineral Rich States to Central Finance Commission.

[23] Public consultation meetings and focus group discussions (FGDs) were conducted around mining villages to understand the concerns and demands of the directly and indirectly affected families.

so that they can be the actual beneficiaries of 'development'. An 85-year-old man said, 'If we are bearing the burnt [*sic*] of development by losing our land, livelihood and by suffering pollution[,] at least we deserve direct benefit from these projects. Just by paying one time land compensation that too inadequate, these companies cannot run away from their responsibilities.'

One distinct observation is the change in the demands of the local people. In previous decades (also in the current phase of land acquisition) the demand was primarily around permanent employment for at least one member of the family. But now the project-affected families have understood that the employment demand is not a feasible option for the project developers as only a few people will get jobs in these projects. So, now, they are demanding a long-term profit sharing in these projects.

In the present study, it is noted that there are two layers of conflicts in the land acquisition and resource development debate. One layer is between the project developer and the affected community and the other is between the state government and the central government. As in the given precarious fiscal situation of the mineral-bearing states, there is a question with regard to the powers exercised by the centre, vide the MMDR Act, in fixing royalty rates for a resource that is, in principle, owned by the states. There is also discontent regarding the manner in which revisions are done by the centre in terms of their periodicity.[24] In the opinion of the state governments, the delay in the revision of the royalty rates by the centre result in significant losses to the state revenue.

Existing Compensation Arrangements and Gaps

An attempt has been made in the study to summarize the findings about existing revenue sharing arrangements and compensation payments and link them to the principles and indicate to whom or where the funds are supposed to go. The gaps identified are the potential new areas of compensation that need to be addressed. These relate to depletion in the case of finite resources and deal with sociocultural impacts of resource development. This is not only to suggest that environmental externalities, loss of land, and health and displacement impacts are being compensated satisfactorily but to make the point that these issues are addressed in the payment system, while depletion and sociocultural impacts are not. Another identified area is the local development fund, which should be targeted at improving the lives of the local people and making investments in the social and physical infrastructure of the region. There is need for much more detailed regional and project-level researches to be able to assess if compensation

[24] Interview, mining officer, MP State Mining Corporation.

payments for environmental and social costs generated by resource projects are fair and adequate. Even if compensation is paid for negative externalities generated, it cannot be said that all of the costs are reflected in the transaction and with the resource in question. Establishing norms for sector-wise social and environmental impacts also requires more detailed research. The study indicates that land sold for industrial and mining projects seems to be inadequately compensated.[25] However, the profitability of PSUs, such as NCL and NTPC, and the resource revenue generated from Singrauli since 2015 (as discussed in Chapter 6) appear to be significant. There has been no considerable change in the socio-economic profile of the local populace.

Minerals

In India, the proprietary title to minerals vests in the federating states. However, this ownership is subject to the legislation governing regulation and control of mining enacted by the parliament.[26] Minerals within the maritime jurisdiction of the country are owned by the central government. The MMDR Act confers upon state governments the right to allow exploitation of minerals by way of granting licence and lease. However, any permission or lease is to be granted in accordance with the MMDR Act and its rules as enacted and notified by the central government. Therefore, although a state may own the minerals, control over it lies with the centre. With respect to major minerals, states have little power except for their possession, receiving royalty and a few other payments. A mining lease is granted by the state but in doing so, the state is subject to the conditions and procedures laid down by the MMDR Act and the Mineral Concession Rules 1960. Neither can the states grant mining leases for Schedule I minerals without the central government's approval nor do they have a role in determining the rates of royalty, the most important non-tax revenue from minerals. However, states can impose certain additional conditions with respect to compensation for damage to the land, felling of trees and restrictions on surface operations.[27]

With respect to minor minerals such as mica, gypsum and so on the situation is different as states can make their own rules and regulations. The Panchayati Raj Extension to Schedule Areas of 1996 provides for a role for even the rural communities.[28] It mandated states to make provisions for obtaining

---

[25] Interview, director of TERI; FGD, district office, Singrauli.

[26] Regulation and development of minerals is a state subject, but it has to be in conformity with the central legislation.

[27] 27(2) of Mineral Concession Rules 1960.

[28] *Samatha vs State of A.P. and Ors.*, AIR 1997 SC 3297, JT 1997 (6) SC 449, 1997 (4) SCALE 746.

recommendations of the *gram sabha* or the panchayats at the appropriate level prior to the granting of prospecting licence or mining lease for minor minerals in Scheduled Areas.

Mining, like other economic sectors, is subject to several fiscal instruments that are used to raise resources to meet various developmental objectives of the government. Internationally, governments get their share of wealth created by mining either in the form of taxes or as non-pecuniary requirements on companies such as requiring them to create local infrastructure (roads, bridges and so on) and use local raw material or human resource. Focusing on fiscal instruments, several different types are levied on the mining sector with varying implications on economic efficiency, division of risks between state and companies, timing of tax flows to the government in the product cycle, ease of administration and other considerations. Further, given the high risk and high investment characteristics of the mining industry (such as long gestation periods, geological uncertainties, large sunk costs, dependence of specialized and imported machinery, long operation periods subject to political uncertainties and social opposition, cyclical nature of revenues, and sizeable social development and closure costs), most governments typically provide some sort of tax concessions to the industry in the form of tax holidays, accelerated depreciation, or concessions on export and other duties.[29]

Compared to taxation of other sectors, royalty is unique to sectors like mining in that it is a payment for ownership transfer of non-renewable natural resources, which in most countries is the property of the state. While it could take several forms, in most nations where minerals are the property of the state or of the people collectively, some sort of royalty is imposed. It thus is critical and often a contentious issue in the compensation debate.

Resource Revenues and Benefit Sharing

To ensure independence and fairness, there is need for a system outside of courts, the centre, or the states' authority to determine royalty rates and decide the allocation of compensation funds between the centre and states and between states and local governments. This could be institutionalized either through the Finance Commission or through an adjudicating mechanism which includes the central and state representatives or through collectives of states. Considering that states are seeking to attract new investments into resource development, compensation payments and revenue sharing need to ensure that they do not make the project unattractive.[30] Industrial agglomerations such as the Confederation of

[29] Interview, commissioner, industries, governmnt of MP.

[30] Interviews, executive director of TERI and director of CSE, Delhi.

Indian Industry (CII) and the Federation of Indian Chambers of Commerce and Industry (FICCI) generally advocate that such propositions can make industrial projects financially unviable.[31] However, review of the literature suggests that across the world, the principle of benefit sharing is commonly practised for sustainable development of the region.

In the context of revenue sharing and management of resource revenue, it is important to clearly demarcate the difference. Revenue sharing addresses (a) the split between the public and the private sectors and (b) the allocation of payments among the central, regional and local government levels; while revenue management refers to how these revenues are utilized to support development at the national and increasingly at the regional and local levels. With regard to revenue sharing, there is no universal percentage or formula; what is appropriate depends on the circumstance and what is acceptable to all stakeholders. With regard to revenue management, the capacity to efficiently use revenue is as important as generating adequate revenue. Particularly in rural regions such as Singrauli, local government may not have the resources and capacity to manage the impacts and social investments in a productive manner.

It is important to internalize in the planning that revenue sharing and compensation payments are based on principles, linked to the issues that they seek to address and have a legal basis for them. Multiplicity of payments to address the same issue needs to be avoided, as should ad hocism and arbitrariness and excessive burdening of the project, which could reduce the competitiveness of the resource vis-à-vis others. It needs to be reiterated here that in selecting an instrument, it needs to be ensured that there are no multiple charges for the same use and that the consumer is not overcharged.

An important aspect of compensation and benefit sharing is to ensure that the right groups of people are compensated. For instance, in Singrauli, there has been an influx of outside population into the region for casual, contractual and permanent employment opportunities. Over the years, a significant outside population has permanently settled in the region for employment reasons. It is important to ensure that the original inhabitants and indigenous populations who have been parting with their lands for resource development and bearing the huge 'cost' of development are identified to be the beneficiaries of such policy. Having a sense of where the funds collected are going, and to what levels, and to ensure transparency of fund movement, it becomes necessary to plan for this in advance through a clear 'follow the funds' approach. Figure 8.1 indicates more explicitly where these funds go or should go. It helps in understanding at what spatial level the revenues and compensation funds should be spent.

---

[31] CSE (2011) report.

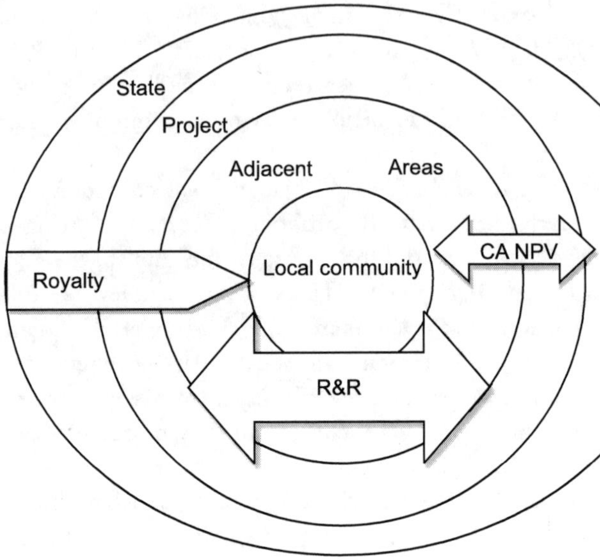

Figure 8.1 Payments and revenue distribution across stakeholder groups and spatial levels

Source: Author.

Notes: CA refers to compensatory afforestation; NPV refers to net present value.

Regional Developments and Institutional Framework for Singrauli

FGDs and public consultation meetings (PCMs)[32] in Singrauli and also the secondary data on social development indicators of the region suggest that the regional or local development so far has been unsatisfactory and local people have not benefitted from the resource development projects. Earlier institutions such as SADAs and their performances were reviewed and it was recorded that, without adequate and sustaining financial resources, institutions, however well-conceived, would not be successful. The design of financing plans is also important for supporting environmental policies, encouraging the development of democratic institutions, and economic and social development of the region. In the Singrauli region, there are different stakeholders who have economic interests: the central government, state governments, PSUs and private corporations, and the district administrations.

[32] FGDs 4 and 5 and PCMs 1 and 2 were conducted in the second phase of projects, particularly in the villages affected by NCL, since these are operational coal mining projects; people were able to respond to enquiries about their past experiences.

The central government is looking at Singrauli to contribute significantly to the development of the power sector where demand is rapidly outstripping supply. It is expected that by 2017, Singrauli would add 35,000 megawatts[33] of thermal power to grid. There is a growing demand–supply gap and peak power shortage is currently at 19 per cent. The state governments have grown accustomed to receiving income from coal royalties. It was studied that during the 1990s, these were accrued to the consolidated account and represented less than 1 per cent of the revenue receipts of the states.[34] The correspondence[35] between the SADAs and state governments during this period indicate that both states (MP and UP) refused to consider remitting all or part of this income to fund local projects in Singrauli. It is also important to note that both the states are populous and among the backward states of India and have several other development priorities as well.

The two government corporations, NTPC and NCL, have very significant stake in the region. More than a quarter of NTPC's electricity generating capacity is installed in the region (out of NTPC's 45,500 megawatt generation, 11,000 megawatts[36] come from the Singrauli region). Coal production by NCL from Singrauli during 2014–2015 was 68.64 million tons, which is more than 20 per cent of the total coal production by CIL from the entire country. The last five-year data (2008–2013) of Singrauli reflects that seven coal mining projects of NCL have paid ₹68,690 million as royalty and tax to the central and state exchequers and generated a profit of ₹131,640 million during this period (see Chapter 5). Similarly, NTPC is also a profitable PSU generating enormous profit from the Singrauli region.

The review of earlier reports[37] suggests that during 1992–1993, ₹1,870 million was paid by NCL to state governments in royalties and further ₹100 million in coal excise duty to the Ministry of Coal. Tax payments by NTPC were significantly smaller but their expenditures on infrastructure were greater than NCL. An analysis of the flow of funds during this period (1993–1994) between the centre, states, big firms and the community suggests that on a net basis, ₹2,500 million of financial surplus leaves the region each year. While some of this surplus will be needed to fund future investment in the area, it is considered that large corporations will have the capacity to fund social and environmental programmes in the area either directly or indirectly through taxes. The data reflects that during 1992–2012, resource revenue generation from Singrauli has grown enormously and it is consistently increasing due to the participation of private projects in the

[33] See www.singrauli.nic.in.

[34] Documents, letters, reports and so on in the NTPC library.

[35] Ibid.

[36] See https://www.ntpc.co.in/en/corporate-citizenship/ntpc-singrauli-region.

[37] NCL reports, Singrauli headquarters.

area. The geostrategic advantage of the region in relation to raw materials means that significant economic rent is earned from operations in Singrauli and there is little risk of the corporations becoming footloose and relocating elsewhere.

The communities in need consist of rural disadvantaged villages, emerging informal townships and impoverished oustees. A dual economy has emerged in which the workers in the large firms are predominantly from outside the region and live in company townships and whatever savings they make are sent outside the region. Oustees and other indigenous inhabitants have often lost their land and other livelihood opportunities as a result of the influx of new firms and are not compensated by an increase in economic activity from which they can benefit. As discussed earlier in this chapter, SADAs were set up in an effort to redress the balance but they failed because of lack of finance and made little impact on the region.

Sources of Funds

The development potential of the region is largely limited to coal-based industries. Considering private investments, it is envisaged that future growth of the region will continue at higher rates than those of the past decades. However, apart from the investments that are already proposed in the power and coal sectors, the region is unlikely to attract further capital from outside in the form of new, large or medium firms. Future development will encourage the growth of small, locally generated industries that take advantage of local linkages. The interview of a DM[38] reflects on the inability of the third-tier local authorities to increase the resource base available to the region. Financial plans must be based on retaining the larger proportion of financial resources that are generated in the region. This would require using the resources of PSUs as well as private corporations to finance development programmes at the local level. However, common but differential responsibility is required from the project developers, as the two PSUs have been operating in the region for last four decades while many of the private corporations are just beginning to operate in the region. The two large PSUs owe a greater responsibility towards the people of Singrauli. Also, the FGD suggests that local representation is such institutions is critical in planning and designing development programmes. Some of the potential sources of revenue generation options were explored and discussed at the local level in FGDs and PCMs.[39]

---

[38] Interview, DM 1, Bhopal.

[39] FGDs 6 and 7 and PCMs 3 and 4; these discussions were conducted at the district office among district officials and village and political representatives. Company officials were invited but there was no representation.

Property Tax

An analysis of the revenue options for local authorities points to the desirability of using property taxation as one of the main sources of funds. The advantage of collecting property tax by the local authority is that it spreads the burden of taxation over those property owners who have the ability to pay. It is capable of generating the amount of finance required through increased collection and assessment efficiency without increasing existing tax rates. The tax will encourage a more efficient use of land and possibly the selling off of surplus land[40] by big firms to the local authority and individuals. However, there are number of difficulties with property tax in India. The question of whether public corporations, such as NTPC and NCL, are subject to the tax is currently being tested in the courts. But in Delhi, the Delhi Development Authority has succeeded in raising taxes from central government bodies, while in many industrial areas of West Bengal, the state government has established notified area authorities instead of municipalities.[41] A holding tax is charged from each individual company based on the amount of land owned. Similar arrangements are made in other states of India, and there is a possibility of some negotiated settlement between the state government of MP, NTPC, NCL and private developers based on the arrangements made in other states. If these project developers in the region are not brought under property taxation, the tax will be perceived to be unfair. It will only be able to generate sufficient resources if the tax net is extended to firms and individuals with marginal ability to pay.

Royalty

The other two major sources of funds are coal royalties and the coal excise duty. Coal royalties are paid to the state governments but a share of the royalty to the local people will contribute in a significant way. The coal excise duty is collected from all coal mines under the Mines (Conservation and Development) Act of 1974 and distributed to environmental, coal conservation and other projects that qualify under the Act. It is apparent that the Singrauli region has not benefitted from this funding (FGD 6), although NCL makes payments from this fund of around ₹100 million per year (NCL reports). There is clear demand from the local community that a share of the coal royalty be set aside for their local development. A major advantage of this source of grant aid funds is that it would be available

[40] PSUs, such as NTPC and NCL, have acquired large tracts of land in the past, which are not in immediate use but kept behind fencing.

[41] SADA correspondence, from the NTPC library.

for pre-financing institution building and activities to increase local revenue generation capacity.

Environmental Taxes and User Charges

Environmental taxes and user charges should be important public finance instruments available to the local government, particularly to the agencies concerned with pollution control and water management and those delivering environmental services, for example, water supply, sanitation and solid waste management. It is recommended that taxes on chemical inputs, water resources and waste products be examined in order to both improve the operations of imperfect markets in the region and achieve the goal of environmental sustainability. These taxes are unlikely to generate substantial net resources (although they should cover the costs of the services provided).

Corporate Social Responsibility Fund

From a policy viewpoint, corporate social responsibility (CSR) is being redefined with the clear shift from philanthropy to a more responsible social development in India. For PSUs, such as NTPC and NCL, this is being undertaken through the central public sector enterprises in India with directives from the Department of Public Enterprises, Ministry of Heavy Industries and Public Enterprises, Government of India. While for the private corporations, the Ministry of Corporate Affairs, Governemnt of India, has introduced an independent law on CSR under Section 135 of the Companies Act of 2013, which mandates allocating 2 per cent of the annual profit for CSR activities in the project area. Considering the profitable corporations operating in Singrauli, such legislation would generate significant fund for local development projects. CSR budgetary provision under the Companies Act came into effect from 1 April 2014, and according to the new law all private and public corporations are covered under this law. The group discussion on CSR in Singrauli highlights that the people are largely dissatisfied with the developers' approach towards CSR projects, which have mostly been superficial and casual interventions in the region. A 28-year-old young man pointed out in the group discussion, 'The company officials are more interested in clicking photographs for their annual reports under their company banner rather than seriously understanding the village issues.' It was clear from the group discussion that the local people expect serious and organized CSR projects rather than the ad hoc activities that the companies have been doing in the past.

DMF Singrauli: Case Study

Over 60 per cent of MP's District Mineral Foundation (DMF) collection comes from just one district, Singrauli – a major coal mining hub. The Centre for Science and Environment (CSE) analysed the DMF plan prepared for Singrauli for 2016–2017. And the analysis has been very useful in highlighting the current trend of budgetary allocations and utilizations of DMF funds. The author also visited the Singrauli district headquarters to interview district officials and mining companies to get an understanding of the ground situation and how the DMF policy is unfolding. The data provided by CSE was also triangulated in the course of the analysis. It is important to highlight that the resource revenue sharing experiences of some of the resource-rich countries also reflect that sometimes these policies do not result in anticipated outcomes and often lead to the issues of corruption.

During the fiscal year 2016–2017, Singrauli received ₹2,730 million as the DMF budget, and 63 per cent of the DMF fund was allocated for physical infrastructure projects, for instance, roads, bridges and so on. It is important to highlight that the state and the central government already have budgets for physical infrastructure purpose and there are already ongoing programmes to meet such requirements. According to the fund utilization guidelines set by the Pradhan Mantri Khanij Kshetra Kalyan Yojana (PMKKKY), the district has allocated 80 per cent of its budget to 'other priority areas'; however, as per the guidelines, not more than 40 per cent of the budget should be spent in 'other priority areas'. In 2018, the National Institution for Transforming India (NITI) Aayog under 'Aspirational District Program' declared Singrauli as the 'third most backward district' of the country, which clearly signifies the poor human development indicators and lack of social infrastructure in the district. The district fares poorly on some of the critical human development indicators, for instance, nutrition, access to clean drinking water, mortality, education and so on. In view of the existing social reality of Singrauli, the allocation of the DMF funds to such physical infrastructure raises concerns about the planning process and the rationality behind such allocations.

Singrauli: The 3rd-Most Backward District – Social Reality

Drinking Water

In January 2010, the Union Ministry of Environment and Forests (now the Ministry of Environment, Forest and Climate Change) had declared Singrauli as the ninth most critically polluted area in the country. Water remains one of the most stressed resources in the district – less than 1 per cent of its rural households get treated tap water. Uncovered wells serve over 58 per cent of the population and hand pumps cater to another 31 per cent – but the water they offer is believed to be severely contaminated and barely potable (Directorate of Census Operations, 2011). Despite this situation, the district has allocated only 0.9 per cent of its DMF budget for drinking water and that too entirely for digging tube wells.

Welfare of Women and Children

With an infant mortality rate (IMR) of 67 and a shockingly high under 5 mortality rate (U5MR) of 112, the district is one of the worst in terms of child development indicators. Close to 35 per cent of the children here also suffer from various symptoms of malnutrition, such as stunted or wasted growth (MoHFW Survey, 2016). The DMF budget, however, chooses to ignore this: a cursory allocation of ₹17 million (0.6 per cent of the budget) has been provided towards Anganwadi Centres (AWCs) and ₹2 million (only 0.07 per cent) for developing fair price centres (under public distribution system).

Healthcare

The health infrastructure in Singrauli adds to the health challenges in this critically polluted area. There is a severe shortage of primary healthcare facilities and resources in the rural areas. According to Rural Health Statistics (2014–2015), there are only 15 primary health centres (PHCs) in the rural areas of the district. Therefore, effectively, there is one PHC per 64,000 people. According to Indian Public Health Standards (IPHS), there should be at least one PHC per 30,000 people in rural areas and one per 20,000 people in tribal areas. The DMF budget fails to account for this extreme shortage. The ₹445 million health budget cursorily mentions construction of trauma and health centres, distribution of health equipment and renovation of waiting rooms.

Education

Access to education and availability of educational infrastructure are challenges in Singrauli. The education sector in the district suffers from the following maladies: acute shortage of teaching staff, with more than half the primary schools in the district having a pupil–teacher ratio higher than 30, which is the prescribed norm under Right to Education; high dropout rates, with nearly 20 per cent of the students dropping out of schools as they reach the eighth standard (Directorate of Census Operations, 2011). The DMF plan does not address any of these gaps and issues. A mere 2 per cent allocation for education vaguely describes projects such as installing green boards, constructing waiting rooms, putting up coolers and so on.

Recommendations

As the DMF enters its third year, it is an important point in time to understand the course and progress of implementation so that necessary measures can be adopted to make it effective for serving the best interests of mining-affected people and regions. The obligation of the DMF to perform well towards its objective is also very high because various government welfare programmes have fallen short of their intended purpose in the past. This is arguably owing to inadequate funds, delay in fund release by authorities, difficulty in processing claims by beneficiaries, and lack of proper planning, to name a few. The DMF comes with some functional advantages which do not have such constraints. These include a non-lapsable and significant financial corpus, targeted beneficiaries, defined areas of intervention and a very precise objective. The job is now to harness all of these to realize the potential of the DMF. The review of the Singrauli DMF indicates that there is a long way to go in achieving its objectives. There are gaps in various fronts, including institutional and administrative issues, DMF planning and fund allocation, and people's engagement in the decision-making process.

Conclusion

This chapter summarizes the importance of sound institutions and governance strategies for local and regional development. Several lessons can be drawn from the experiences of SADAs, which can guide the development of future institutions in the region. The establishment of the new district highlights the strength of private capital in reorganizing the space according to its own need. It substantiates the resource–capital relationships, valorization of resources and mobility of capital. The manner in which some of the land acquisition tasks have been executed raises serious questions about the role of the state. The blurred lines of administration and encroachment into the functioning of the district administration represent the emergence of 'crony capitalism' where the state has been reduced to performing the role of a managerial workforce for the capitalists. In order to create an 'investment climate' and facilitate the entry of private investment into the region, the state has undermined its regulatory functions.

Some of the measures suggested in the study need to be translated into law or may require amendments to existing laws to create a greater financial and institutional capacity. On the part of the companies, it will require integrating such payments and claims into project planning from the outset. It is important that project developers conceptualize these costs and transactions as part of production costs. Such claims will involve a clear share in economic rents earned from the resource. If the state is the resource owner, the cost should accrue to the state, and if the resource is an attribute of other resources which belong to the local people or communities (for example, land, in case of minerals), then they should have a right to a part of the rent over and above the land, R&R, and compensation payments that are made for transfer of rights over the land.[42] As states have a right to the royalty from mineral production, as owners of the mineral, similarly, the local people in the mining region too should have the right to royalty. It is, therefore, fiscally, ethically and politically correct to give them a share in the royalty. It is particularly important that the payments are not cornered by stronger groups but used to empower those who have been hitherto marginalized. The portion of the royalty thus collected has to be earmarked for development of human capital in the mining area and for an intergenerational fund as this is a finite resource. The rationale for earmarking the fund for development of human capital in the mining region is to convert natural capital that is used up in the form of minerals to human capital, thereby implementing the weak sustainability principle. The case for setting up an intergenerational fund is to share the benefits of this depleting resource with future generations. Until these local issues are addressed at their very source and the immediate population and the region start benefitting from such projects, the problems of uneven development cannot be countered.

[42] For similar arguments, see Rothman (2000: 5) and Cernea (2007: 1035–1036).

9

Land Acquisition and Its Socio-economic Implications
Field Survey

This chapter documents the socio-economic impact of land acquisition and displacement processes and particularly focuses on the project-affected families (PAFs) of the third phase of land acquisition projects in Singrauli. The land acquisition and PAF details were collected from the district headquarters and respective project developers' offices. The experience of the land acquisition process and challenges faced by the PAFs were documented. From the third phase of land acquisition in Singrauli, six private sector projects spread across 26 villages were identified and the PAFs from each project were selected for the household survey. The broad objective of the survey was to understand the impact of land acquisition on lives and livelihood patterns of the PAFs, the adequacy of the compensation amount, utilization of the compensation amount, coping strategy of the PAFs and to identify the gaps in the land acquisition policy. The chapter also demonstrates the project-specific data on cost of private land acquisition vis-à-vis the total project investment. It studies the issues of community forest rights and total forestlands being diverted for industrial purposes in the last five decades. Issues related to land entitlement to receive compensation were studied and analysed. To holistically understand the multiple views, all the concerned stakeholders (district administration, project developers, the PAFs and civil societies) were identified and interviewed.

Land Acquisition and Displacement, Third Phase

As discussed in Chapter 6, Singrauli has a long history of displacement (multiple), and it is a 'space of dependence' which is serving national interest since 1960 bearing huge social and environmental costs. After the formation of this district in 2008, around 31,619 acres of land has been acquired and allotted for various projects,

Table 9.1 Details of land acquired and allotted for various projects in Singrauli between 2008 and 2015

Land category	*Area in acre*
Private land (acquired)	10,351
Government land (allotted)	6,282
Forest land (allotted)	14,230
Revenue – forest land (allotted)	756
Total	31,619

Source: Singh (2015: fieldwork data of 2015, collected from District Revenue Department, Singrauli).

out of which around 10,000 acres of private land (see Table 9.1 and Figure 9.1) has been acquired displacing more than 15,000 families in the district. Undoubtedly, it is one of the few districts of India which have made such phenomenal progress in acquiring land during this period despite the country-wide social protests and large-scale dissatisfaction with the colonial Land Acquisition (LA) Act of 1894. The government of Madhya Pradesh (MP) has paid the least attention to amending its own state resettlement and rehabilitation (R&R) policy; however, the priority has been on attracting private investments to the region. It appears that the government has not incorporated the learning from the earlier phases of displacements and the previous rehabilitation experiences of the PAFs. Otherwise, along with the establishment of the district headquarters, the state would have also set up a rehabilitation department at the district level to oversee the large-scale displacement and R&R process. The government and the developers need to understand that R&R is a 'project within project' and requires equal effort and attention as given to acquisition of land. However, the primary focus of the district administration has been the acquisition and transfer of land to private developers.

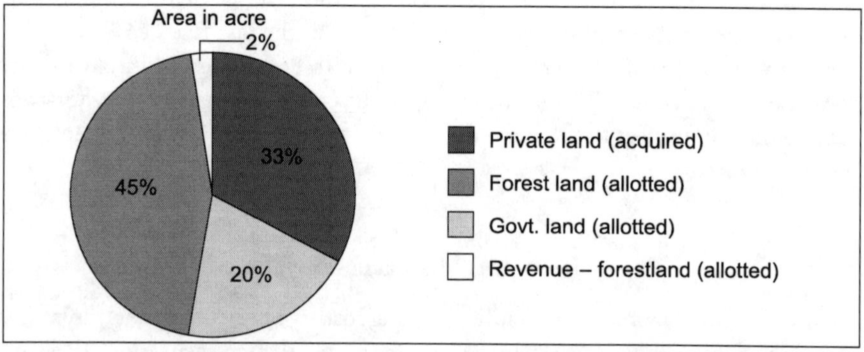

Figure 9.1 Percentage share of land acquired for various projects in Singruali, 2008–2015
Source: Singh (2015: fieldwork data from 2013 to 2015).

Revenue Forestland

As discussed in Chapter 3, the recognition of rights under Forest Rights Act (FRA) and community forest rights (CFR) remains a major concern in Singrauli, regarding identification of beneficiaries and compensating them under the land acquisition process. In the Singrauli region, the category of revenue forestland creates another set of complexities for the PAFs to claim their entitlements for compensation in land acquisition projects. As the name indicates, it is neither purely revenue land nor forestland; it is that category of land which does not have the forest density of 226 trees in 1 hectare of land to be declared as forest areas (Forest Conservation Act of 1980) but contains shrubs and small trees demarcated in the revenue land. According to Upadhya et al. (2006), who term this as 'Orange Area', this is a result of lack of coordination between forest and revenue departments, ambiguity in understanding of the Zamindari/Malguzari Abolition Act of 1950 and State Land Revenue Codes, and faulty adoption of administrative and political mechanisms to give effect to the rights of the people, especially tribals.

As per the LA Act of 1894, the requisition of land under project-notified area (Section 4 of the LA Act) is made to the respective department of the government and the project developer deposits the acquired land value into the revenue and forest department treasuries. For the acquired forestland, net present value (NPV) is calculated per hectare of forestland as per the government guidelines and the project developers deposit the amount to the forest department. Along with this, the project developer also deposits the amount for compensatory afforestation on twice the area of the forestland acquired for that particular project.[1]

The problem originates when a few occupants (generally poor landless households) who reside and till this particular land parcel (revenue forestland) for subsistence come under the process of land acquisition. At the government level, disputes arise between revenue and forest departments for claiming compensation for this patch of land. In most cases, the forest department gets the priority for compensation but sometimes the developer has to make double compensation to both the revenue and the forest departments. The interview of revenue officials[2] reflects that no department wants to lose the revenue in the land acquisition process and that is the reason behind claiming this compensation. However, it is the responsibility of the state government to conduct periodic land regularization but that does not happen due to inefficiency and corruption, which is why this complexity exists in Singrauli. The occupants on the revenue forestland are most affected as they are compensated in an ad hoc manner in the

---

[1] Interview, district forest officer, Singrauli, 2014.

[2] Interview, revenue inspector (RI) and *tehsildar*, Singrauli, 2014.

form of rehabilitation packages. Because if the government declares overtly that the forest department has been compensated for that patch of land, then, under FRA, a survey procedure has to be conducted to identify those occupants and the area of land that they were tilling before the land acquisition process so that they can be fairly compensated for their lost assets.

The review of revenue documents and interviews indicates that 92 hectares of revenue forestland was acquired for the Reliance Sasan project and 67 hectares of revenue forestland was acquired in the Moher coal mining project (data collected from Revenue Office, Singrauli, by the author). In both projects, approximately 40 PAFs were officially recorded as occupants who were residing and having a homestead in the project-notified area. These PAFs were only provided with the rehabilitation allowances but not compensated for their land. The families whose homesteads were outside the project-notified area but were tilling the revenue forestland for livelihood were excluded from any benefit.

Private Land

The state of MP is India's second largest state in terms of geographical area, that is, 0.308 million square kilometres, which is 9 per cent of the total geographical area of the country. The state has a decent forest cover of around 9.5 million hectare area, constituting about 30.88 per cent of the state's geographical area. According to agriculture census 2010–2011, the average size of landholdings declined from 2.22 hectares (2000–2001) to 1.78 hectares (2010–2011). Marginal and small farmers account for 71 per cent and hold 34 per cent of the total area (Census 2011).

Similar to the state profile, Singrauli has fragmented and small landholdings, and a large number of farmers are involved with subsistence agriculture. The majority of respondents in the survey, that is, 64 per cent of the sample, were recorded to have less than 2 acres of land in their possession (see Table 9.5). This clearly indicates that these families get minimal produce from the land and interviews suggest that there is significant dependency on forest. Subsistence agriculture alone cannot meet the economic or nutritional needs of the people of the project villages, particularly of the tribal families. The title to the land is tenuous, especially of the families residing on revenue or forestland; more than 40 per cent of the tribal respondents (Singh, 2015) did not have any title to their land, nor were their individual forest rights recognized under the FR Act. And hence, most of these tribal families (poorest of the poor) did not receive any compensation for the land that they were tilling prior to land acquisitions. More than 95 per cent of the respondents in the survey used firewood as their primary source of fuel during the pre-displacement period. Other sources, for instance, kerosene and gaslights, were used in a limited way due to economic reasons. Such practices clearly indicate the existence of dependency on forests.

Singrauli has a long history of land acquisition and multiple displacements (see Chapter 6), and this is also one of the reasons that families have been consistently losing their land for different projects under different land acquisition phases. This has resulted in a continuous decline in the landholdings of the households, turning many small and marginal farmers into landless families.[3] In the majority of the cases, the PAFs were jointly holding the land in name of one title-holder; however, two to three PAFs (as per the definition of R&R policy) emerged out of a single land title. The field interviews, analysis of district land records and Census 2011 data suggest that one land title consisted of two to three family units and one family unit consisted of five to six individuals in the district. Table 9.2 demonstrates the quantum of private land acquired after the formation of the district (between 2008 and 2015), which has affected 119 villages in different parts of the district. This land was acquired for various purposes such as thermal power plant sites, coal mining, coal conveyer lines, project townships, approach roads, pipelines and so on. The data suggests that more than 10,000 acres of only private land has been acquired from 10,267 title-holders, which turns out to be more than 20,000 PAFs spread across 119 villages in the district. Along with the private land, 20,000 acres of government land and forestland have been acquired during the same period. Another significant observation is the land acquisition award[4] for this private land acquisition; the private developers deposited ₹5.3 million in the government treasury for the acquisition of 10,411 acres of private land. In relation to the quantum of private investment of these projects, the private land acquisition cost is less than 1 per cent of the total project investments.

Singrauli is one of the most backward and poorest regions[5] and due to its geographical remoteness, it has a suppressed circle land rate for these villages and that is the prime reason behind the low land acquisition award. Unfortunately, when such land falls under acquisition, the only legal provision is to pay the prevailing circle land rate of those areas. But it has been observed that post-land acquisition, due to the rise in industrial and economic activities, the land prices suddenly shoot up and most of the farmers fail to purchase land or restore their landholdings with the received compensation amount.

---

[3] Interview, project-affected person (PAP), Gm third phase, 2014.

[4] Land acquisition award is the money spent on acquisition of land and other immovable assets, under Section 11 of LA Act of 1894.

[5] On the basis of socio-economic and developmental indicators, Singrauli is listed under Backward Region Grant Fund of the Ministry of Panchayati Raj.

Table 9.2 District level private land acquisition detail, 2008–2015

Quantum of land acquired (acre)	*Number of land title-holders*	*Affected no. of villages*	*Land acquisition award amount (₹ million)*
10,411	10,267	119	5,302.80

Source: Singh (2015: fieldwork data of 2015, collected from District Revenue Department, Singrauli).

Considering the quantum of land acquisition during this short period and the massive dissent with the LA Act in other states of India, Singrauli stands out in its 'performance' and 'efficiency'. It raises a critical question, at the time when 804 projects are stalled across India due to land acquisition and environmental clearances issues: how has Singrauli managed to perform this complex task with the already challenged and outdated land acquisition (1894) law?

Household Survey

The household survey was executed on the PAFs of the third phase of the land acquisition process in Singrauli district. Six ongoing projects of the private sector were selected for this purpose to understand the approaches adopted by different corporations for compensation and rehabilitation programmes of the PAFs. Following the research methodology, a total of 401 households were interviewed (see Table 9.3), out of which 273 (69 per cent) households were private landholders (who lost privately owned land for the projects) and 128 (31 per cent) households were government land or forestland occupants (families who were residing and cultivating the government land or forestland before land acquisition) (see Figure 9.2). The household survey and field interviews were conducted in 30 project villages and resettled hamlets in the district to gather information about the land acquisition process. The PAFs who settled in far-off places in search of arable land were not covered in this survey due to time and resource constraints.

Table 9.3 PAFs' land title, government/private, by various projects

Project names	*Government land/forestland (PAFs)*	*Private land (PAFs)*	*Total (PAFs)*
Jaypee Nigri Thermal Power, Reliance Chitrangi Coal Mining, Reliance Sasan Power Thermal Power, Reliance Moher Coal Mining, Hindalco Thermal and Aluminium Smelter, Essar Thermal Power	128	273	401

Source: Singh (2015: fieldwork data of 2015).

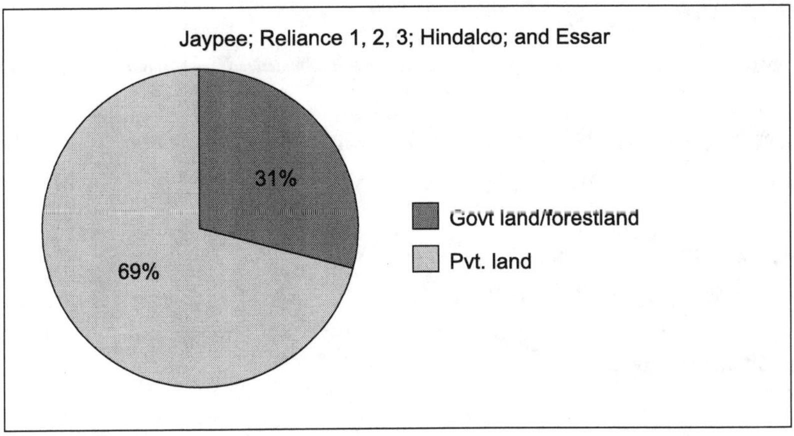

Figure 9.2 Ratio of PAFs in the household survey, government and private lands
Source: Singh (2015: fieldwork data of 2015).

PAFs' Categorization and Landholdings

The land acquisition process has differential impact over different categories of PAFs, and it affects their social and economic well-being during the post-displacement period in different capacities. To understand the severity of the impact of land acquisition on households and their coping mechanism, categorization was done on the basis of their lost property and land (see Figure 9.3).

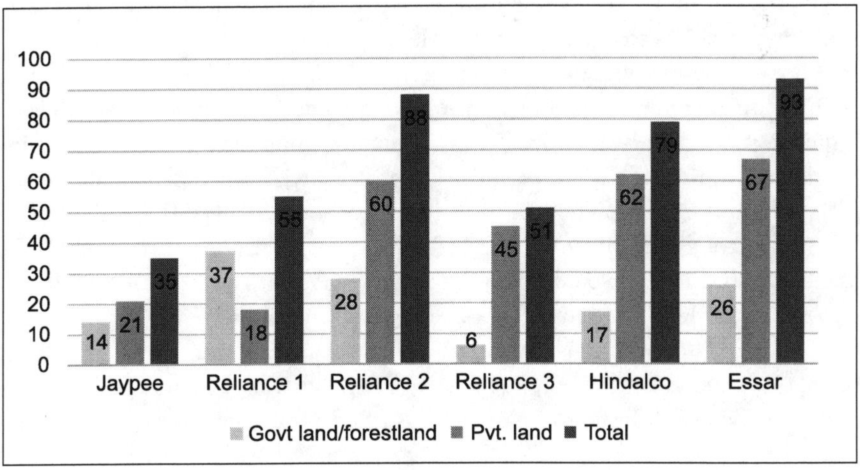

Figure 9.3 PAFs' land title, project wise
Source: Singh (2015: fieldwork data of 2015).

Table 9.4 Land acquisition status of PAFs

Project name	*Both land and house*	*Homestead only*	*Land only*	*Total*
Jaypee; Reliance 1, 2, 3; Essar; Hindalco	352 (88%)	27(7%)	22(5%)	401

Source: Singh (2015: fieldwork data of 2013).

Out of 401 households, 88 per cent of the households lost both their house and land for the project, 7 per cent of the households lost only their homestead and 5 per cent of households lost only their agricultural land for the project while their homesteads remained unaffected (see Table 9.4).

Private Landholding Profile

As discussed earlier, the landholding pattern in Singrauli is highly fragmented and small. For the purpose of survey and to draw insights on the quantum of landholdings, categorization was done on the basis of the quantum of land acquired for a project. The survey reveals that 40 per cent of the households lost between 1 and 2 acres of land for different projects and 11 per cent of the households lost between 51 decimals and 1 acre of land. In land categories E (2–3 acres) and F (3–5 acres), respectively 13 and 12 per cent of the households were found (see Table 9.5). The survey also indicates the existence of very small landholdings, which was further investigated in semi-structured interviews with villagers and the district administration. There were 13 per cent households in categories A and B who lost less than 50 decimals of land for the project.

The interviews revealed that in categories A and B, some of the households were genuinely poor and owned only less than 50 decimals of land prior to land acquisition, but there was also an influx of squatters into the project villages prior to the notification of the land acquisition process, who purchased small parcels of agricultural land (which is technically not economically viable for agriculture due to its size) to benefit from the R&R allowances, jobs and other benefits that potentially the project would offer to the affected families (see Figure 9.4). It was also recorded that hundreds of non-residential structures were built overnight on such parcels of land to claim habitation and residency in the project villages so that they could become eligible for the R&R benefits. The interviews of the revenue officials[6] indicate that the officials faced a real challenge in segregating

[6] Interviews, subdivisional magistrate, land acquisition officer and *tehsildar*, Singrauli, 2014.

Table 9.5 Landholding status of private landowners

Land code	*A*	*B*	*C*	*D*	*E*	*F*	*G*
Land category	0–10 decimals	11–50 decimals	51 decimal–1 acre	1–2 acres	2–3 acres	3–5 acres	5 acres and above
No. of PAFs	9	31	47	111	38	36	1

Source: Singh (2015: fieldwork data of 2015).

genuine from non-genuine PAFs so that the R&R benefits could be given to the actual entitled beneficiaries. The R&R managers[7] of the project developers said,

> The number of PAF's has gone significantly high, when we published the section 4 notification under L.A. act in August 2006, there were limited number of households who were genuinely residing in the project notified area, but since government failed to monitor the encroachments today we are struggling with so many people. This has also affected our R&R budget.

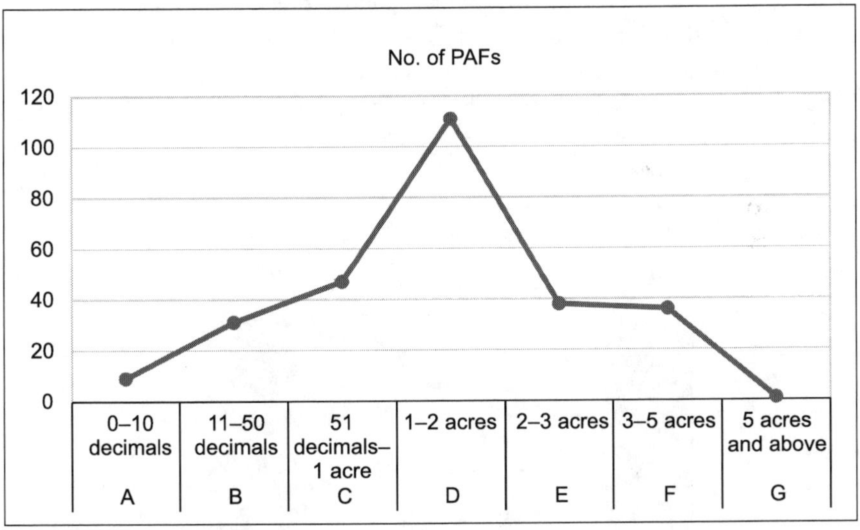

Figure 9.4 Landholding status

Source: Singh (2015: fieldwork data of 2015).

[7] Interviews, R&R manager (Essar Power), CSR head (Reliance Power) and R&R manager (NTPC), 2014.

Table 9.6 Pre-acquisition land details

	Land acquired (acres, private + government)	*Total private land (acres)*	*Government land/forestland (acres)*
Land	1,654.44	789.06	865.38
PAFs	401	273	128

Source: Singh (2015: fieldwork data from 2013 to 2015).

Government Land Occupants and Their Entitlements

One significant observation that emerged from the survey was the engagement of government land occupants with the forest and government land for livelihood. In terms of engagement with land, the survey recorded that 69 per cent of the private land respondents were cultivating 789 acres, that is, 47 per cent of the total land; however, 31 per cent of the government land/forestland occupants were tilling 865 acres, that is, 53 per cent of the land recorded during the survey, before acquisition in the pre-displacement period (see Table 9.6). From the legal viewpoint, under the state regularization policy, many of the landless tenants or occupants who are tilling government land or forestland for a certain period (25–30 years; this period varies in different states) are entitled to allotment of that particular parcel of land, since it is the only source of livelihood for such families. Unfortunately, land regularization and allotment are subject to corruption and many poor households fail to access these benefits due to lack of resources,

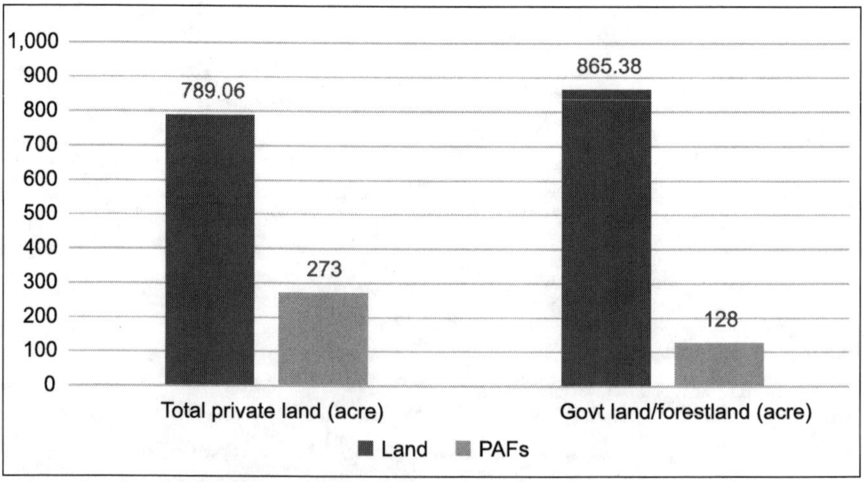

Figure 9.5 PAFs tilling private and government land

Source: Singh (2015: fieldwork data from 2013 to 2015).

awareness, power and information. According to the LA Act of 1894, only private landowners are entitled to receive any form of monetary compensation in the land acquisition process. The law completely excludes any other entities, for instance, government land or forestland occupants, to receive any benefits. Following the LA Act, the government land occupants in Singrauli were not considered for land compensation irrespective of their tenure or association with the land. The only benefit that was extended to these families was a one-time lump sum rehabilitation assistance to the tune of ₹0.15 million and a resettlement plot in the R&R colony. From the legal viewpoint, in the land acquisition process, government does not acquire the government or revenue land falling in the project-notified area; rather the government resumes its title, which is 'resumption' of land and not acquisition. In such cases, those occupants have no standing in the socio-economic survey to be considered for land compensation.

Land Appropriation and Private Interests

The third phase of land acquisition in Singrauli district started in 2008, immediately after the formation of the district. However, the land acquisition procedure, for instance, Section 4 preliminary notification, signing of memorandum of understanding (MoU) and so on, for most of these projects started in 2006. It was also highlighted in some of the interviews that one of the primary reasons behind redrawing of geographical boundaries and formation of Singrauli district was to create an 'investment climate' and facilitate private investments in the region. However, this need was not felt earlier as the National Thermal Power Corporation (NTPC) and Northern Coalfields Ltd (NCL) (Government of India corporations) were already operating in the region for the last four decades. This does reflect the role of the state and the power of private capital in influencing the decision-making process and path of development.

The land rate for the project villages were determined following the guidelines of the LA Act of 1894 on the basis of prevailing circle rates of the revenue villages. As per the guidelines, the Section 4 notification year is taken as the base year for circle land rate and the land award is finalized on the basis of these prevailing rates. However, in case of Singrauli, in the third phase projects, the physical displacement started in 2010 as there was a time lag and delay in the land acquisition process. But land rate was determined on 2006 prices (Section 4 notification year) and in many instances, it was not revised according to the current year circle land rate, because of which PAFs incurred losses. Following the procedure, the land transactions between 2003 and 2006 of nearby project villages were collated and the average land rate was recorded as the circle land rate for the project villages to be acquired. Due to generic conditions of the rural land market, fewer land transactions and remoteness of the region, the land rate was naturally low. This led to the determination of a low land acquisition award.

Analysis of the revenue records of the district and interviews reveals that agricultural land transactions in the villages were very few and limited before the announcement of the projects. During the pre-project period, the villagers used to sell land only in a situation of crisis, for instance, to pay back loans, for urgent medical treatment, marriages and so on. Due to the geographical remoteness of Singrauli and the predominance of the rural agrarian community, land transactions in the Singrauli region were very limited, which was the reason for suppressed land

Table 9.7 Circle land rate in project villages

Name of project	*Corporation*	*Name of village*	*Land rate (million per hectare)*	
			Unirrigated	*Irrigated*
Sasan Ultra Mega Power Project	Reliance Power	Sidhikhurd	0.30	0.450
		Sidhikala	0.25	0.357
		Tiyara	0.30	0.450
		Jhanjhitola	0.30	0.450
		Harrarwah	0.25	0.357
Essar Power MP Power Ltd	Essar Group	Bandhwa	0.292	0.530
		Nagwa	0.292	0.530
		Khairahi	0.292	0.530
		Karsualal	0.292	0.530
Mahan Aluminium and Captive Thermal Power Project	Hindalco	Barainia	0.239	0.40
		Dhaurar	0.239	0.40
		Odgari	0.239	0.40
		Gidher	0.157	0.267
J. P. Power Ltd	Jaypee	Nigri	0.20	0.374
		Katai		
		Hardi		
		Niwas		
Chitrangi Power Ltd	Reliance Power	Badgadh	0.450	0.710
		Bagaiya	0.450	0.710
		Kokhawa	0.913	1.369
		Jamhitwa	n/a	n/a
		Kapurdehi	n/a	n/a
Muher Coal Mines	Reliance Power	Muher	n/a	n/a
		Amlori	n/a	n/a
		Navgarh	n/a	n/a

Source: Singh (2015: fieldwork data of 2013, collected from District Revenue Department, Singrauli).

prices. Undoubtedly, the private players have been the beneficiaries of the prevailing cheap land prices of the Singrauli region. Land being one of the unique and important factors of production, has been transferred to the private corporations at throwaway prices. Table 9.7 represents the circle land rate of respective project villages at which it has been transferred to the private corporations.

Project Cost versus Land Cost

Review of literature on land acquisition and rehabilitation has pointed towards the inadequacy of compensation and the meagre amount paid to the affected families that is not sufficient to restore their lands and livelihoods in the post-displacement period. During the fieldwork, individual project-wise data on private land acquisition and compensation was collected and compiled to understand the ratio of private land cost to total project investments. This exercise was done in order to understand how much private developers actually pay for the land component in the project. Land being an important factor of production becomes extremely critical for any project due to its special characteristics, for instance, geostrategic value in case of minerals, immobility, scarce resource and so on. In this context, an attempt was made to understand the dynamics behind preference for state-mediated transfer of land from farmers to private developers under the LA Act of 1894. The individual village-wise land acquisition award was quantified in relation to the total project investment (see Table 9.8). As per the law, 10 per cent of the land award is charged additionally from the developers by the district administration as administrative and service expenses for executing the land acquisition process. It is critical to note that the total cost incurred by the developers for private land acquisitions has been around 1 per cent of the total project cost. However, in case of a few projects, for instance, J. P. Power, D. B. Power, and Sasan and Chitrangi Power, the private land acquisition cost is not even 1 per cent of the total project investment. Another significant observation is the land cost of the Chitrangi Power project; it is cheapest due to the existence of tribal villages and, hence, the circle rate of these project villages were naturally low or suppressed due to very limited land transactions.

The study also reveals that there has been differential approach for compensation within the same district and by the same developer (see Figure 9.6 and Table 9.8). As discussed earlier, in the Sasan Power project, the government land occupants were not paid any compensation as there is no such provision in the LA Act for compensating such categories of families. But in the case of the Chitrangi Power project, all government land occupants who were tilling the land before the land acquisition process began were identified, a special survey was

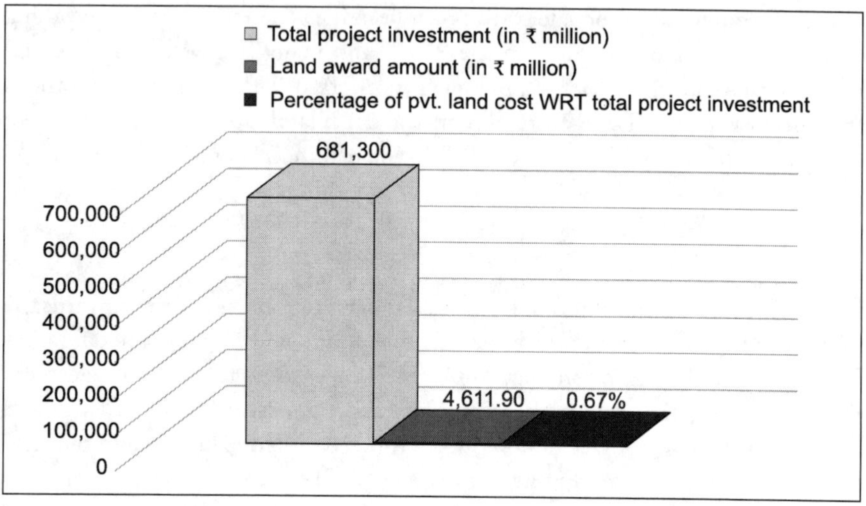

Figure 9.6 Project cost versus land award amount

Source: Singh (2015: fieldwork data of 2015).

conducted by the revenue department with the 'assistance' of Reliance executives, and were compensated for the non-titled land. The Chitrangi project villages were predominantly occupied by tribal populations, particularly Gonds and Baigas. One striking question that arises in the process is, why was such an approach not adopted by Reliance for their Sasan project? Interviews of stakeholders suggest that there was enormous pressure from and urgency shown by the state government to acquire and transfer this land to Reliance. It is important to highlight that simultaneous to this process, a case was filed by Tata Power in the Supreme Court concerning the irregularities in the allotment of coal blocks to Reliance.

Land Categorization and Valuations

Following the procedure of the LA Act of 1894, under Section 6 of the Act, a detailed survey of the land and immovable assets is conducted to prepare an inventory of each PAF. A detailed measurement of each parcel of land falling in the project-notified area is done and the land quality is categorized as irrigated and unirrigated. The categorization is done on the basis of the existing source of irrigation for that particular parcel of land, such as well, canal, tube well, river and so on, and it is recorded in the survey. Analysis of the field survey suggests that in many project villages, 40 per cent of the acquired land was irrigated land (see Figure 9.7). However, during the course of the interviews, it was recorded that many PAFs (20 per cent of the sample) complained that despite having sources of irrigation in their field, the land acquisition survey team registered their land as unirrigated. Some respondents indicated that the revenue officials deliberately made such errors during land surveys so that they could take bribes later for correcting those mistakes in order that people could receive their genuine compensation for irrigated land. There are several features that are attached to land, and more importantly, the human labour that is invested to make the land productive is significant in case of the rural agrarian community. Interviews of the government land occupants suggest that the PAFs invested years of human labour to make the land fertile and developed sources of irrigation in the undulating and unfertile government land. They were tilling this land for more than 30 years but, due to lack of awareness and information, failed to register this land in their names. Developing sources of irrigation and making bunds in the field were significant tasks that took years to accomplish in order to make the land suitable for productive use. But the government did not compensate for those activities on government land. During the pre-displacement period, 237 households had some sources of irrigation in their fields (see Table 9.5). During the land acquisition process, a survey of property is conducted under Section 6 of the LA Act of 1894 to register the type of land – irrigated/unirrigated – and accordingly, valuation is done for the acquired land. The interviews of small landholders (87 households lost less than an acre; see Table 9.5) indicated that even though their agricultural fields did not have any source of irrigation, with understanding among the community, they were

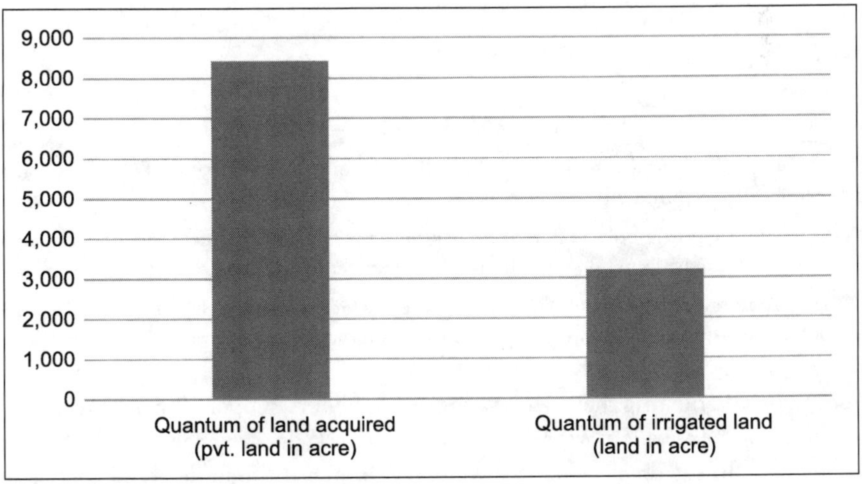

Figure 9.7 Quantum of irrigated land in the total amount of land acquired

Source: Singh (2015: fieldwork data between 2013 and 2015).

Table 9.8 Details of land acquisition – private sector projects, third phase

Project name	*No. of villages affected*	*No. of title-holders**	*Quantum of land acquired (pvt. land in acre)*	*Quantum of irrigated land (acre)*	*Land award amount** (₹ million)*	*Total project investment (₹ million)*	*Percentage of private land cost WRT total project investment (%)*
Sasan Power Ltd (Reliance)	23	2,037	1,984.83	831	889.80	160,000	0.55
Chitrangi Power Ltd (Reliance)	4	751	948.51	103	218.50	160,000	0.13
Mahan Super Thermal Power project – Essar Group	4	751	761.55	676.58	618.80	50,000	1.2
J. P. Power Ltd	8	634	972.82	413.23	281.90	52,800	0.53
Hindalco Aluminium Power Plant	8	2,059	2,777.25	927.85	797	78,000	1.02
NTPC Stage 4 ash dyke	2	400	490.87	73.77	1,127.10	40,000	2.81
D. B. Power MP Ltd	1	151	269.32	108.16	132.60	85,000	0.15
MP J. P. Mineral Ltd	2	332	231.16	70.39	5.97	5,500	1.08
Moher Coal Block	3				486.20	50,000	0.97
Total	55	6,619	8,436.34	3,204	461,190	681,300	0.67

Source: Singh (2015: fieldwork data of 2015, collected from District Revenue Department and project developers, Singrauli).

Notes: * Number of title-holders indicates the number of individuals who were possessing land at the time of acquisition; it does not indicate the number of affected families.

** Land award amount indicates the compensation, which includes value of land and all the property, for instance, house, well, trees and so on, on the acquired private land.

continuously irrigating their fields with the neighbours' support. Their requests for valuation of their fields as irrigated were rejected by the government and the project developers. In the displacement process, it is important to understand and value the social cohesion and support structures that exist in the community. Though it was a meagre amount for consideration, no attention was given to these concerns.

Compensation and Land Restoration

The research attempted to study the complexities involved in the compensation process from the viewpoints of different stakeholders. The objective was to assess the 'fairness' in the compensation design and its impact on the households. In the survey questionnaire, information was collected on the landholding status of the PAFs in the pre- and post-displacement periods. Out of the 401 respondents from different project villages, only 91, that is, 22 per cent of the households, were able to buy some land in the post-displacement period (see Table 9.9 and Figure 9.8). However, it is important to note that only private landholders were provided with acquired land compensation and government land occupants were not considered for land compensation as per the provisions of the LA Act of 1894. In order to further investigate and analyse the inadequacy of compensation, the landholding status of every household (pre- and post-displacement) who purchased land were compared and studied. Out of 91 households, only 22 households (that is, <10 per cent of the total private land PAFs) were able to purchase an equal amount of land they lost for the project (see Table 9.10). The interviews of these respondents indicate that these land purchases were not in the host or adjoining villages but in distant villages within the same district. Of the remaining, 35 households were able to regain only partial amount of agricultural land with the compensation money and the rest of the 34 households could purchase only homestead land (that is, for house construction).

As discussed in Chapter 3, the circle rate declared by the revenue department is not the correct indicator of true market value of land due to several reasons. The land acquisition for the third phase of projects in Singrauli district was done under the similar, repeatedly challenged and contentious LA Act of 1894 which does not prescribe any sound (rationale) methodology for the determination of land price. Interviews of the key persons also reflected that local businessmen from Waidhan (district headquarters town) and nearby districts already started purchasing large tracts of land around project-notified areas much before the displacement happened. These local politicians, spectators and businessmen have access to information about proposed project locations, and they start investing in land much before the project initiation. It is a known fact and observed across states of India wherever land acquisition has happened that land prices around project areas shoot up enormously during the post-displacement period and the immediate affected families fail to restore their land. Apart from the inadequacy of compensation in the land law, asymmetry of information and lack of support from project developers and the district administration could be other reasons for failing to restore the lost land.

Table 9.9 PAFs' post-displacement land transaction status

Total no. of PAFs	*PAFs who could purchase land*	*PAFs who failed to purchase land*
401	91 (22%)	310 (78%)

Source: Singh (2015: fieldwork data from 2013 to 2015).

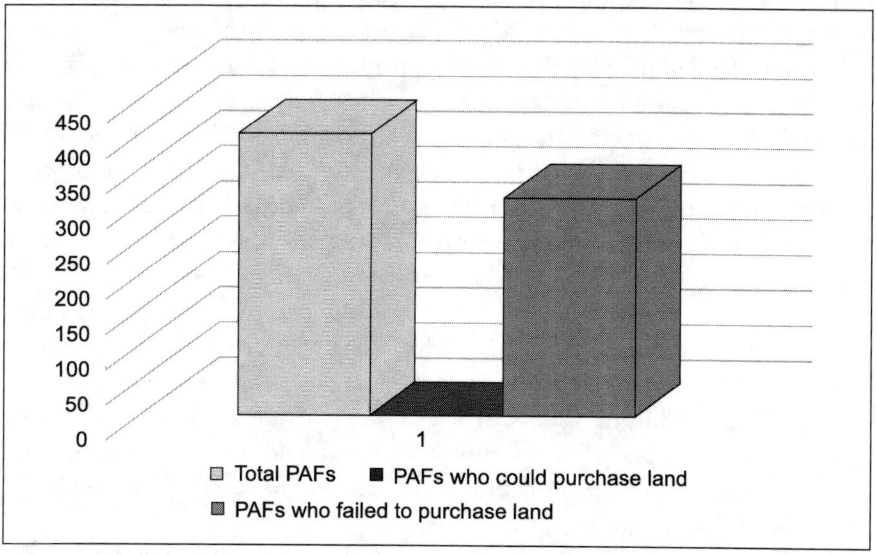

Figure 9.8 PAFs' land transaction status post displacement
Source: Singh (2015: fieldwork data of 2015).

Table 9.9 demonstrates the actual and predicted land purchase in the post-displacement period. On the reasoning of compensating the PAFs on the basis of market value (under land law), all the land purchases would have been on the linear line. However, only a few households (22) were able to regain equal quantum of land during the post-displacement period.

Table 9.10 Landholding status, small/marginal/landless, in pre- and post-displacement periods

No. of families that purchased equal amount of land post acquisition	*No. of families that purchased less amount of land post acquisition*	*No. of families that almost became landless (purchased less than 10 decimals of land only for homestead construction)*
22	35	34

Source: Singh (2015: fieldwork data of 2015).

Land Acquisition and Differential Impact

The socio-economic impact of land acquisition on the households varies on the quantum of land and property lost in the process, land title status and the present social status of the households. Poor households (particularly, the Scheduled Caste [SC] and the Scheduled Tribe [ST] categories in case of Singrauli) are the most affected categories of PAFs in the land acquisition process. Another peculiar concern of the Singrauli region is the issue of multiple displacements, as there have been series of land acquisitions in the past (see Chapter 6). Multiple displaced households are severely affected, and there are no legal or policy safeguards to provide additional support for rehabilitation to such households. The survey results indicate that out of 401 households, 76 per cent of the households lost all their land for the project. For this purpose, both private landowners and government land occupants were considered who were tilling the agricultural land for their livelihood. As most of the PAFs were involved with subsistence agriculture during the pre-displacement period, it severely affected the livelihoods of the PAFs. The 97 households who lost partial land for the project continued to live on the remaining land to avail the employment and other economic opportunities (shops, vendors, contract labour and so on) from the project. But the remaining land post acquisition became economically unviable for agriculture, so they had to explore other livelihood options. It is observed that PAFs who had to relocate from their past habitation were the most affected category in the displacement process as they had to undergo physical, economic and social rehabilitations – particularly, the families who lost all their landholdings for the project and became landless.

Settlements

The relocation of habitation has severe impact on the lives and livelihoods of the affected communities. The affected families belong to poor rural agrarian communities and the tribal families in particular are the worst affected in the process, as their lives and livelihoods are primarily dependent on land and the nearby forest resources. The field survey indicates that out of 401 households, 304 (75 per cent) had to relocate to other areas from their host villages (see Table 9.11). Out of 401 households, 188 (47 per cent) households chose to resettle in the host

Table 9.11 Displacement status

PAFs residing on remaining land (partial acquisition)	*PAFs moved away from past habitation*
97	304

Source: Singh (2015: fieldwork data of 2015).

and adjoining villages and 77 households occupied the nearby government land and built their houses on the barren land (see Table 9.12). However, the number of families who reoccupied government land post displacement is much higher; some families chose not to answer this question and their opinion was respected during interviews. It was observed that a large number of government land occupants were again in the process of encroaching upon nearby available government land and developing it for cultivation.

Most of the tribal families decided not to relocate to the R&R colonies, as they could not imagine their lives without forests primarily due to livelihood association. However, the decision for relocating (or not relocating) to the R&R colonies varied across projects. Out of the total sample, 136 households were residing in the R&R colonies and the PAFs have different reasons for relocating in different projects. In the Sasan Power project, education and health facilities were two reasons for the families to relocate to the R&R colony. However, the majority of the Other Backward Class (OBC) PAFs (Vaishya and Sahu caste families) were residing in the colony but that was not their primary residence. The Sasan PAFs unanimously pointed out the site of the R&R colony as the main reason for not relocating to the colony. The respondents reflected that the R&R colony was located at a significant distance from the host villages and the selection of the colony site was not done in consultation with the community.

The interviews of revenue officials[8] suggest that the R&R site (Majhauli and Chachar villages) in the Sasan project case was barren land (undulating terrain and infertile soil) with low circle land rate and it was the main reason for the company to select this land for establishing the R&R colony. In case of Essar Power's R&R colony (Nagwa village), it was said that the site was actually not suitable for settlements as it fell under the coal-bearing zone and the coal would be exploited in the future and the families would have to relocate again. A local activist[9] pointed towards the selection of the Essar R&R site and said,

> The site is not suitable for the settlements as it's a coal bearing zone and the site has coal beneath it and also under the adjoining hills of the R&R site and in the near future the coal will be mined and these people will have to shift again. This is a result of flawed planning as the district does not have a regional planning map and the only focus of the government is to mine the coal and generate thermal power. The trauma of the local people and loss of livelihood is of least priority to the government.

[8] Interviews, sub-divisional magistrate and *tehsildar*, Singrauli, 2014.

[9] Interview, Upendra Pandey, Udvasit Kisan Mazdoor Samiti, 2014.

Table 9.12 Post-displacement residential status of PAFs

PAFs withown house on own site	*PAFs constructed house on encroached land (govt/forest)*	*PAFs living inside the R&R colony*
188	77	136

Source: Singh (2015: fieldwork data of 2015).

Community consultations and participation of the affected community in rehabilitation planning are given the least importance, which affects successful rehabilitation in the long run. It is important to note that out of the 5,672 square kilometres of geographical area of Singrauli, 2,200 square kilommetres have been demarcated for coal mining; this data reflects the concentration of huge reserves of coal within a small region, and hence the importance of proper regional planning.

Forest Resource

As discussed in Chapters 3 and 6, the Singrauli region has a rich forest density with diverse flora and fauna. Singrauli also inhabits significant indigenous populations; the Baiga, Gond, and Kol populations in particular are large in terms of number. The survey data suggests that out of 401 households, 206 (51 per cent) respondents were recorded as having some association with forests (see Table 9.14). To understand the forest dependency and diversified livelihood patterns of the PAFs, data was collected in the survey to further investigate the household income and livelihood supporting mechanism in the lean seasons. It was recorded in the survey that a variety of non-timber forest products (NTFPs), such as *tendu* leaves, *mahaua, amla, harra, chakawada, bella*, mushrooms, sal seeds and so on, are collected across the year, and it provides livelihood support to the poor, rural households (see Table 9.13). Besides their household consumption they also sell some of the forest produce for earnings during lean seasons. Table 9.14 summarizes the annual income from the sale of forest produce and the number of PAFs involved with this activity. It was recorded in interviews that the availability of NTFPs, including that of firewood, is a critical support system for these households. It is important to highlight that most of the PAFs involved with the sale of forest produce were the SCs[10] and the STs, who were the poorest households in the survey. However, these livelihood associations were not studied in the socio-economic survey (SES) or during social impact assessments study prior to the land acquisition process. The Sasan SES report (2006) contains generic information about the potentially affected villages and most of the analysis in the

[10] The SC PAFs denote Dalit families, who are recognized as a socially and economically backward class according to the Constitution of India.

Table 9.13 NTFP collection pattern in Singrauli

Jan.	*Feb.*	*Mar.*	*Apr.*	*May*	*Jun.*	*Jul.*	*Aug.*	*Sept.*	*Oct.*	*Nov.*	*Dec.*
Amla	Harra	Tendu	Bella	Tendu	Tendu	Mushroom	Mushroom		Medicinal plants		Amla
		Bella	Mahua			Dori	Chakawda	Chakwada	Chakwada		

Source: Singh (2015: fieldwork data from 2013 to 2015).

report is based on secondary data, which does not completely represent the ground reality or a situational analysis of the region. The land acquisition procedures or rehabilitation policies have no provisions for compensating for or restoring the common property resources of the affected communities.

Livelihood Patterns during Pre- and Post-Displacement Periods

The land acquisition process has significant impact on the livelihoods of the affected families; an attempt was made to study the transformations in the livelihood patterns of the PAFs. However, it was an extremely challenging and complex task to quantify the income from various sources, as the PAFs were deriving income from diverse sets of livelihood activities during the pre-displacement period. The objective was to understand the transformations and livelihood changes during the pre- and post-displacement periods. The survey indicates that prior to displacement, it was primarily a rural agrarian community dependent on agriculture or allied activities. But post displacement, the PAFs have undergone massive transformation with regard to livelihood engagements.

During the pre-displacement period, 265 (66 per cent of the sample) out of 401 households were directly involved with farming activity (see Table 9.15) and 55 households were earning their livelihood through agricultural labour work.

Table 9.14 Income from NTFP – forest dependency during lean period

Income range, ₹/year	*No. of families*
500–1,500	38
2,000–3,500	76
4,000–5,500	44
6,000–8,000	22
8,500–12,000	18
12,500–15,000	7
15,500–20,000	1
Total	206

Source: Singh (2015: fieldwork data from 2013 to 2015).

The data substantiates the predominance of an agrarian set-up in the project villages. The majority of the PAFs were utilizing their human labour for earning their livelihood. The interviews of the project officials[11] indicate that they failed to engage people in formal project employment as they lacked skills required for the project development. But, as secondary employers, the officials engaged many project-affected persons (PAPs) via construction agencies. The majority of the PAFs, that is, 235 (58 per cent) PAFs, were working as casual construction workers during the post-displacement period with different construction companies hired by the project developers (see Table 9.16). There has been an increase in the per day income of the PAFs due to the industrial wage rate for the labour work compared with the pre-displacement period. A senior electrician, also a PAP from one of the project villages, said, 'Since the projects are not offering us permanent employment, we are presently working with these construction companies and hopefully the employment will continue for 4 to 5 years.' It is important to note that this employment is temporary and will be available only until the time of construction of the power plants.

In the second phase of the project, that is, operation and maintenance, most of these PAPs will not find any suitable place for long-term employment. This problem arises because the affected people are not immediately 'employable' as the only marketable commodity they possess, in the absence of skills valued by the market, is their labour. And this alienates the peasantry from their traditional means of livelihood and, more often than not, results in social turmoil and unrest. Only 15 (0.03 per cent) respondents got permanent employment in the projects and they were General caste and OBC candidates who were politically connected and affluent enough to assert their demands. The other form of project employment was recorded in the form of labour cooperatives; 36 PAPs were working at the project sites under labour cooperatives formed by the PAFs. However, there were irregularities in the allocation of work awarded to these cooperatives by the project developers. The cooperatives have to struggle and protest to receive work awards from these developers. The interviews of project executives[12] indicate that the involvement of PAFs in project work is troublesome as they form unions and assert demands which are deemed to be unreasonable. The issues of land acquisition and R&R are brought into these protests and discussions repeatedly, which developers have nothing to do with. 'We have paid compensation as per the law and there is no legal binding for employment.'[13] However, the PAFs feel that since it was involuntary land acquisition, which has taken away their livelihood, the project authorities are bound to give them employment in some form.

---

[11] Interview, M. K. Parameswaran, Project Director, Sasan Power, 2014.

[12] Interview, project operations, Reliance Power, 2014.

[13] Interview, K. K. Tripathi, Legal Head, Sasan Power Ltd.

Table 9.15 Livelihood pattern – main and subsidiary occupations (pre displacement) – and per day income range (in ₹)

Occupation	*Farming*	*Agricultural labour*	*Non-agricultural labour*	*Self-employed artisan/ technician*	*Self-employed shop owner/ businessmen*	*Salaried service person (in govt)*	*Traditional occupation (other than farming and artisan/ technicians)*
No. of families	263	55	25	6	37	3	12
Income/ day	25–275	50–150	50–200	150–200	50–300	300	50–100

Source: Singh (2015: fieldwork data of 2015).

Compensation and Uncalculated Stress

R&R is a slow and continuous process; to understand the challenges faced by the PAFs during the resettlement process, information was collected on the utilization of the compensation amount and how it was perceived by the PAFs. As discussed earlier, the target population was predominantly an agrarian community either involved with farming or working as labourers for their livelihoods in the pre-displacement period (see Figure 9.9). Post displacement, the PAFs faced several challenges during the transition period from the time of eviction until the construction of their houses at the new site. As the PAFs were involved with the construction of their new houses, they failed to work during this period to earn their livelihood. As a result, the compensation amount was used during this period to support this gap. The survey reflects that 328 households (81 per cent of the sample) used their compensation money to support their families during the period of transition. However, it is important to note that there was no provision in the

Table 9.16 Livelihood pattern – main and subsidiary occupations (post displacement) – and per day income range (in ₹)

Occupation	*Direct project employment*	*Labour cooperative*	*Shop*	*Contractual construction labour*	*Agricultural labour*	*Salaried service person (govt)*	*Traditional occupation*	*Salaried service person (non-govt)*
No. of families	15	36	26	235	74	3	4	8
Income/ day	200–300	100–300	100–300	150–300	100–300	300	100–150	200–300

Source: Singh (2015: fieldwork data of 2015).

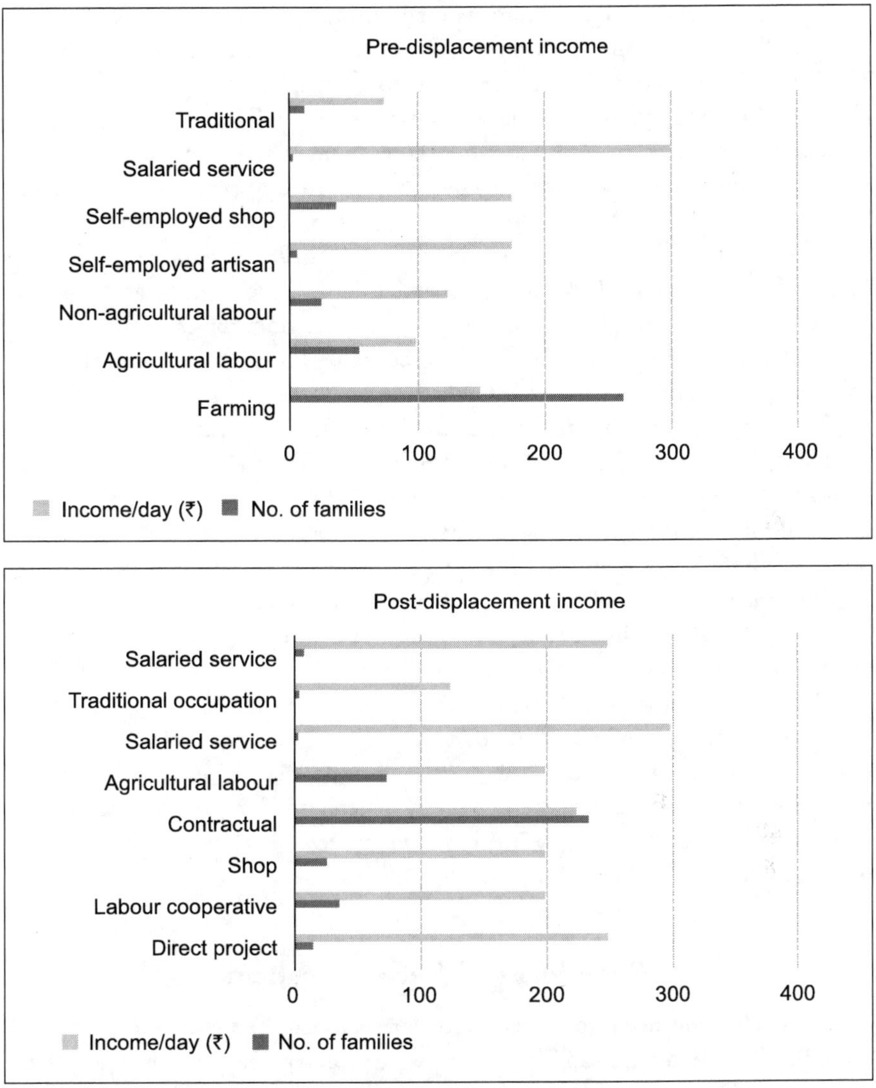

Figure 9.9 Pre- and post-displacement occupations and income

Source: Singh (2015: fieldwork data of 2015).

law to provide this additional support in the land award or rehabilitation package. This was 'uncalculated stress' for the PAFs, and the received compensation amount for the lost land and property was diverted towards meeting this requirement during the transition period, which further compounded their impoverishment.

During the survey, an attempt was made to study the responses of the PAFs towards the received compensation amount and its utilization. It was recorded that 129 respondents, that is, 32 per cent of the total sample, purchased some vehicle (Jeep, car, bike and so on) out of the compensation money. This trend of purchasing vehicles out of the compensation money is more popular in peri-urban or urban areas. However, interviews of the key persons indicate that 'many of these vehicles purchased by the poor households, particularly the SC and ST families, are no more used as they don't have money to buy petrol for these vehicles'. It has been observed across states in India that PAPs fail to utilize the compensation amount in a productive manner. There has been no assistance from the government or the project developers to provide financial literacy to productively utilize the received compensation amount by the affected families.

The changing economic dimensions and capitalist transformations in rural areas are affecting the poor rural households in different aspects. Today, rural India is seen as a large source of consumers of the capitalist production process. But in Singrauli project villages, a new trend was recorded during the land acquisition process. The PAFs who received monetary compensation were targeted by the insurance agents of various private companies, for instance, Reliance Money, Bajaj Alliance, Shri Ram Finance and so on, to invest in their mutual fund policies which involved market risks. Despite knowing the profile of these poor households (subsistence agriculturalists) who were not in the position of taking any market risk, they were mobilized and manipulated to buy these policies. The survey indicates that 45 households invested in the mutual fund policies. The interviews of key persons suggest that this number would have been much higher had the district administration not stopped the insurance agents from entering and selling their insurance policies in the project-affected villages.

Compensation Utilization Pattern

The compensation received by the PAFs for their acquired land and property is disbursed by the district administration as monetary compensation as per the procedure in Section 11 of the LA Act of 1894. The utilization of the compensation amount is critically important for restoration of their lands and livelihood. To study the compensation utilization pattern of the PAFs, data was collected during the survey. The information on land and property valuation was also cross-verified with the revenue department. However, most of the PAFs possessed the copy of Section 9 notice which contained the amount due to the title-holders, which helped in recording the exact value in the survey.

The received compensation data of 401 households was compiled and studied in aggregated form. The expenditure pattern was summarized into five sections:

Table 9.17 Dwelling pattern

House type, pre-displacement		*House type, post-displacement*	
Kutcha *house*	Pucca *house*	Kutcha *house*	Pucca *house*
364	17	81	320

Source: Singh (2015: fieldwork data of 2015).

(a) land purchase, (b) house construction, (c) subsistence during transition, (d) vehicle purchase and (e) bank deposits. The survey data reveals that 41 per cent of the total received compensation amount was utilized by the PAFs to reconstruct their new houses (see Figure 9.10). It is important to note that this money was not spent only on constructing their primary houses but also on investing strategically around other proposed project villages (see the section 'Investment in Land: the Singrauli Way' and Table 9.9). It was observed that a significant amount of the compensation money was utilized for building *pucca* (house structure built with bricks and cement) houses during the post-displacement period (see Table 9.17). The PAFs used 12 per cent of the compensation amount to buy land, as only 91 households bought some land during the post-displacement period. Amounts used for subsistence during transition and vehicle purchase were 9 and 8 per cents respectively. The compensation amount that was deposited in banks was 30 per cent of the total received amount. The compensation amount used during the period of transition was unaccounted cost that was not budgeted in the model of compensation and which added to the households' stress during

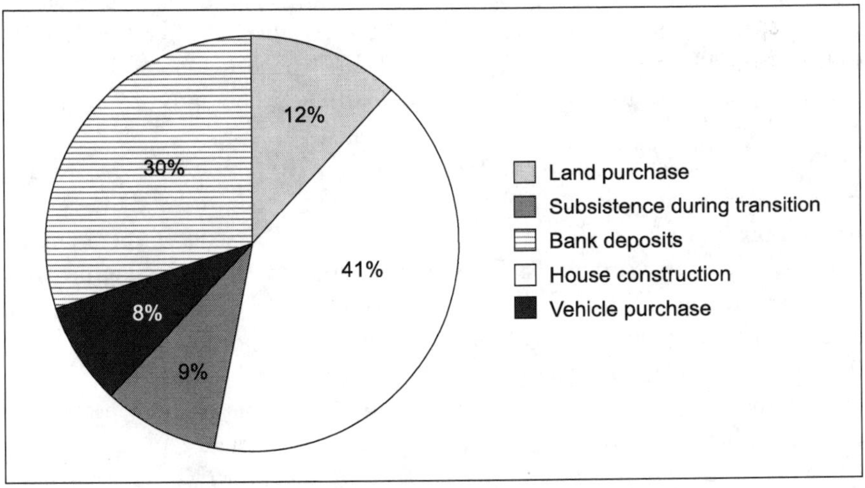

Figure 9.10 Compensation utilization pattern

Source: Singh (2015: fieldwork data from 2013 to 2015).

the post-displacement period. The expenditures on vehicles further diverted the compensation amount into unproductive activities. Considering the socio-economic profile of the rural, agrarian affected community, who were not equipped with managing the large sum of money, they ought to have been but were not provided with any assistance (financial literacy/awareness) by the district administration or the project developers to utilize the money in a productive way. The other two stakeholders – the project developers and the district administration – considered their job done by disbursing the compensation amount.

Multiple Displacements

In Singrauli, development and displacement commenced with the construction of the Rihand reservoir. The dam proved to be a boon for a limited number of people in the Singrauli region, especially the farmers. The land turned fertile, particularly on the banks of the reservoir (Verma, 2004: 97). This process also led to the submergence of various villages located on the banks, which has not been documented sufficiently. A number of studies across the country have documented multiple displacements of people and successive displacement of the same families from one place to another following execution of development projects in those areas. As one of the studies points out, in the early 1960s, the displaced people of the Rihand Dam had to face displacement from their new place of habitation for the second time in the 1970s and 1980s because of coal mining projects and again due to the setting up of a number of industries, particularly the NTPC projects. In each time of their displacement, they were progressively pauperized (Lokayan and Environmental Defence Fund, 1987, quoted in Thukral, 1996, cited in Pandey and Rout, 2004: 2002). Post 2008, after the formation of the district, a third phase of displacement started, which affected thousands of families for the third and fourth time.

During the survey, 82 households (20 per cent of the sample) were recorded as multiple displacement oustees, who were displaced for the third and fourth time in the Singrauli region. These families were particularly concentrated around Sasan and Essar Power projects. The interviews indicate that these families were the most affected in the displacement process. And there were no policy or legal safeguards or provisions to provide any additional support for R&R to these families. Additionally, there were a few respondents (five) who were Rihand project oustees and were allotted 5 acres of agricultural land plots as compensation for their rehabilitation. These plots were not registered in their name (or *patta*) as they failed to record these agricultural lands in their names at the revenue department due to lack of resources. During the third phase of land acquisition, such families were not paid any compensation for their land as it was surveyed as a revenue land.

These Rihand oustees repeatedly raised their concern to the district administration but, unfortunately, their case was not considered for compensation. A 95-year-old Ram Charitra Baiga, displaced by the Reliance project, narrates,

> I have been displaced three times in the last five decades, all forests are disappearing, now I do not know where to get settled in Singrauli, in fact, now I do not want to build my house on land, I just want to become a bird so that no one can displace me.

Some of the multiple displaced families from the NTPC projects were identified and particularly women were interviewed to gather perceptions on displacement and livelihoods. These narratives are discussed below.

One of the female respondents, Bauhri Devi, a 90-year-old widowed Brahmin woman who has lived through 50 years of displacement, narrates,

> I have seen Singrauli turn from a jungle to an urban one. I was married into this village when I was fifteen, and since then I have lived here. Initially we lived close to Rihand reservoir, we went to hear Nehru when he came to inaugurate the dam in sixties. With whatever compensation we received at that time we got settled in Harai village, but in the year 1988, NTPC came and acquired our land and we were asked to move again. It took us 10 years to settle with our house and farming land. Yet again no one asked us; just commanded us to leave. Now we live in Navjivan Vihar but I don't know if they ask us to move again. Now I just want to die in peace in one particular place.

Mangli is a 60-year-old woman, who lives in Sector 1 of the Navjivan Vihar resettlement colony of NTPC. She points out the extent to which they were engaged in agriculture,

> I helped my husband [Purushottam] in all agricultural activities. I helped him in land preparation, sowing, applying manure, harvesting along with performing domestic chores. Moreover, I took care of the livestock-washing, grazing, collecting fodder, milking, etc. Agriculture provided us with minimum sustenance. Now there is no money left, even to buy food.

Phoolan Devi, a 60-year-old woman from Sector 2 of Navjivan Vihar, points out, 'In the past before displacement we produced our own food. Now, we are dependent on ration shops. The government ration shops do not even identify us as poor because we have a *pucca* house. But inside the *pucca* house, there is no food.'

Ramkali, a 70-year-old woman, has been living in Sector 4 of Navjivan Vihar for the last 20 years. She points out,

> My daughter-in-law has to go inside the NTPC Vindhyachal Township to collect fuel, twigs for the house and fodder for the cattle. However, the guards do not let her enter and keep asking her to show a card for entering the colony. They abuse her and we have to constantly fight with the guards? Can't we just enter the colony to collect fodder lying around?

The pain and trauma of multiple displaced families is enormous and, unfortunately, the district administration and project developers are least concerned about these aspects. The non-recognition of these aspects in the R&R policy demonstrates that the state has not incorporated the experiences or lessons from the past.

Investment in Land: The Singrauli Way

During the course of the research, an unusual practice of buying a small parcel of land and constructing a house (which the administration called *dabba*) in the proposed project area was noticed in Singrauli. According to the district administration, there were around 2,800 such non-residential structures found in and around proposed project areas (see Figure 9.11). The livelihood trajectories of families indicate that investing in land (buying a small parcel of land for homestead construction) around proposed power plants and mining projects was a widely utilized strategy among OBCs (particularly, Sahus and Vaishya) and SCs to get access to compensation and rehabilitation benefits of other projects. It is important to note that not a single tribal family, either Baigas or Gonds, were involved in this practice. The compensation amount used for house construction as indicated earlier, 41 per cent of the total compensation (see Figure 9.10), accounts for both their primary house construction as well as the secondary house developed on homestead land in the nearby proposed project villages for future benefits. However, not all lower caste families had the means to buy land and many SC and ST families claimed they were unable to purchase any land. Nevertheless, the presence of multiple thermal power plants and coal mines in the region meant that people could strategically choose to buy lands in particular areas to further their opportunities for securing some compensation, R&R benefits or employment opportunities. There are approximately 14 coal mines and power plants in Singrauli district and most of these are located in Mara and Singrauli *tehsils*.

At the level of general conversation, one sensed high levels of awareness about where it was best to purchase land for acquisition, the facilities offered by the different plants and the opportunities one could garner based on land location. While NTPC offers higher salaries compared to NCL, even for a low-level job such as that of a clerk, they no longer offer permanent jobs. Thus, a number of

Figure 9.11 Non-residential structures built on small parcels of land for claiming R&R benefits

Source: Author.

people were keen to have their land acquired by NCL as it offers permanent employment. They were also keen on buying small parcels of land in and around private projects to extract maximum benefits.[14] Interviews with the PAFs indicate that 'it is mainly a one-time extraction strategy, as they know that in long run they could not derive any benefits from the project. Initially everyone makes promises to offer several benefits but once the land is acquired the project security guards would stop them from even entering into the project boundary.' To seek land and house compensation along with the R&R benefits has become a popular strategy in the Singrauli region. The narrative of Ramlal Shah, recorded during oral history interviews, reflects this.

> People are compelled to do illegal activities and everyone in Singrauli even the District Magistrate of Singrauli is fairly aware about this trend. Tell me what's wrong in this? If you would not allow people to resettle properly and keep displacing people again and again, they are bound to do such activity. It takes over 100 years for a village to establish and you have [the government] displaced thousands of

[14] While discussing the construction of non-residential structures in the proposed project notified areas, it was highlighted in one of the interviews that these constructions were funded by Maoist groups from the adjoining Chhattisgarh state, particularly to the poor households who could not afford to build such structures at short notice.

> families 3 or 4 times over last 5 decades. The government keep saying that all these are happening in national interest but tell me who will look after our interest; the people of Singrauli are forced to die in the name of national interest.

Conception about Land and Diversified Livelihood

During the course of the research, the affected people were asked to express their conceptions of land use and importance. However, complete reliance on narratives of land served to reinforce a romanticized construction of land. Thus, it was deemed relevant and useful to examine both the narratives around land and the material livelihood strategies people were engaged with. It was thought that this approach would yield a more comprehensive understanding of contemporary land use and its contribution to diversified livelihoods.

While conducting in-depth interviews, people stressed, in both functionalist and romanticized terms, the use value of even a small parcel of agricultural land that could be utilized for subsistence agriculture. Maintaining access to some form of agriculture appeared economically important, as it entailed low input costs and allowed respondents to engage in small-scale agriculture to produce items for everyday family consumption. Moreover, there was a strong negative connotation attached to purchasing food from the market. Most respondents across the caste groups appeared invested in facilitating subsistence agriculture to 'meet one's everyday needs'. With respect to demography, a number of the younger respondents perceived agriculture as an undesirable pursuit. These youths were either upper-caste or OBC men seeking a shift from rural livelihoods towards professional employment or SC men that have historically not had agricultural land in their family.

Ramlal Shah is a 24-year-old Sahu man who has a bachelor of commerce degree and is in the process of completing his ITI (Industrial Technology Institute) diploma and seeking employment opportunities. When asked about people's preference for employment over agriculture, he says, 'People want a job that is the best, agriculture should also be there but if one is able to get a job somewhere then it is better everybody wants that their son is well educated and gets good posts and does well in life that is why people move from the village to the city.'

Significantly, Ramlal's immediate family does not practise agriculture. His father's brothers live in a village close to the Essar plant and practise agriculture on 5 acres of land. Ramlal's grandfather bought this land in the 1990s, 10 years after their displacement from NTPC. He thought that not everybody would get jobs to earn their livelihoods, so some people will have to do agriculture to make a living. Thus, the family's livelihood strategy indicates that agriculture served as a backup strategy that one conceded to in the absence of other opportunities rather than the occupation that one aspired to. This was confirmed by Ramlal's response to the question about whether his father asked him to be involved with the family's agricultural activities. Ramlal said, 'No he hasn't; I have studied and if I get settled somewhere, its good but if that doesn't happen then one will have to go and work on the land.' Thus, Ramlal's narrative underlines that a move away from agriculture is associated with an aspirational drive towards urbanization and professional employment. This narrative is representative of the younger generation of Sahus whose immediate families do not contemporarily practise agriculture. Among Sahu families engaged in agriculture, the younger generation also perceived it as being important.

It was observed during interviews that across castes, respondents that had previously either owned or worked on agricultural land as sharecroppers were inclined to maintain agricultural land. The younger generation has this aspiration of getting jobs in projects but the older respondents stressed engagement with agriculture simultaneously because of the sustainability of livelihoods. The older respondents (from their previous displacement experiences) also believe that everyone does not get employment in projects, so agriculture is important. For instance, despite making a more concerted move towards professional employment and regardless of generational status, previously landowning upper-caste Brahmins perceived the maintenance of agriculture to be important. Among the middle castes, Sahus depicted this tendency. Also, the SCs who practised agriculture on government land or were sharecroppers prior to their displacement echoed a similar narrative of land use.

For instance, Chameli, a 45-year-old Dalit woman who lives in Sector 3 of Navjivan Vihar (NTPC R&R colony), whose family owned 2–3 acres of land prior to displacement, vociferously points out,

> We had less land but it was ours. Our identity comes from our land. We were autonomous and could do whatever we wanted on it. Now look at our situation in this 40 by 60 plot (the land plot given by NTPC post displacement for house construction). Left with no land, we are naked now.

Nevertheless, Chameli's idealized construction of agricultural work stands in stark contrast to her emphasis, later in the conversation, upon social mobility and development that has been facilitated through land acquisition and compensation money.

There was greater concurrence on the usability of subsistence agriculture. None of the respondents, with the exception of one upper-caste family, indicated engaging with commercial (this was also technically deemed productive) agriculture. For most respondents, it did not seem to be something that they had really considered.

Small landholders especially expressed the opinion that commercial agriculture was an unfeasible option due to the logistical and financial commitments it entailed. Also, Suresh Tiwari, an upper-caste Brahmin man who worked at the Essar plant as deputy manager, indicated the difficulty of managing full-time employment with agriculture due to time constraints. Another upper-caste Brahmin respondent who was permanently employed with NCL expressed that he did not have enough helping hands to extensively pursue agriculture as his children were still schoolgoing. These upper-caste respondents tended to enter into sharecropping arrangements for the land they currently owned, as this enabled them to set aside the land for the time being so that in the future once the fathers retired and children grew older, they can engage with agriculture more substantially.

The respondents depicted the propensity to maintain subsistence agriculture; this was not the primary preoccupation for any of the families. Most of the respondents pursued diversified livelihood trajectories that centralized simultaneous involvement in various activities, such as employment, setting up one's own business, or becoming a contractor and purchasing land for investment.

In Singrauli, broadly, the livelihood patterns of respondents combined urban employment, either permanent or contractual, with land investments and maintenance of agriculture, wherever it was feasible. In fact, the livelihood strategies depicted by the Brahmin and Dalit families discussed above represent ideal livelihood patterns in the context of Singrauli, as they effectively combine and utilize opportunities in the rural and urban landscapes.

Empowered Bargaining

In this 'third' phase of displacement in the region, a significant change is visible. This change is perhaps due to the nationwide protests against land acquisition projects, which led to the stalling of hundreds of industrial projects in the country. On the contrary, despite the nationwide protests, the Singrauli region did not encounter that many local and regional protests (in relative terms). The affected people are no longer 'taken for granted' either by the projects' managements or the government. On the contrary, their entitlements and R&R have become crucial not only for mitigating the adverse impact of these projects on their lives but also for the very success of these projects. Civil society groups and the affected people make this possible through sustained agitation across the country. Those business groups who ignore this changing environment are, in fact, struggling to see their projects take shape. The overall impact of such movements is that the central government was compelled to revise the LA Act of 1894 and integrate the rehabilitation policy into a unified law to develop comprehensive R&R policies for mitigating the ill effects of such displacements. Several business groups in the private sector are, in fact, offering generous compensation (and rehabilitation) packages to the oustees so that the implementation of their projects can proceed smoothly.

One significant change that is visible in Singrauli now is the mechanism for addressing the issue of livelihood. For instance, the project developers at Essar Power assessed that providing employment to all the PAFs was not a feasible option, considering the skill sets that were required for the project employment. To address the issue of employment, the company announced its policy of unemployment monthly allowance[15] to every adult PAP (only males) in the age group of 18–50 years. During the survey, 93 households were surveyed from the Essar project villages and 40 out of 93 households were receiving the monthly unemployment allowance from the company. The unemployment allowance was only given to the homestead oustees and not to the families who lost land for the project but whose homestead remained unaffected. The land oustees were agitated and demanded the allowance to be extended to everyone affected by the project. It is important to highlight that Essar Power announced its company's unemployment allowance policy only after violent farmers' protests at their construction site office, when people's outburst led to the destruction of the site office and expensive machinery and equipment were set on fire. According to the Essar officials, this led to the loss of ₹100 million to the company and even the district administration was not able to stop them. However, after these protests 20–25 men were arrested from the villages and a case was filed against them. One can draw an inference that the company took a reactionary approach to this policy rather than being progressive in the very first incidence in addressing the concerns of the PAFs' employment and alternative livelihoods.

The 40 households surveyed were from the SC (Dalits) and the ST communities and were residing in the R&R colony. To study the response of unemployment allowances on the households, information was gathered on expenditure pattern and alternative livelihood engagements. There has been significant change in the expenditure pattern compared with the pre-displacement period; in some of the households, increased alcohol consumption was recorded and almost all the PAFs had purchased motorbikes. The female counterparts were still engaged with the management of livestock and collection of firewood. The recent field data shows that each adult PAP was receiving ₹7,500 per month as unemployment allowance. The interview of Essar officials indicates that the company has decided to pay the industrial wage rate with 10 per cent annual increment to the PAPs. It is difficult to comment on the socio-economic and cultural impact of such allowances on

[15] Essar Project office, Singrauli. Interviews, Essar officials, 2014.

the PAFs and it requires an in-depth study. However, such an approach adopted by the corporations indicates that they no longer take the affected families for granted on the issue of restoration of livelihood.

Conclusion

The third phase of land acquisition in Singrauli started with the formation of the district in 2008 and a large quantum of private land and forestland has already been acquired and diverted for the projects. Undoubtedly, the quantum of land acquisition in this short period demonstrates the efficiency of the district administration in managing this complex task. However, many projects are still in the process of acquiring land and setting up various coal mining and thermal power projects in the Singrauli region. For the private corporations interested in establishing coal mining or thermal power projects, Singrauli has become the ultimate destination for their investment. Even with the resentment against the land acquisition law and the outdated MP R&R policy, the district administration has been successful in acquiring and transferring large tracts of land to the private developers. There have been constant protests by the affected families to ensure fair compensation and rehabilitation in the district. The project developers have been reactionary towards this issue and responding to these concerns on the basis of the severity of the protests and demands. The project developers have been adopting differential approach for mitigating PAPs' concerns in their respective project villages. There is no uniform policy in the district regarding R&R.

Considering the large-scale social protests across the country concerning the provisions of the LA Act of 1894 and Singrauli's own painful rehabilitation experiences of five decades, the state government of MP could have acted in a progressive manner to revise the land award and adopted 'just' principles to compensate the affected families. But, unfortunately, in the race for creating a conducive investment climate and attracting private capital into the region or in the process of competing with other regions, the focus has been to provide more and more benefits to the private corporations. The formation of the district and providing administrative support for land acquisition for the private projects is one such example.

The analysis of the land cost in the project's total cost clearly demonstrates the cheap availability of land in rural India and the preference of state-mediated land acquisition over direct land purchase by the private developers. It further highlights that the amount paid under the LA Act of 1894 is not the true 'market value of land' as only 10 per cent of the respondents were able to regain an equal amount of the land as they had lost. The decision of not relocating to the R&R colonies also demonstrates the lack of consultations and participation of the PAFs in the planning process, which is critical for any successful rehabilitation programme. The field survey indicates that there is a massive livelihood transformation of the PAFs from primarily agrarian to industrial workers. It also suggests that casual employment with construction agencies is not a sustainable livelihood option. The information on compensation utilization patterns highlights that simply disbursing the compensation in cash does not address impoverishment of the PAFs. The enhancement of compensation, as suggested in the new law (RFCTLARR, 2013), by multiplying the circle rate four or two times or by payment of monthly unemployment allowances needs to be seen from their end results. The society (rural agrarian) that is not used to managing large sums of money needs to be handled in their way. Making one-time disbursement of compensation appears to be escaping the state's and the developers' legal and moral responsibilities.

The Singrauli region, because of its geographical remoteness and lack of civil society, has suffered enormously to raise the people's voices and concerns to the mainstream national media and to the courts. At the same time, when there are nationwide protests regarding unfair land acquisition and rehabilitation laws, Singrauli district stands out in facilitating acquisition of large-scale private lands and forestlands. It was the need of the private capitalists, and the state acted merely as a facilitator or simply performed the managerial functions for the 'bourgeois'. The creation of the district or redrawing of the geographical boundaries of Singrauli clearly signifies the motive of private capitalists and the role of the MP state government.

Part III
Analysis

10

Understanding Development

Politics of Growth

As discussed earlier, land policy in India has been a critical subject of public debate since Independence but, in the last one decade, the land acquisition issue has become unprecedentedly central to India's political economy. The introduction of the New Economic Policy in 1991 significantly impacted the growth-oriented model of development. It marked a complete transformation in the policy agenda of the government from closed-door economic policies to a market-oriented, investment-friendly environment for private business – an end to the monopoly of public sector enterprises. The economic logic behind such action was the stagnation in industrial and infrastructural growths accruing from sick and untenable public sector companies. The process of structural change had already begun in the early 1980s but it reached its culmination with the adoption of the Structural Adjustment Programme in 1991 in response to the loan received from the International Monetary Fund to overcome the balance of payment crisis. Thereafter, the government continued to remove structural constraints that impeded private investment, such as licensing, heavy taxation, import restrictions and tariffs (Ahluwalia, 1999). In addition, the government laid down a propitious business environment for foreign companies by creating avenues for both foreign direct investment (FDI) and portfolio investment.

The economic logic is, however, not sufficient to explain the policy transition during the early 1990s. If this was so in the 1990s, then it would have been possibly easy to do the same in the 1980s, which did not happen. What has indeed determined the trajectory of economic policies since Independence is the political environment prevailing at different points of time. In this view, it becomes imperative to acknowledge the political contextualization of economic and social policies. The political context may include both internal and external political purviews. Implicit in this political framework are also the ideological and interest imperatives that govern the nature of policies to be formulated and implemented by the government.

The politics of economic growth, in essence, has redefined the nature and strategic choice of the government in economic policy matters since the 1990s. It is less a variant of the laissez-faire state that Friedman (1980) envisages in his theory on the role of government that creates conditions for voluntary exchange by not interfering in a freely functioning market. Rather, the new model approximates well with Jagdish Bhagwati's perspective, that the government that play a positive role in business by carrying out three vital functions: creating incentives for exports by ensuring that the effective exchange rates for exports are higher than the effective exchange rate for imports, promoting selective industries on the criteria of comparative advantage, and providing fiscal advantages for trade promotion but not substantial excess of incentives to exports (Bhagwati, 1993: 94–100). The neoliberal state that assigns the highest value to economic freedom and yet ensures government's presence and intervention in the economy in a positive way gives the greatest priority to the objective of economic growth.

The ideological preferences have changed since the 1980s and the support for capitalism and growth-oriented model of development has become more firm after 1991. The Congress party since Rajiv Gandhi had abandoned the socialist model and embraced market economy. A new generation of leaders in both the party and bureaucracy with pro-market leanings replaced the older ones who had socialist commitments. Kohli (2009: 201) observes that advisors with pro-liberal proclivities and the World Bank or multinational company backgrounds, such as Arun Nehru, Arun Singh, Montek Ahluwalia, Abid Hussaain, Bimal Jalan and Manmohan Singh, were in sharp contrast with the left-leaning advisors in earlier regimes, such as Pitambar Pant, P. C. Mahlanobis, I. G. Patel, Vishnu Sahay, Tarlok Singh, Ashok Mehta and V. T. Krishnamachari.

Liberalization, privatization and globalization became the watchwords of the new economic policy adopted in 1991. The internal political dynamics that propelled globalization and privatization during the reform period is marked by a shift in political perceptions and power bases of the prominent industrial bodies in India. Kohli's analysis of relative strength of the various business organizations is apt in this regard. In his view, the pro-protectionist organizations such as the Federation of Indian Chambers of Commerce and Industries (FICCI) and the Associated Chambers of Commerce and Industry of India (ASSOCHAM) lost ground to the newly constituted Confederation of Indian Industries (CII) in terms of their political influence. The latter, in contrast with FICCI and ASSOCHAM, has been a vocal advocate of export-driven businesses, FDI and portfolio investment. It developed closer ties with the bureaucracy and the erstwhile Planning Commission (Kohli, 2009: 168). A more authoritative advocacy for global integration, special economic zones (SEZs) and software technology parks (STPs) was made by another powerful business organization, the National Association of Software and Service Companies (NASSCOM), which is the umbrella body for the software and service companies in India. NASSCOM was established in 1988 and was able to develop close links with various central ministries and state governments. Its insistence in the early 1990s led to the creation of STPs, and now its proximity to the government has led to the fulfilment of one of its basic demands – a flexible land acquisition policy.

Consultation with such powerful business organizations while amending economic policies is now a well-established practice. For instance, NASSCOM has been working closely with the Ministry of Commerce to identify the specific requirements of SEZs so that the new changes will reap maximum benefits to the fast-growing information technology (IT) and business process management industry. NASSCOM's position on the proposed Land Acquisition (LA) Bill became crystal clear when its president, Som Mittal, avowed, 'We are delighted that the government recognizes IT exports as a key growth driver for India's exports and the SEZ scheme. Removing the minimum land requirement and reducing the built up area will enable the SEZ scheme to realize its true potential.'[1] He further added, 'The new land policy with these most awaited changes will be specifically beneficial for the growth of small and medium enterprises and provide incentives for setting up SEZs in Tier II/Tier III locations.'[2]

Hence, business expansion has served as the basic driver for land acquisition. The growing strength of business lobbies and their closer engagement with the government since the 1990s has resulted in a policy architecture that comes closest to the interest of private businesses in India. Moreover, the government, since the early 1990s, itself felt convinced of the need to open up the economy and encourage both private and foreign investments. The ideational change is well explained by the tipping point model given by Rahul Mukherji (2014), which suggests that ideas favouring economic globalization were well established by the early 1990s but had gradually developed since the late 1970s when the government realized the weakness of the import substitution model of industrialization.

The mining and extractive industry is a significant sector, which has led to massive land acquisitions in the past and, with the opening of the economy, the demand for land is consistently increasing. The mining sector in 2014 contributed around 1.2 per cent to the gross domestic product and is expected to grow by 5–6 per cent in the next few years. In 2012, the Indian mining sector was valued at US$28 billion, and it can generate an additional output of US$44 billion by 2025

---

[1] See www.nasscom.in.

[2] Tier II and Tier III locations refer to the small and medium towns in India away from the metropolitan cities.

under a business-as-usual scenario and has the potential to grow to US$70 billion under an accelerated reforms regime, which the new ordinance is expected to herald (CII, 2014). The Government of India has allowed 100 per cent FDI in the mining sector under the automatic route. The Mines and Minerals (Development and Regulation) (MMDR) Act of 2015, passed by the parliament, aimed to provide a better legislative environment for investment and technology. Generally, the mining leases for resource development projects are granted for a long duration of minimum 20 years and up to 30 years. This policy move indicates that the Government of India is laying emphasis on resource development projects and expecting significant investments in the next decade.

Land Acquisition: Changing Regimes of Dispossession

In India, for four decades (1950–1990), the government largely dispossessed land for public sector projects to meet the requirements of industry and infrastructure projects. And the 'development' and displacement experience of Singrauli broadly illustrates the development trajectory of the country during this period. The land acquisition was primarily done for public sector dams, mines, thermal power generation and so on. Although the LA Act of 1894 had the provision for land acquisition for private companies, this was done in a limited capacity before liberalization. It cannot be said that dispossession in this period actually served 'public interest', but it had, by and large, public legitimacy in the post-Independence period. So, on the one hand, dispossessing land for these projects made possible accumulation that disproportionately benefitted the public sector elites, industrial bourgeoisie and dominant agrarian classes (Bardhan, 1984; Dwivedi, 2006; Nilsen, 2010). On the other hand, this accumulation was a distributional regression as it led to the impoverishment of 50 million people (Fernandes, 2008), that is, 'marginalisation of the marginalised'. The adequacy of compensation and rehabilitation was also challenged under this regime, but these projects had a high degree of legitimacy for being public sector projects. This legitimacy was also linked to the fact that a large number of people believed that they would benefit from the irrigation projects or receive employment in the public sector industries. It was mainly in the 1970s and 1980s that strong social movements started challenging this model of development; the Narmada Bachao Andolan challenged the legitimacy of 'destructive development' and pioneered anti-dispossession politics in India. These movements were successful in highlighting the concerns around land acquisition and displacement, but they were less successful in stopping or halting the projects.

The second regime of dispossession started post liberalization, after 1991, and unleashed increasing private demand for land for industry, infrastructure and real estate. Due to the decision to liberalize private investment and to reduce the public sector's role in the economy (Chandrasekhar and Ghosh, 2002), the share of private capital in the economy steadily increased and became dominant by the end of the decade (Kohli, 2012: 45). While liberalization did not affect all sectors uniformly, it did, for instance, unleash dramatic growth in India's service sector, particularly IT, IT-enabled services and business process outsourcing (Bardhan, 2010; Kohli, 2012). This IT boom was also reflected in the number of SEZs that were approved by 2009; 63 per cent of the approved SEZs were in IT and IT-enabled service sectors (Ministry of Commerce, 2017), leading to the growth of hi-tech IT parks and STPs in peri-urban frontiers. Land acquisition for SEZs resulted in nationwide protests by farmers and the civil society.

Another sector that attracted significant FDI and private capital was the extractive industries, which raised demands for land in mineral-rich states. This segment of projects also gave rise to a lot of public protests around land acquisition issues. Many significant investments, such as the POSCO and Vedanta projects in Odisha and the ArcelorMittal and Reliance coal mining projects in Jharkhand, were held up because of land acquisition protests. One significant difference noticeable between these earlier phases and the present regimes of dispossession is that the earlier phase of dispossession was mainly led by public sector projects and civil society movements were unable to stop the projects from displacing people, whereas the present phase of dispossession is led primarily by the private sector and the civil society intervention is much more organized, strong and impactful in stalling the projects. So, the land conflict issues and social unrest due to land acquisitions have widened in the present time.

Politics over the LA Act of 2013

The politics of growth favoring commercialization triggered the most recent land acquisition drive. And particularly during 2005–2015, the pace of land acquisition increased exponentially, mainly for private corporations. The last decade also witnessed large-scale public protests against land acquisition drives, which led to massive restructuring of the land acquisition law. The United Progressive Alliance (UPA) government, in its second term (2009–2014), emphasized on the revision of the already challenged LA Act of 1894, and a comprehensive legislation was prepared which, for the first time, brought land acquisition and rehabilitation under the purview of a single piece of legislation. Land, which was the most basic requirement for doing business, was not easy to acquire under the draconian LA Act of 1894. Therefore, it was imperative for the government to amend the legislation so that land could be made available for private investments.

But more importantly, such action had to be legitimized by providing necessary safeguards against displacement and the resulting vulnerability. To begin with, necessary changes were made in the land law under the UPA government to ensure legitimate transfer through popular consent and substantive compensation to the displaced people. However, when the Bharatiya Janata Party (BJP) government came to power in June 2014, it introduced land ordinances to dilute the UPA land law by exempting certain projects from the social impact assessment (SIA) study and the landowners' consent clause. These ordinances faced massive opposition from several political parties, including some of BJP's own allies. As a result of this opposition, BJP had to withdraw these amendments.

It is important to note that there were no cabinet meetings regarding introduction of these land ordinances; also, there was no evidence of challenges or complexities faced by the state governments or developers while executing the new land legislation. The alarming question is that without even executing the law and understanding its effectiveness on ground, what was the need to revise it? Undoubtedly, the private sector was dissatisfied with some of the provisions such as the consent clause and so on that had been introduced by the UPA government.[3] So, the only conclusion one can draw is the pressure from the corporate sector to amend the UPA law. Also, there was an argument by an RTI activist, Venkatesh Nayak, that only 8 per cent (*Economic Times*, 2015a) of the total stalled projects were held up due to land acquisition issues, so one could not blame the UPA Land Bill for that. However, it is difficult to rely on this data as land acquisition has been a major concern for stalled projects, and there have been massive protests regarding existing provisions under the LA Act of 1894.

The Right to Fair Compensation and Transparency in Land Acquisition, Rehabilitation and Resettlement (RFCTLARR) Amendment Ordinance, promulgated on 31 December 2014, brought 13 central Acts in conformity with the land acquisition legislation of 2013 only in terms of the rehabilitation and resettlement (R&R) package. However, the actual rigours laid down by the land acquisition legislation, including survey of land, identification of beneficiaries and SIA, were not made mandatory under the 13 central Acts. Between January 2015 and June 2015, the central ministries overseeing the development projects made 219 acquisitions (*Economic Times*, 2015b) and not a single acquisition was done under this ordinance. Land was purchased for four sectors – railways, coal, petroleum and natural gas, and highways – across 1,584 villages in 141 districts of 22 states. The most number of acquisitions was for national highways (137) under the National Highways Act of 1956, 44 land acquisitions were for petroleum and

[3] Interview, additional secretary, Ministry of Rural Development, New Delhi, 2015.

natural gas under the Petroleum and Minerals Pipelines (Acquisition of Right of Users in Land) Act of 1962, 31 were for railways under the Railways Act of 1989 and 7 were done by the coal ministry under the Coal Bearing Areas (Acquisition and Development) Act of 1957. If these acquisitions had been done under the RFCTLARR 2013, it would have created precedence for other developers. The reluctance to use the RFCTLARR for acquiring these new lands raises questions about the internal dynamics of the government.

Politics of Resistance

Politics inherent in the growth model seeks to maintain dominance of the capitalist class and buttresses a laissez-faire variant of government. Contrarily, the politics of resistance is inbuilt in democratic structures and processes that serve as an antidote to the politics of growth. Even core capitalist governments sometimes fall short of pursuing unregulated capitalism when they face resistance from political opponents, civil society and social movements. In this way, an ideological force is inherent in the politics of resistance. It involves public activism to challenge the existing social and economic order that appears to be genuine and overarching. The Indian democracy offers multiple sites to voice contestation and dissent. At the societal level, it has taken the form of civil society activism, farmers' struggles, tribal movements, candlelight marches or even state demonstrations. At the institutional level, the parliament serves as the most prominent spot for political resistance. Critical positions over the Land Bill have been stated and expressed at both institutional and societal levels.

Resistance against relentless land acquisition has drawn public attention in the last two decades. State governments have acquired huge tracts of land for carrying out private or public–private partnership (PPP) industrial or infrastructural projects. State development authorities more often acquire these lands to establish large industrial estates and SEZs through the involvement of private developers. In many cases, they fail to search for prospective entrepreneurs to utilize the facilities. Ultimately, all such lands remain vacant and unutilized for a long period. Many such lands fall in areas that are predominantly inhabited by tribal populations (Asif, 1999: 1565). Consequently, land acquisition in such cases results in large-scale displacement and vulnerability of poor farmers and tribals, on the one hand, and fails to fulfil its intended purpose, on the other. These vulnerable communities pay a heavy price for this failure of the government.

Local movements against land acquisition for establishing industrial estates and SEZs have received nationwide attention in the recent past. As observed, 'Land acquisition has become the single most contentious issue surrounding SEZs. It has led to vigorous anti-SEZ movements varying in methods from protest marches to violence against the state' (Aggarwal, 2012: 229).

Resistance has often taken the form of violence or even bloodshed in states such as West Bengal. Many a time, state authorities have resorted to armed coercion to suppress such movements. For instance, when land acquisition by the left government in West Bengal in 2007 for the Tata Nano project was met with massive protests by farmers in Singur and Nandigram, the government reacted by using arms against innocent protestors – many of whom were killed. The movement that was spearheaded by Krishi Jami Raksha Committee at Singur and Bhoomi Ucched Pratirodh Committee at Nandigram received the political backing of Trinamool Congress (TMC) under the leadership of Mamata Banerjee (*Hindu*, 2007). Ultimately, the left government had to withdraw and Tata Motors was compelled to transfer the project to Gujarat.

Land acquisition in Odisha has witnessed similar reactions from farmers and tribal inhabitants. The issue of land transfers to POSCO, a South Korean steel giant at Jagatsinghpur, was one of these. When farmers resisted the demolition of their betel leaf vineyards by the district administration, they were beaten up. The protest against the arbitrary land acquisition and state violence was led by POSCO Pratirodh Sangram Samiti, which strongly condemned the anti-poor initiatives of the government to assist multinational companies. Finally, the government had to suspend the project under social pressure and the insistence of international human rights bodies such as the International Human Rights Clinic, US, and the International Network for Economic, Social and Cultural Rights (*Hindu*, 2013).

Protests and political opposition against the bauxite mining project of Vedanta Group, the British mining giant, at Niamgiri Hills, Odisha, is yet another example of the politics of resistance. Tribals predominantly inhabit Niamgiri Hills situated in the Kalahandi and Rayagada districts of Odisha. The area was found to be rich in mineral resources, especially bauxite, and hence was a suitable site for establishing a massive industrial project. Acquisition of land at Niamgiri was not only a violation of tribal rights but also of basic environmental laws. Tribals, including Dongri Kondhs, living on the hilltop, came out in protest against the state action. In response to opposition by the tribals, the Supreme Court came to their rescue by directing the state government to empower the *gram sabha*s of the affected areas to take the final decision on the project. Twelve *gram sabha*s unanimously took a decision against the project, as a result of which it was withdrawn by the government (*Statesman*, 2015).

These three cases of protest against land acquisition exemplify the power of dissent in a democratic nation. In all of them, the people's action against arbitrary land acquisition is common, in addition to the support and assistance of political and civil society organizations. As pointed out, 'Political parties are quick to cash in on these movements and civil society is not far behind' (Aggarwal, 2012: 229). While TMC, the main opposition party in West Bengal, backed the social struggle against the Tata Nano project in the displaced community's land, local and international civil society organizations played their respective roles in the protest at Jagatsinghpur. In the case of Niamgiri, the Supreme Court provided necessary safeguards against compulsory land acquisition. The Land Bill that seeks to legitimize compulsory acquisition has also faced stiff resistance in the wake of political assertion at the institutional level and social mobilization on the ground.

Democracy provides multiple avenues to voice political dissent at both the societal and the institutional level. The recent political turmoil over the passage of the Land Bill has brought the two houses of parliament at loggerheads with each other. It exemplifies the politics of resistance taking place at the institutional level. Amidst strong opposition from the Congress, the left and other political parties, the Bill was finally passed in Lok Sabha where BJP enjoyed an overwhelming majority. It was, however, met with an undesirable fate in Rajya Sabha where the Congress could assert well with its majority position. The Bill was henceforth chastened in Rajya Sabha and is now being referred to a joint parliamentary committee as a result of this institutional deadlock. The Land Bill that galvanizes the prospects of private and foreign investments, and thereby buttresses the politics of growth, gets a heavy dose of public resentment and political antagonism. Politics of resistance, thus, acts as a check on the pro-corporate stance implicit in the new land policy. It triggers political contestation by offering several sites of democratic dissent.

Resource Developments and Reorganization of Space

This section briefly discusses the findings of the study and examines the potential policy reforms. The resource development process and the experiences of Singrauli, along with the revenue data between 2008 and 2013, suggest that the existing mining operations generate significant profit from the region. For instance, the existing Northern Coalfields Ltd coal mines generated ₹131,650 million between 2008 and 2013 and considering the proposed MMDR (Bill) profit-sharing provision, the district would have received ₹6,845 million annually for its regional development. After analysing the district annual budget of ₹8,000 million, which is allocated by the state government, it was found that the mining profit share alone (as proposed in the MMDR Act of 2015) is significantly high in relation to the district budget. It is important to note that resource revenue generation from Singrauli will increase in the forthcoming years, once the third phase of ongoing mining projects begin their operations. The data on resource revenue generation, annual district budgetary allocation and social development profile substantiates the argument that Singrauli has been strategically used as a 'space of dependence' and kept deprived in the name of 'public purpose'.

The redrawing of geographical boundaries according to the accumulation of natural resource and formation of Singrauli district indicates the role of the state in facilitating private investments into the region and to provide better administrative support for resource development projects. As discussed earlier, the Singrauli region straddles the border between Madhya Pradesh (MP) and Uttar Pradesh (UP), but the major coal deposits are concentrated within the MP state jurisdiction. The Sonebhadra district (adjoining Singrauli district of MP) in UP has coal deposits but these are not comparable to those in the Singrauli district of MP and that is the reason behind concentrated industrial investment in Singrauli district. The role of the state in a neoliberal framework raises serious concerns about its position in 'facilitating' development and still ensuring justice to the people. The experiences of Singrauli highlight the failure of the local people to realize justice in the land acquisition process. The lack of participation of the local people in the public sphere in meaningfully understanding and articulating their interests is a matter of serious concern in backward regions such as Singrauli.

The individual household experiences of the project-affected families (PAFs) in Singrauli of earlier phases in general and the third phase in particular demonstrate that the land acquisition and compensation policy fails to address basic concerns, for instance, restoration of sustainable livelihoods of the PAFs post displacement. Failure to regain an equal amount of land with the compensation money in the post-displacement period reflects the inadequacy of the existing compensation practices. The study also suggests that the disbursement of a one-time compensation in cash is not productive for most of the PAFs and should be replaced with recurring benefits or staggered payments over time.

An increasing flow of new investment in resource development projects in less developed regions of India is evident as the country further liberalizes its investment policies. Resource-rich states seem to be competing for investment in resource development projects. So, while on the one hand they are making demands for more compensation for resource development in order to augment revenues from such development in the form of resource revenue sharing, on the other hand they seem to be ready to provide large fiscal concessions or tax benefits via SEZs and other tax concessions in the name of creating a better 'investment climate' for potential investors. In trying to promote economic growth and short-term development in the state, they run the risk of losing out on promoting sustainable development and intra-generational and intergenerational equity. There is increasingly sharp competition emerging between coal mining companies and steel producers in the iron ore belt. They are competing against each other for a bigger slice of the mineral market and are driven by a strong need to acquire low-cost properties. These dynamics are leading to undervaluation of social and environmental impacts and lower returns to mineral-bearing states, and hence the requirement for careful monitoring and implementing significant changes at the policy level. I would argue that it would be in national and state interest to have efficient mining companies, and states should aim at encouraging the most socially and environmentally responsible mining and advocate for desired changes in the policy framework.

Resource Developments and Resource Federalism in India

Compensation payments may be backed by legislation and based on general principles of law such as torts or those developed by the judiciary as in the case of compensatory afforestation. Besides their treatment in the constitution and laws, the nature of the resource also has an important role in determining any liability that arises from the use or depletion of the resource or the environmental or socio-economic externalities created thereby. The ownership and control rights are clearly defined in some of the resources, while some amount of conflict in interpretation may exist due to qualified ownership and control as in the case of minerals. The exercise of rights to own, control, use and levy a charge on a resource are all dependent on another right of the government, that is to legislate on these matters. In India, the proprietary title to minerals vests in the federating states. However, this ownership is subject to the legislation governing regulation and control of mining enacted by the parliament.[4]

Analysis through my research reflects that there is a certain level of encroachment into the state's domain in case of mining minerals through the MMDR Act. Thus, ownership rights in minerals held by states is a qualified and conditional one, given that while states have a right to the share of revenues from mining in the form of royalties and dead rents to reflect ownership, they (a) have no right to decide on the method of fixation of royalty, its rate and its periodic revision; (b) have no right to decide on the granting of mining lease in cases of major minerals without prior clearances from the central government and (c) are unable to tax mineral resources in any way they see fit.

The research analysis and demands by the mineral-bearing states suggest that the key issue that is voiced by states is about augmenting the revenues from the sources of wealth that states have in order to promote development. At the local

[4] Regulation and development of minerals is a state subject but it has to be in conformity with the central legislation.

level, however, the concerns of the local communities with resource development are the impact that it has on their lives and livelihoods, with the need to address externalities when they arise and to increase the sharing of benefits of resource development with them. For resource federalism to work well, the focus needs to be on the relevant institutions and their interactions to manage inter-jurisdictional conflicts and to ensure greater accountability and transparency. There is also need for a greater role for intergovernmental instruments to address many of the cross-level jurisdictional issues that arise in the context of resource development and inter-ministerial cooperation to make fiscal departments aware of sectoral concerns and avoid the disconnect that is observed with the social and environmental policies. The experience of the Special Area Development Authority (as discussed in Chapter 7) in the Singrauli region suggests that institutions in mineral-rich regions need a sustainable flow of funds and professional expertise to productively utilize the mineral funds for the development of the local area. The international experiences of multinational corporations operating in resource-rich economies also indicate that corporations can take progressive steps by establishing their own foundations and trusts and contributing towards the welfare of the people in

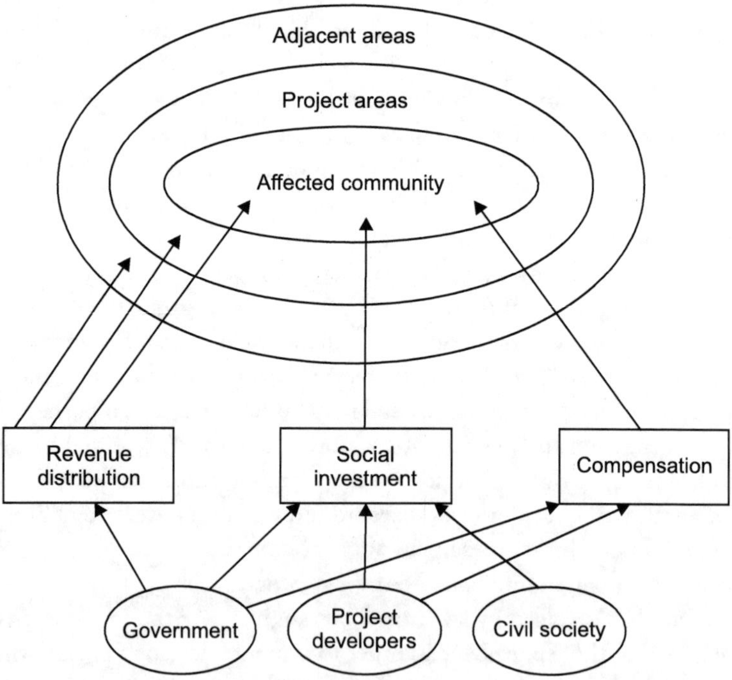

Figure 10.1a Approaches to benefits distribution – parallel contribution

Source: Author.

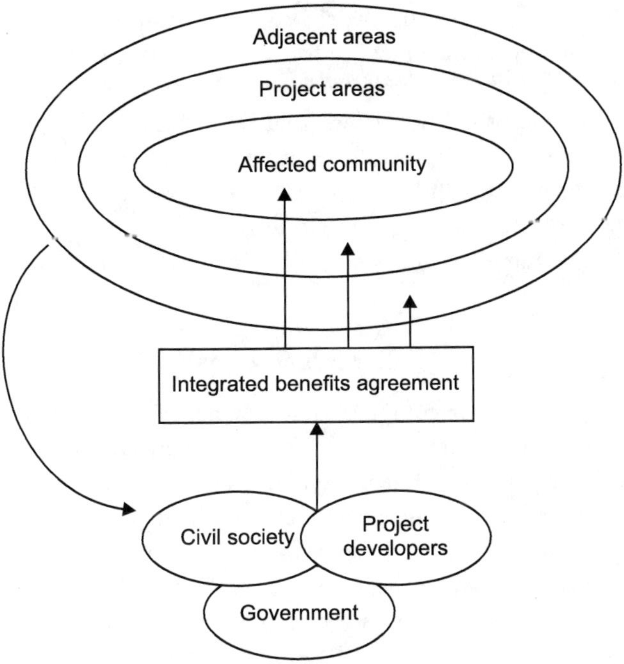

Figure 10.1b Approaches to benefits distribution – partnership approach

Source: Author.

such regions. However, the most sustainable and rational approach would be both local governments and project developers collectively owning the responsibility and contributing towards the welfare of the region.

As we have seen in earlier chapters, there are various ways to share the benefits of resource development across agents and spatial levels. Parallel contributions by various stakeholder groups and partnership approaches best summarize the various arrangements observed internationally. Parallel approaches involve a share of revenues across government levels through social investment programmes in partnership with civil society as in the case of corporate foundations and through compensation by government and private companies as reimbursement for incremental costs created by development projects (see Figure 10.1a). This is also the more common form of benefits distribution in India. More integrated benefits distribution arrangements can be drawn up in partnership arrangements to reflect a greater integration of stakeholder values and concerns (see Figure 10.1b). The international experiences are just to indicate that there are various existing practices (at least at policy level); how much successful they are on the ground requires a detailed analysis.

International experiences suggest that without increased resources going to the local government, development will be mismanaged, negative impacts will not be mitigated and the potential benefits will be largely lost. This will further generate public animosity and dissent that will ultimately cause the resource development to fail or, at best, to be much less successful than it could be in generating development. While some of the resources to address the impacts will have to come from the company, if the local government has no resources (as in case of the Singrauli region), it has no bargaining power to create improvements.

Policy Suggestions

The various rationales for compensation and benefit sharing linked to land acquisition and resource extraction and the current status in India with respect to each stream have been summarized in earlier chapters. As discussed earlier, some of these issues have been addressed but not all. The issues which have not been addressed are related to depletion in case of minerals and many sociocultural impacts of resource development; where mechanisms do exist to address issues, they are not always adequate or enforced. My research has brought out that compensation and revenue sharing should address the following: (a) a fair replacement value of land and assets, and one-time compensation should be replaced with recurring benefits in the form of share in the project benefits to improve productive base for the PAFs, (b) payments for all social and environmental externalities, and these costs must be accounted for in the cost of production by the developers, (c) payments for use of resources that are owned or over which use rights exist and (d) funds to provide for sustainable development of the local area once the resources have depleted.

The research suggests that the key to bringing consensus amongst stakeholders for resource policy is for it to be people centred. It must have a 'representation strategy' that incorporates multiple dimensions of resource valuation of key groups; the rights and responsibilities of the various stakeholders should form the underlying 'perimeter' of planning, where the 'criticality' of some resources in terms of uniqueness and future uses is acknowledged. Such a strategy will allow for trade-offs between different interests where possible; where no compromise is possible, there will be need to legislate 'no-go-areas'. Resource development creates risks, costs and benefits which do not occur in other activities in the economy and which need to be addressed through special fiscal provisions. Land acquisition and resource development policy has so far ignored the centrality of project-affected persons (PAPs) and the creation of institutions for equitable distribution and sharing of project benefits. This is ethically and politically problematic. Policy has to make PAPs better off as a result of the project than they were before.

They need to have a clear prior claim on the revenue streams of the project, beyond just payments for lost land and the resultant displacement. Policy needs to recognize the role and value of land and share project benefits with owners, beyond compensation and replacement value of land. It is evident that people in project areas contribute to a project by giving up their land and that the project is not possible without access to this land. And yet, payments made to them are only for the damage created or for losses incurred (that too not completely); they do not create a benefit. Payments do not make communities or individuals stakeholders in the project and do not recognize the loss of opportunity by the affected people in benefitting from enhanced land values as a result of resource development.

Understanding the issue of compensation, as I have argued in my book, requires both a multifunctional view of resources (both material and non-material values) and a multidimensional perspective (spatial, agency and temporal) of resource development. In the context of land acquisition for resource development projects, land emerges as an important and highly volatile issue at many points during the life cycle of the project. Corporations and project developers need to secure access to land and community consent, and communities need to secure that land rights are properly recognized – free prior informed consent is obtained and appropriate compensation policy is in place where land is lost or affected. As discussed earlier, the numerous resource development and infrastructure projects which are held up across states in India due to land acquisition and environmental clearance issues and extensive farmers movements and civil society protests demonstrate that, for a long period, these concerns have been ignored by the project developers and the concerned state governments.

Ambitious Land and Mining Act to Be Delivered by 'Weak Institutions': Is India Ready?

On 25 May 2019, after winning the second consecutive parliamentary election, Prime Minister Narendra Modi came up with the slogan of 'NaRa' (National Ambition and Regional Aspirations) to transform the geographically backward regions of the country and pull a significant population out of poverty by 2022. There was a strong emphasis in his town hall speech to transform the nation in his second term, when India will complete 75 years of its independence. Undoubtedly, if the country has to achieve this target, then these 100+ 'aspirational districts', as declared by the National Institution for Transforming India (NITI) Aayog, will have to be given special attention for their 'regional development'. Many of these aspirational districts are also 'resource rich' (mining districts) but fall poor in socio-economic indicators.

During UPA II (2009–2014), on policy fronts, there were significant amendments in the LA Act of 1894 (the Act was repealed by the RFCTLARR Act of 2013) and the MMDR Act of 1957 to introduce principles of fair compensation and provisions of fiscal decentralization by adopting a mechanism for profit sharing (MMDR Amendment Act of 2015) with mining districts through 'District Mineral Funds'. Global experiences suggest that there are varied experiences of resource revenue sharing and a mere revenue allocation does not yield desired outcomes. The institutional framework governing these funds needs professional expertise and representation from all stakeholders in decision-making and requires sustainable flow of funds. The representation from stakeholders will guide the expenditure of funds as per the 'need' of the local population. Both the LA Act and the MMDR Act depend heavily on local institutions for its successful implementation and to achieve desired social development outcomes.

The Journey

Land Law

In India, the colonial LA Act of 1894 was used by the state for 120 years to acquire land for 'public purposes'. The colonial law was challenged several times in the court of law due to its inadequacies and its detrimental social and economic implications on the project-affected communities. It was questioned on several grounds, starting from the very definition of 'public purpose' to determination of 'fair compensation' and for being inhumane on the issues of R&R. The colonial Act nowhere mentioned R&R to be a legal obligation of the land acquiring body. Of course, the colonial government was under no obligation to justify its acts, as the very purpose of land acquisition was to create business opportunities for the colonial government and extract profits out of India.

However, from the colonial era to the Indian 'welfare state', the government took long to realize that every 'citizen' is important and the local project-affected communities in the rural hinterland (already vulnerable ones) cannot be taken for granted for the 'larger common good'. There are no official statistics on the total number of displaced persons in India; by some estimates (Fernandes, 2000; Cernea, 2005a; Mathur, 2005a, 2005b; Padel and Das, 2008), more than 60 million people have been displaced in the last six decades for various 'developmental projects' undertaken in the name of 'public purpose'. Out of these, 40 per cent are tribals and dalits who are the most vulnerable social groups in India (Amnesty International, 2016). This also signifies the reasons behind 'unsuccessful rehabilitation', and there are hardly any successful case studies that can be showcased. The UPA government, during its second tenure (2009–2014), started deliberating on the new land acquisition law and after long parliamentary deliberations, the Land Act was passed in 2013. The subsequent National Democratic Alliance (NDA) government continued with these legislations by giving independent powers to the state governments (under federal polity) to move ahead with their own amendments.

Mining Law

With regard to mining, there has been a long-standing demand from mineral-rich states (MP, Jharkhand, Odisha and so on) to the central Finance Commission for developing a fair resource revenue sharing mechanism between the centre and state governments to fairly compensate the latter for the losses (social and environmental externalities) that they incur due to mining projects. The role of the civil society has been very crucial in highlighting the socio-economic and ecological concerns of the mining regions. In 1997, the Supreme Court, in its landmark 'Samtha Judgment', indicated certain duties and obligations on the part of the mining leaseholder, who would have to henceforth set aside 20 per cent of the net profit from the mining operations which would be allocated for local area development so that the local indigenous people could benefit from these projects and their socio-economic status could be improved. The Supreme Court judgment initiated a discussion at the central government level and between 2006 and 2010, the Ministry of Mines started deliberations to draft a new MMDR Bill to replace the MMDR Act of 1957. In 2011, the MMDR Bill detailed out the provisions of sharing mining benefits through the District Mineral Foundation (DMF), and there was unanimous agreement among the Group of Ministers. However, the Bill lapsed in February 2014, and the subsequent NDA government passed the law in 2015. The revenue allocations under DMF to the mining districts have been very significant and if the objective is to transform these backward areas, then institutions need to be strengthened and dedicated independent departments are required to carry forward the provisions of the Act. Currently, in most of the mining districts, the district collector, who is already responsible for steering dozens of committees in the districts and oversee the line departments, has been given this additional charge. Map 10.1 gives a sense and a magnitude of revenue allocation in some of these states.

Conceptualization of a 'Just' and 'Fair' LA Act

In UPA II, after long parliamentary deliberations and civil society consultations, the RFCTLARR Act of 2013 was passed that came into effect from 1 January

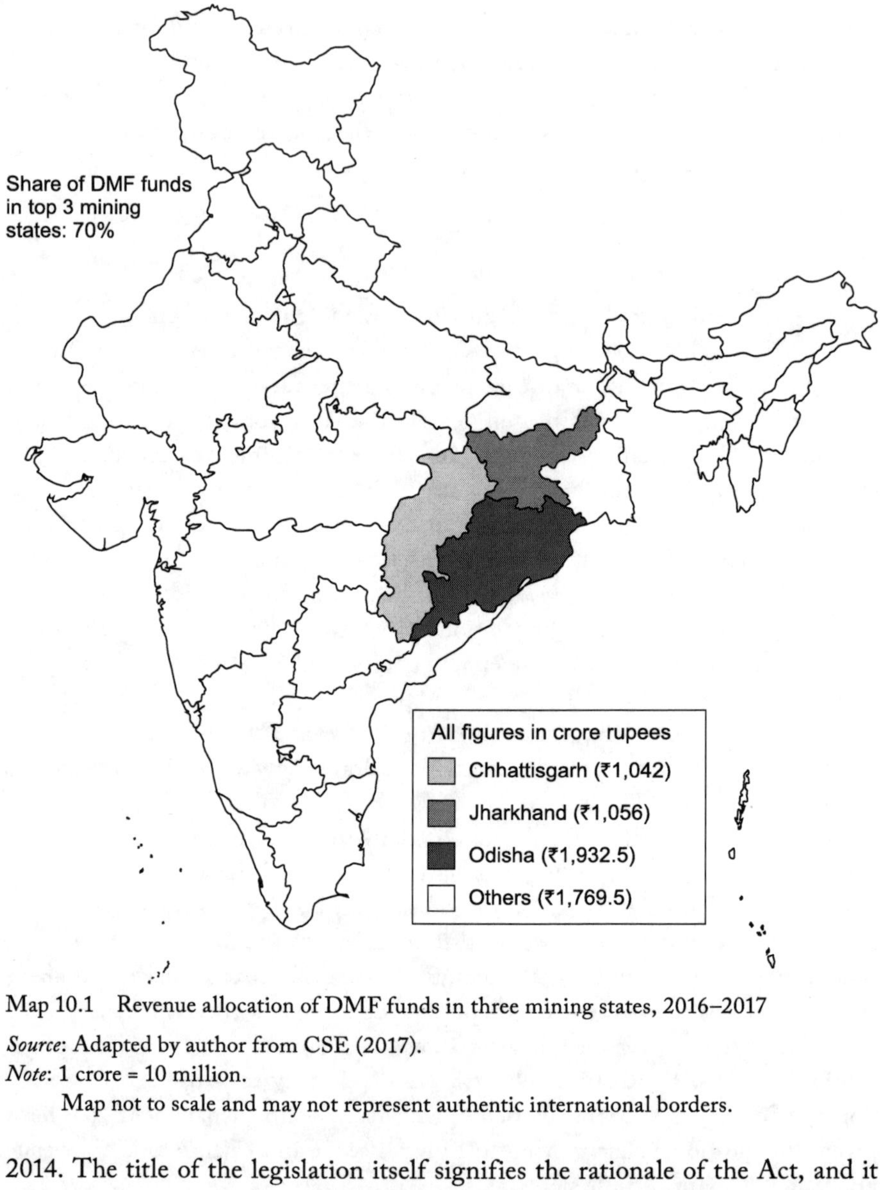

Map 10.1 Revenue allocation of DMF funds in three mining states, 2016–2017

Source: Adapted by author from CSE (2017).
Note: 1 crore = 10 million.
Map not to scale and may not represent authentic international borders.

2014. The title of the legislation itself signifies the rationale of the Act, and it attempts to create a robust legal framework to ensure that the project-affected families (PAFs) are provided with enough 'social safeguards' to protect their socio-economic interests and that they are not deprived in the post-displacement period. The Act has a detailed pre-land acquisition notification procedure and starts with a mandatory execution of an SIA study (to be conducted by an independent agency appointed by the district administration) and review by an independent 'expert committee' (EC) at the state government level. Only after the detailed evaluation of the 'social implications' of the project and overall 'cost-benefit analysis' of the potential project can the EC decide to 'decline' or 'approve' further land acquisition procedures. The Act also has a mandatory requirement of obtaining 'free prior informed consent' (FPIC) of the landowners and R&R provisions for 'livelihood losers'. In order to address the issue of 'inadequate compensation', the Act increases the solatium to 100 per cent (which was 30 per cent under the colonial law) and introduces a multiplication factor of 1–2 to be applied on the prevailing government circle land rate (1 for urban and up to 2 for rural land acquisition projects). Section 11(5) of the Act requires the administrator to update the land records after preliminary notification in the project-notified area within a period of two months so that potentially affected families with unclear land tenure become eligible for compensation and rehabilitation benefits. Overall, the Act touches on all prominent issues that have been major reasons behind land conflicts across the country, and the government anticipates that the central Act will be implemented in its true spirit to address the historic injustice embedded in the colonial Act.

Ordinance Showed the 'Way'

In 2014, the BJP government came to power and attempted to bring two ordinances to dilute the provisions of the SIA and the consent clause to exempt certain categories of projects. Undoubtedly, the pressure to introduce these ordinances came from the industry as there was a unanimous position that such an 'impractical' 'over ambitious' Act would create unnecessary hurdles and would delay the land acquisition process. These ordinances faced massive opposition from several political parties, including some of BJP's own allies. And as a result of this opposition, the BJP government had to withdraw its amendments in the central law. It is important to note that no cabinet meetings regarding introduction of these land ordinances were held; also, there was no evidence of challenges or complexities faced by the state governments or developers while executing the new land legislation. The alarming question is, without even executing the law and understanding its effectiveness on ground, what was the need for amending it?

Undoubtedly, the private sector was dissatisfied with some of the provisions of the Act such as the consent clause and the SIA that had been introduced by the UPA government. So, the only conclusion one can draw is the pressure from the corporate sector to amend the UPA law. After the strong opposition on the proposed ordinances in the parliament, the BJP government decided to leave it to the discretion of the state governments to make their own land acquisition rules. The ordinance allowed the government to exempt five categories of projects from provisions such as SIA, prior consent and limits on acquisition of irrigated multi-crop agricultural land. These five categories are (a) national security or defence, (b) rural infrastructure, (c) affordable housing, (d) industrial corridors and (e) infrastructure projects, including PPP projects where the central government owns the land. One significant amendment, as part of the ordinance promulgated on 31 December 2014, brought 13 central Acts in conformity with the land acquisition legislation of 2013 only in terms of the R&R package. However, the actual rigours laid down by the land acquisition legislation, including survey of land, identification of beneficiaries and SIA, were not made mandatory under the 13 central Acts.

Since then, several state governments have come up with their own state-specific legislation, and the state-specific amendments revolve primarily around the issues of exemption of certain projects from SIA compliance, FPIC and determination of multiplier factor, among others. On 10 December 2018, the Supreme Court issued notices to five state governments (Gujarat, Andhra Pradesh, Telangana, Jharkhand and Tamil Nadu) on a plea challenging state amendments to the central land acquisition law following arguments that the states cannot make changes to a central law. These state-specific amendments were to exempt land acquisition provisions (FPIC, SIA, participation of local bodies and return of unutilized land) in these states for infrastructure, industrial corridor and housing projects. The Supreme Court cited the landmark *Kesavananda Bharati Case* of 1973 and held that the basic structure of the constitution cannot be changed through a constitutional amendment. Similarly, a central Act passed by the parliament also has a basic structure and it cannot be amended by passing an ordinance under Article 254 (2) of the constitution. States such as Tamil Nadu, Gujarat, Telangana and Jharkhand, from time to time, have approved amendments to the centrally legislated RFCTLARR Act of 2013, doing away with SIA and consent clauses required to be fulfilled for acquisition of land for public projects. The petition filed in the Supreme Court indicated that it has resulted in dilution of the central law.

In 2015, central rules were notified to develop a guiding framework for the RFCTLARR Act of 2013. Since then, 14 state governments have notified their own rules under Section 109 of the central Act. These rules have adopted certain provisions of the 2015 Land Ordinance too, thereby circumventing the scope of the 2013 Act. Four states (Goa, Madhya Pradesh, Punjab and West Bengal) have not notified any rules or state Act.

Social Impact Assessment (SIA) – Stumbling Block or a Useful Tool?

The execution of an SIA study is a standard practice across the world, and it is a critical tool to assess the potential impacts of projects on the local community

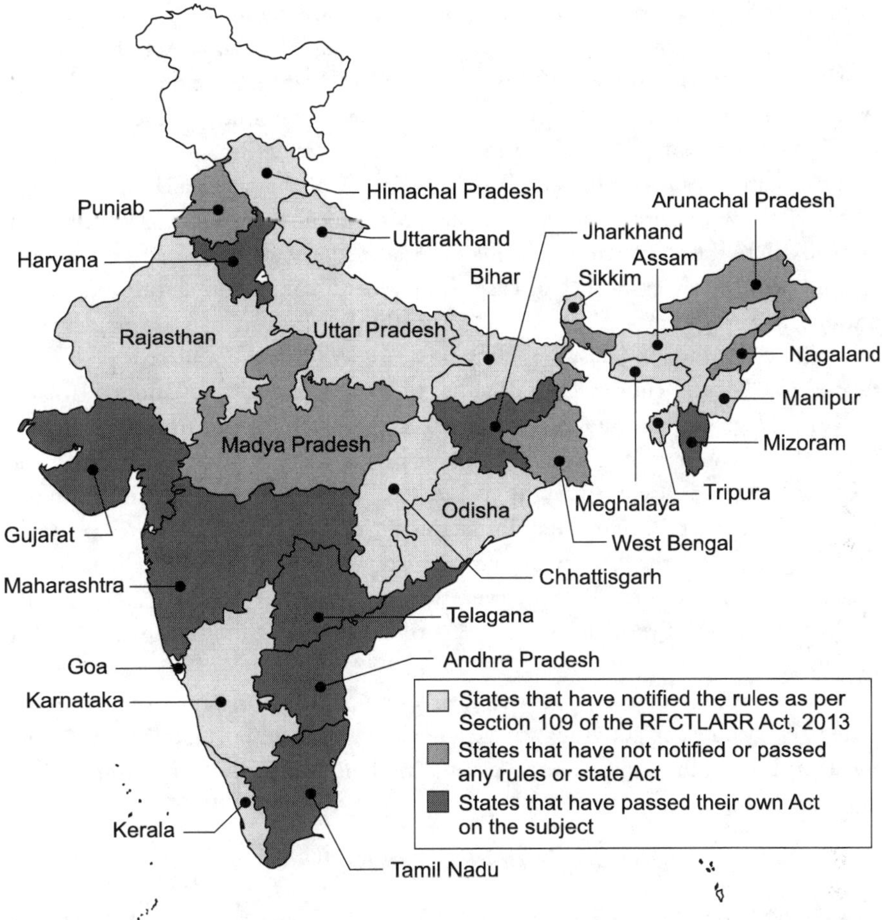

Map 10.2 Approach of state governments towards land acquisition amendments

Source: Adapted by author from CSE (2019) (information obtained through RTI).
Note: Map not to scale and may not represent authentic international borders.

and develop a plan in advance to mitigate adverse effects of those projects. It is a rehabilitation tool that helps in developing a realistic plan for successful R&R of the PAFs. Since its introduction in the central law, SIA has been perceived as a stumbling block in the process of land acquisition. And therefore, states such as Andhra Pradesh, Gujarat, Maharashtra, Telangana, Tamil Nadu and Jharkhand have removed the requirement of conducting an SIA in their state-specific laws for those five categories of projects (see Map 10.2). The Maharashtra government has moved further and exempted projects under industrial areas and estates too. The Tamil Nadu government has also exempted three more Acts from the requirement of conducting SIA and obtaining consent – the Tamil Nadu Acquisition of Land for Industrial Purposes Act of 1997, the Tamil Nadu Highways Act of 2001 and the Tamil Nadu Acquisition of Land for Harijan Welfare Schemes Act of 1978. A significant number of land acquisitions are carried out under these three Acts.

The government of Gujarat, in order to maintain its image of an 'industry friendly state', has incorporated all the provisions of the ordinance into its state Act of 2016 and, according to the statement of object and reasons, this amendment aims to dilute the stringent provisions and make the lengthy and difficult process of land acquisition 'smooth and easy'. The amendment exempts projects under national security, rural infrastructure, affordable housing, industrial corridors and other infrastructure projects, including those under PPP, and, thus, the provisions related to SIA and consent do not apply to such projects. The Union Ministry of Rural Development and the Union Ministry of Home Affairs have recently noted that the amendments in the Gujarat Bill are very similar to those that the NDA government has been trying to pass and, therefore, referred the Bill to the Joint Parliamentary Committee. Pursuant to that, the Union Ministry of Rural Development and the Union Home Ministry refused to send the Bill to the president for his assent. This, however, was overlooked as the Bill did eventually find its way to the President of India. As of 8 August 2016, it has become a law in Gujarat.

The exemption to SIA provisions clearly indicates the 'un-preparedness' of the state to carry out such activities and lack of clarity on its importance in developing successful rehabilitation plans and mitigating land conflicts on the ground.

Existing Institutions and Reality Check

The land acquisition procedure, at the district level, is carried out by the officials of the revenue department (*patwari*, revenue inspector or circle officer, *tehsildar*) and further administered by the sub-divisional magistrate and district magistrate. The state revenue department is primarily responsible for land acquisition notification procedures and issues necessary approvals to carry forward the work at the district level. So, primarily, it remains the prerogative of the district administration to 'successfully' or 'unsuccessfully' carry forward the land acquisition activities. The RFCTLARR Act of 2013 is highly ambitious in its expectations from the district administration to conduct activities such as updating land records within a period of two months, assessing and identifying livelihood losers and sharecroppers, facilitating SIA, obtaining FPIC and so on. Undoubtedly, both the LA Act and the Mining Act emphasize fair identification of beneficiaries and distribution of benefits to the local people. However, to realize the objectives of these Acts and achieve their implementation in true spirit, the local institutions need to be oriented

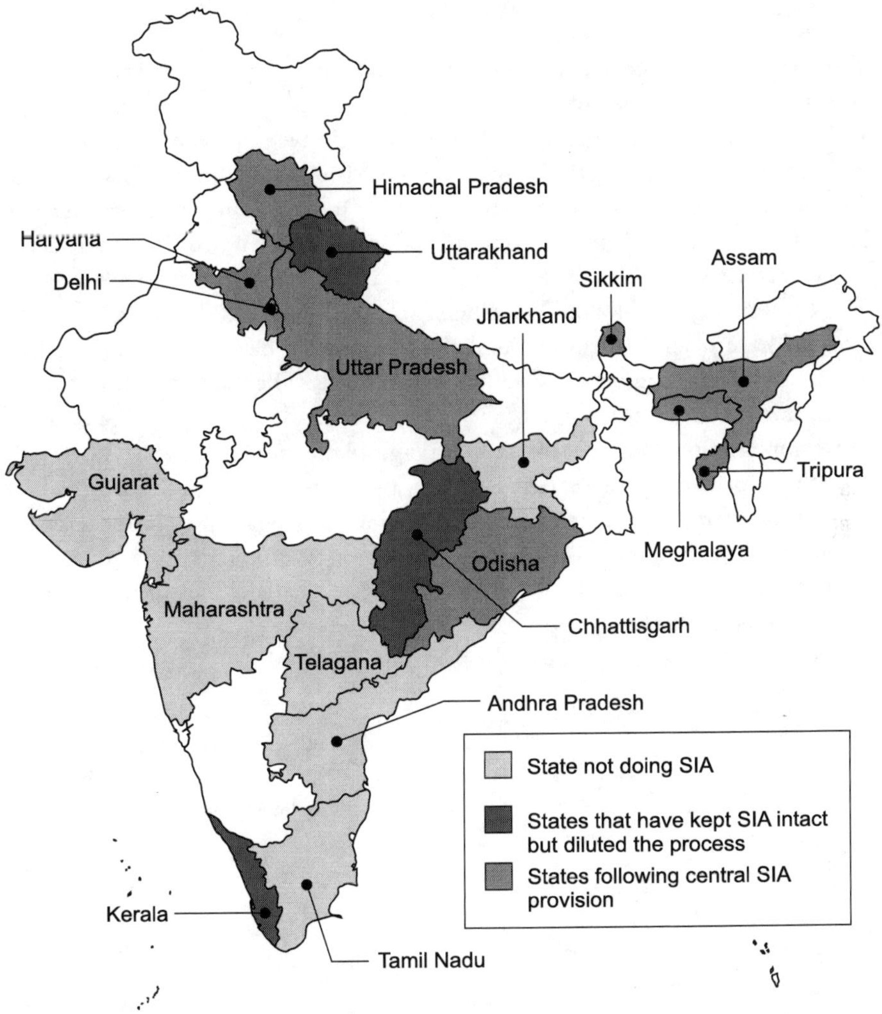

Map 10.3 Status of SIA in states

Source: Adapted by author from *Down to Earth* (2018).

Note: Map not to scale and may not represent authentic international borders.

and strengthened. It is easier at the state level to make strategic amendments and get rid of these progressive provisions of the central Act (see Map 10.3), but that does not resolve the reasons for land conflicts on the ground. The challenge is to work with these institutions and prepare them to take up new roles for the betterment of the local community and regional development.

Way Forward

If the nation has to move ahead with the agenda of a fast-growing economy and meeting local aspirations of underdeveloped regions, then we must prepare our institutions to take up larger roles to deliver 'inclusive development'. Instead of exploring ways of escaping these progressive provisions of the central Act, it is high time we start realizing its importance, which is inclusive, participatory and fair. The last decade has witnessed hundreds of unresolved land conflicts across the nation that have significantly delayed (or withdrawn) many infrastructure projects from their timely completion. For a long time, the 'social costs' in 'developmental projects' have been undermined and the assessments have not been done in a realistic manner to compensate people for their losses. The state governments need to understand the fact that one has to first understand the 'damages' to design a 'fair compensation and rehabilitation package'. And a tool like the SIA precisely does that. As discussed in earlier chapters, the past six decades of displacement experience of Singrauli clearly demonstrates the sufferings of people and a flawed development paradigm. It is high time that state governments stopped diluting the central Land Act, if the governments have to truly achieve the agenda of 'inclusive development'.

11

Conclusion

Development projects in India since Independence have resulted in large-scale involuntary displacement of people from their habitation, livelihood and environment, which is the direct consequence of forced land acquisition. The case of Singrauli, which has been studied in this book, illustrates various 'regimes of dispossession' and has a long story of displacement and deprivation, neglect, and underdevelopment. Loss of livelihood and displacement have become a recurring feature for the people of Singrauli due to dams and power and mining projects over the last five decades. During 2005–2015, the state government has received a large number of proposals from private companies to establish resource-based industries in Singrauli. Communities are again in the process of being displaced, with private players setting up four mining projects and five super thermal power projects in the area.

However, there is no official figure on total displacement from the Government of India, but an unofficial figure shows that nearly 60 million people have been displaced until 2000 (Cernea, 2000b; Fernandes, 2008). The economic reform in the 1990s and the spree of market economy brought large-scale foreign direct investment into sectors such as mining, industries, infrastructural projects and special economic zones, and it accelerated the number of involuntarily displaced people to a great extent. Among the displaced, the tribals are the most affected group, who constitute 8 per cent of India's population but miserably account for 40 per cent of the total displaced in the country. Development projects also affected huge areas of productive agricultural land (including irrigated and multi-cropped), which had adverse impacts on the food security of the people. The dignified self-employed farmers turned into landless labourers overnight in the name of 'public interest'. Such marginalization has been erupting into a number of protests and movements against developmental projects since Independence and it has increased manifold, especially in the era of economic reforms, and, thus, many of the high-profile projects have been halted or delayed. It forced the government to promulgate a new Act in 2013, called 'the Right to Fair Compensation and

Transparency in Land Acquisition, Resettlement and Rehabilitation Act, 2013, replacing the Land Acquisition (LA) Act of 1894. Although, an amendment was made by the present National Democratic Alliance government through an ordinance to bring certain changes in the Act, the tough resistance from key political parties from the opposition sides forced the government to bring back the original provisions of the Act.

Growth is the watchword of the new economic policy. Driven by the capitalist agenda that has a global outreach, the government is committed to achieving high growth through private and foreign investment. As land appears to be the most vital requirement for new investment ventures, the government intends to streamline land laws by initiating certain amendments. The Land Bill is thus a logical culmination of the pro-business agenda of the government. It mainly accrues from its unwavering ideological convictions about global capitalism. Farmers, village artisans, tribals and fishermen, however, face the brunt of the new land policy.

From a political and economic perspective, the nuances of the new land policy could be understood under three concluding points. First, the new politics of growth redefine the relationship between the state and capitalism. The emerging close alliance between the government and the corporate sector leads to fundamental restructuring of economic policies. The new amendments in land policy are a necessary outcome of this trend. Second, political preference for privatization, and flexible land acquisition law acting as a booster for this, is inherent in the politics of growth. A politics of growth reinforces the state's appeasement of business forces and exclusion of marginalized communities from the growth-oriented development agenda. The new land policy, for instance, removes social safeguards and minimizes the scope of people's consent in matters concerning land acquisition. People's participation and opinions are also given little attention. Finally, the neoliberal agenda implied in the land policy is being interrogated in the public domain. The power of resistance that is offered by democracy opens several channels of dissent. These channels could be located at both formal and informal levels. Resistance against the Land Bill was offered in the parliament as well as on ground in the form of public protests and farmer's rallies led by the Congress and other opposition parties. The politics of resistance is antithetical to the politics of growth and the present Land Bill is caught between the two political opposites. Its passage and fructification are ridden with challenges and political contestations.

A few points that have emerged from this work are that the power of eminent domain has now been questioned and countered by the landowner's consent clause in the Land Acquisition, Rehabilitation and Resettlement Act of 2013. This raises the classical debate between the powers of the state versus individual rights.

However, in a vibrant functional democracy such as India, this is a progressive step that provides a safeguard mechanism to protect the individual's land and livelihood or to better negotiate a compensation package with the land acquiring agency. The 'public purpose' clause, which has been misused for a long time for all kinds of projects, is now under scrutiny, and it is critical to quantify regional benefits under the broad umbrella of national interest. The fieldwork data clearly indicates that the decisions taken by the central government while granting a mining lease for particular resource development projects in concerned states do not incorporate the views of the local communities. The regional dissatisfaction and public dissent as we have seen in the case of resource development projects are not going to stabilize until the immediate affected people and the local community become stakeholders in such projects. Another fact about the mineral-rich regions is the presence of Maoist cadre and Naxal movement in these districts, which has become the biggest internal security challenge (as termed by former prime minister Manmohan Singh) for the country. However, in my opinion, this crisis is state created, as for a long time, the people in these regions and their rights have been neglected and the benefits of development have not trickled down in these regions. These mineral-rich regions have been contributing to the national wealth through significant revenues and taxes. The central government's approach of providing 'development packages' to the Naxal-affected districts raises questions in itself.

The inadequacy of the compensation amount, which has been challenged in the court of law time and again, is another aspect that needs a careful policy analysis. The research findings demonstrate that mere enhancement of the compensation amount by a few times the circle rate is not the only solution for the restoration of livelihood and ensuring well-being of the affected families. The fieldwork data suggests that the one-time compensation practice must be replaced with a recurring payment method by which the affected families can productively utilize the amount for their economic, physical and social rehabilitation. Considering the case of resource development projects, the affected families must have a clear stake in the revenue stream of the project so that they can become stakeholders in the true sense.

The governance of mineral funds and relevant institutions in resource-rich regions is another aspect that this book has highlighted. The principle of benefit sharing with the local communities is practised in some of the resource-rich economies, for instance, Canada, Australia and so on, and the government of India needs to endorse this policy. The amount and percentage of profit-sharing vary from country to country and for India, a deeper analysis is needed. The institutional framework governing this fund needs professional expertise and representation from all stakeholders in decision-making and requires a sustainable flow of funds. The representation from stakeholders will guide the expenditure of funds as per the needs of the local population. This has already been discussed in Chapters 7 and 8 that there are different approaches (parallel and partnership) for integrating resources and to achieve the desired social impact. For India, the socio-economic and cultural reality varies from state to state, so the approach will depend on the local situations.

The five decades of 'developmental' experience of Singrauli demonstrates that in a federal democratic polity, it is critical to consider 'regional interests' while determining 'national interest'. With regard to resource development projects, it is important to quantify 'public purpose' in relation to regional benefits. The 60 years of 'planned development' in India have ignored this aspect, and the mineral-rich backward regions with their high incidence of poverty, the presence of Maoist cadre and massive public dissent are the evidence of this unfair development approach. To address the geographical fulcrum of unevenness, it is critical to shift the developmental approach and adopt fair practices to address the concerns at its source. The role of the state is critical for the welfare of society and it must act as a 'regulator' rather than 'facilitator' of the development process. In the era of neoliberalism and with new economic policy interventions, we have witnessed in the past decade that corporations failed to own their social and environmental responsibilities, which led to massive protests and dissent. The proponents of free market and capitalism argue that limited state control and free market encourage open competition among corporations, which in their opinion is the best economic scenario where the consumers are at the benefiting end. Unfortunately, this logic has failed with regard to India and the withdrawal of the state from basic regulatory functions has created further crisis and dissent. It is a proven fact that it is the inherent tendency of capital to create 'spaces of dependence' in order to flourish on such 'spaces' and develop unevenness, as the only motive that drives corporations is profit. Singrauli is one such 'space' that has become a 'space of dependence' in the name of 'public purpose' and is serving national interest at the cost of regional and individual exploitation.

This book attempted to understand the perceptions of different stakeholders from the lens of justice and fairness. The fieldwork data suggests that for the affected families, 'just compensation' is equivalent to the restoration of lands and livelihoods. One-time cash compensation on the basis of some calculations (methodology) fall short of their aspirations. For project developers, 'just compensation' is delivered by implementing the law of the land (even if the legislation is underdeveloped) and they feel no social or moral obligations beyond the law. The book highlighted that it is critical for the state to perform the 'regulatory' functions rather than merely act as a 'facilitator' of development and ensure that fair policies are in place to address the concerns of the stakeholders, particularly of the affected families.

Another significant aspect of 'realization of justice' in the land acquisition process is correcting inequalities in the public sphere and ensuring true participation of project-affected individuals in the public hearing procedures. Liberal political theory assumes that it is possible to organize a democratic form of political life on the basis of socio-economic and sociocultural structures that generate systemic inequalities. The institution or domain of public sphere is an offshoot of this thought process. Thus, socio-economic structures of capitalist societies create boundaries for the functioning of the public sphere as well. This is true even in case of the public sphere in India. The public sphere in India is not giving much scope for inclusion of interests but rather causes exclusion and marginalization of several interest groups. The interest that overpowers others is the one pertinent to the dominant class. The interest that emerges in the name of 'national interest' serves private interest and, in most cases, does not recognize the plural character of the population. The resultant form of democracy is thus quite lopsided, inherent with the unequal structures of the stratified society. Though liberal political theory guarantees (that is, a public disclosure/platform) in the nature of a public sphere, to propagate common good, the emergence and pattern of the same challenge the 'common good' aspect.

The major challenges that the public sphere is facing probably can be answered by the doctrines of 'critical theory'. First, it is very important to address the issues of socio-economic inequalities rather than proposing for 'equal members'. The public sphere needs to take into account systemic inequalities. Second, a single public sphere in India is not efficient enough to understand the pluralism in India and then deliver the common good. A stratified society creates fragmented space within the idea of a unitary sphere. So, there is a need for multiple policies. Third, the delivery of a common good depends on the quality of participation guaranteed by the public sphere and how far 'public interests' are recognized and respected over 'private gains'. Therefore, the Indian public sphere should identify the loopholes which generate marginalization and respectively address them. Finally, civil society needs to play a pivotal role by catalysing a greater democratic participation of the people.

A democratic set-up with a neoliberal system will have its own share of limitations. But definitely it is time to unlearn a lot of the given assumptions of the public sphere and transform it structurally to achieve the goal of 'common good' and to respect the 'general will'. But one definite insufficiency that needs to be addressed is the crisis of governance, be it at a macro-level state functionary or at the grassroot level. The tandem needs to be achieved in the form of a stronger political will. Probably, in such a case, the three socio-economic institutions of governance along with the agents of change (people *per se*) can strive to provide an effective meaning to the public sphere, as opposed to what has been the outcome of liberal political theory.

Land will remain an important and unique factor of production due to its special characteristics – immobility, geostrategic value and so on. How much it actually constitutes the total project investment and the amount of compensation from the restoration and rehabilitation point of view are crucial questions. And the initiatives taken by the UPA government in amending the LA Act are highly appreciable, but, first, considering its special characteristics and as a factor of production, there is need to go beyond this 'linear, technocratic, economistic' understanding of land and, second, considering the relationships between land and the state, one cannot overlook the question of 'sovereign rights of state' over land, especially regarding the so-called public land.

Land has been and will continue to be a central fault line in the near future and has the potential to radically alter the existing fault lines in politics and in development policies. As discussed earlier, almost all Maoist violence is sourced and concentrated in the forestland or mining land where compensation and rehabilitation have become a sham. And the approach of providing 'development packages' from the centre to the mining districts at a time when there is an incident of violence or a crisis is highly absurd; why are such spaces kept deprived in the first place? I return to compensation: no amount of compensation is enough when a robust and inalienable right to livelihood is not inbuilt in the quantified models of compensation. Some would prefer 'monetary compensation' based on 'informed consent', whereas many would still prefer to transvalue the compensation in terms of 'who they are, where they are coming from and what they will be in future' – the classical communitarian questions are not amenable to easy resolution. This shows why democracies are often vulnerable to pressures from land struggles, whereas authoritarian political systems often offer swift answers. I strongly believe that the classical political economy question of 'land' still remains unresolved; perhaps modernity's future rests on the resolution of this question, though the proponents of neo-age economy would not like to believe that land still matters!

Appendix

Memorandum from Mineral-Bearing States

Demands from the mineral-rich states (memo to the 12th Finance Commission [FC]), Jharkhand, Madhya Pradesh and Odisha, are as follows.

Jharkhand

> The state government is of the opinion that Jharkhand has to be treated as the special case. In any devolution formulae, there will be states where the formula just 'doesn't fit'. Jharkhand has a heavy preponderance of natural resources, which are exploited by the central government, but at the same time give a faulty picture of the per capita GSDP of the state. In these special cases an alternative to the formula must be considered. (Finance Commission of India, 2004: 19)

Specifically with regard to mining, the memo to the 12th Finance Commission says,

> Incessant mining by the central government agencies has had 3 adverse effects on the state:
>
> - The land used for mining cannot be put to any productive use once the mining is complete;
> - Human suffering because of displacement is a tremendous burden that needs to be compensated through an adequate rehabilitation package;
> - The ecological and environmental impact of mining is irreparable and the state should be compensated for the same.
>
> At present there is no national programme to compensate the states for the irreparable damage caused by mining activities. The royalty that is paid to the state government is inadequate considering the huge loss that the state is suffering. The necessity to arrive at a fair royalty is critical for the state and should not be dealt as a commercial activity only, but should also consider the ecological and social aspects of mining. (Ibid.)

Madhya Pradesh

Views on coal royalty:

> We would like to examine and refuse the popular counter arguments that have so far been used to resist correcting this gross injustice to coal bearing states. One popular counter argument against increase in the rate of royalty has been that it leads to an increase in the landed price of coal. The landed price comprises the pithead price, royalty, other cess, freight and taxes. The share of royalty in the landed price of coal is not very significant. The economic impact of increase in landed price due to any of its components is same on the performance of the coal consuming industries. However, it is not clear, why the same argument is not extended when the landed price of the coal increases due to increase in the basic coal price (cost of production) or due to increase in the railway freight charges or other levies. The truth of the matter is that coal prices are frequently increased to benefit the CPSU's without increasing the royalty. (Finance Commission of India, 2004: para 12.7)
>
> It has already been stated that royalty forms a small proportion of the landed price of the coal. Industries like thermal power stations, which use coal directly, will be affected only marginally by the increase in royalty. Thus, adverse impact of any increase in royalty is very small and its incidence on the final consumers insignificant. (Ibid.: para 12.10)
>
> It has traditionally been argued that major consumers of domestic coal in the country being the State Electricity Boards (SEBs) increase in coal royalty in turn has a deleterious effect on revenues of the state because coal is used by the SEBs. In Madhya Pradesh, SEB produces 60% of the coal based thermal generation while NTPC and other produce the balance 40%. The argument therefore is that why should more royalty collected from SEBs to be paid to state governments who pay for these SEBs. It is more like a balancing entry. However, this contention is not true. For instance, NCL (Northern Coalfields Ltd) sells coal to NTPC (Shaktinagar and Vindhayachal) which in turn sells power not only to SEB of MP but also to SEBs belonging to UP, Punjab, Haryana, Delhi, Maharashtra and so on. These are not coal producing states. The fact of the matter is that coal producing states actually subsidise cost of power of other states by keeping the coal price low. (Ibid.: para 12.11)
>
> Another argument has been that revision of rates will also have impact on exports and imports, on the process of privatization of coalmines and on the foreign investments in the coal sector. It is strongly argued that rise in the price of the coal due to increase in the royalty rates makes the domestic coal industry lose its market to the foreign coal. Here again the facts are otherwise. The price effect on the market of coal and the economic impact of increased royalty very much depend upon the demand and supply position of coal in India. The public sector which controls the major portion of coal reserves in India enjoys a monopoly

position. The supply side is having stronger forces than the demand side. Planning Commission estimates that coal supply is actually short of demand for coal and the trend is likely to continue in future. (Ibid.: para 12.12)

'Need to move to ad valorem based compensation':

As argued above the revenue and economic impact of royalty on coal clearly reveal the shortcoming in the royalty system prevailing in the country. From the above it is seen that fixation of coal royalty has been ad hoc and the arguments to continue this dispensation are without much economic rationale. Coal producing states have been continually requesting frequency in the revision of royalty rates or fixation of these rates on ad valorem basis. The GoI has introduced ad valorem based compensation for states producing natural gas, which is expected to benefit Assam, Gujarat and Andhra Pradesh. Considering the fact that mineral rich states Jharkhand, Orissa, Ch[h]attisgarh and Madhya Pradesh are among the relatively backward states of India, ad valorem for coal is long overdue measure. The eleventh finance commission had also appreciated this point and suggested that if for any reason (the counter arguments that mention downstream implications we have considered and rebutted here) mineral royalty cannot be revised, the Centre should compensate the states through an equivalent grant-in-aid.

Bibliography

Adams, J. 1998. *Risk in a Hyper-Mobile World.* London: University of London.

ADB (Asian Development Bank). 2003. *Involuntary Resettlement Operational Manual.* Manila: ADB.

———. 2007. *Compensation and Valuation in Resettlement: Cambodia, People's Republic of China and India.* Manila: ADB.

Agarwal, B. 1992. 'The Gender and Environment Debate: Lessons from India, Feminist Studies'. *Feminist Studies* 18(1) Spring: 119–158.

———. 1994. *A Field of One's Own: Gender and Land Rights in South Asia.* Cambridge and New York: Cambridge University Press.

Aggarwal, A. 2012. *Social and Economic Impact of Sezs in India.* New Delhi: Oxford University Press.

Ahluwalia, M. 2000. 'Economic Performance of States in Post Reforms Period'. *Economic and Political Weekly* 35(19): 1637–1648. Available at https://www.epw.in/journal/2000/19/special-articles/economic-performance-states-post-reforms-period.html. Accessed 6 April 2020.

Ahluwalia, Montek Singh. 1999. 'India's Economic Reforms: An Appraisal'. In *India in the Era of Economic Reforms*, ed. Jeffrey D. Sachs, Ashutosh Varshney and Nirupam Bajpai, Nirupam. New Delhi: Oxford University Press. Available at https://pdfs.semanticscholar.org/c852/bfeca4c7d7c1f572537938abab7a5730ba25.pdf. Accessed 10 April 2020.

Ali, A. 2001. 'Evolution of Public Sphere in India'. *Economic and Political Weekly* 36(26): 2419–2415.

Ambrose, P., ed. 1969. *Analytical Human Geography.* London: Longmans.

Amnesty International. 2016. *When Land Is Lost, Do We Eat Coal? Coal Mining and Violations of Adivasi Rights in India.* Available at https://www.amnesty.org/download/Documents/ASA2043912016ENGLISH.PDF.

Arora, B. and B. Verney, eds. 1995. *Multiple Identities in a Single State: Indian Federalism in Comparative Perspective.* New Delhi: Konark Publishers.

Asian Indigenous & Tribal Peoples Network (AITPN). 2008. *Reports about Land Alienation of the Tribals in India*, vol. III, no. 4, October–December. New Delhi: AITPN.

Asif, M. 1999. 'Land Acquisition Act: Need for an Alternative Paradigm'. *Economic and Political Weekly* 34(25): 19–25.

Atkinson, Giles and Kirk Hamilton. 2003. 'Savings, Growth and the Resource Curse Hypothesis'. *World Development* 31(11) November: 1793–1807.

Austin, Granville. 1966. *The Indian Constitution: Cornerstone of a Nation*. New Delhi: Oxford University Press.

Auty, R. M., ed. 2001. *Resource Abundance and Economic Development*. Oxford: Oxford University Press.

Bajpai and Sachs. 1999. 'The Progress of Policy Reform and Variations in Performance at the Sub National Level in India.' Development Discussion Paper, 730, 25 September 2009. Earth Institute, Harvard Institute for International Development, Harvard University. Available at https://academiccommons.columbia.edu/doi/10.7916/D81V5MT2.

Balakrishnana, R. 2004. *Jharkhand Matters: Essays on Ethnicity Regionalism and Development*. Delhi: Konark Publishers.

Banerjee-Guha, S. 1991. 'Who Are the Beneficiaries? Evaluation of a Public Housing Project for the Poor in New Bombay'. *Ekistics* 58(346/347): 55–64.

Bardhan, P. 1984. *The Political Economy of Development in India*. Oxford: Basil Blackwell.

———. 2011. 'Space, Spatiality, Human Geography and Social Sciences: Politics of the Production of Space'. *Transactions of the Indian Geographers* 33(1): 3–22.

Bardhan, P. 1997. 'Corruption and Development: A Review of Issues'. *Journal of Economic Literature* 35(3): 1320–1346. Available at www.jstor.org/stable/2729979. Accessed 8 April 2020.

———. 1998. *The Political Economy of Development in India*. New Delhi: Oxford University Press.

———. 2010. *Awakening Giants, Feet of Clay: Assessing the Economic Rise of China and India*. Princeton, NJ: Princeton University Press.

———. 2011. 'Land Acquisition: Currently a Major Stumbling Block for Development Policy'. *Development Outreach*, World Bank. Available at http://emlab.berkeley.edu/users/webfac/bardhan/papers/WBILand\%20Acquisition.pdf.Accessed 15 October 2012.

Basu, M. 1996. 'Basic Needs Approach in Displacement Situations'. *Mainstream* 24, July–August: 34–49.

Baum, F. 1995. 'Researching Public Health: Behind the Qualitative-Quantitative Methodological Debate'. *Social Science and Medicine* 40(4): 459–468.

Baviskar, Amita. 1995. *In the Belly of the River: Tribal Conflicts over Development in the Narmada Valley*. New Delhi: Oxford University Press.Baviskar, A. 2003. 'For a Cultural Politics of Natural Resources'. *Economic and Political Weekly* 38(48): 5051–5056.

Baxi, U. 1989. *Notes on Constitutional and Legal Aspects of Rehabilitation and Displacement: Development, Displacement and Rehabilitation: Issues for National Debate*. New Delhi: Indian Social Institute.

———. 2008. 'Rehabilitation and Resettlement: Some Human Rights Perspectives'. In *Social Development Report: Development and Displacement*. New Delhi: Oxford University Press.

Becker, E. and T. Jahn, eds. 1999. *Sustainability and the Social Sciences*. London: Zed Books.

Bell, M. 1980. 'Taking Justice Seriously: Utilitarianism and Compensation'. *Urban Law and Policy* 23(3).

Berger, P. L. and T. Luckmann. 1966. *The Social Construction of Reality: A Treatise in the Sociology of Knowledge*. New York: Garden City.

Berlin, I. 1961. *Two Concepts of Liberty*. Oxford: Clarendon Press.

Bettelheim, B. 1968. *India Independent*. New York: Monthly Review Press.

Bhagwati, J. 1993. *Protectionism*. Cambridge, MA: MIT Press.

Bhargava, R. and H. Reifeld, eds. 2005. *Civil Society, Public Sphere and Citizenship: Dialogues and Perceptions*. London: Sage Publications.

Bhattacharya, H. 2005. 'Federalism and Regionalism in India: Institutional Strategies and Political Accommodation of Identity'. Working Paper no. 27, Heidelberg Papers in South Asian and Comparative Politics. Available at http://www.hpsacp.uni-hd.de. Accessed January 2012.

Bhushan, C. 2008. *Rich, Lands, Poor People: Is Sustainable Mining Possible*. Delhi: Centre for Science and Environment.

Bialasiewicz, L. 2003. 'Many Worlds of Difference and Dissent'. *Reports from the Third International Conference of Critical Geography*. London: Blackwell Publishing.

Billon, L. P. 2001. 'The Political Ecology of War: Natural Resources and Armed Conflicts'. *Political Geography* 20:561–584.

Borras, S. M., Jr, P. Michael and I. Scones 2010. 'The Politics of Biofuels, Land and Agrarian Change'. *Journal of Peasant Studies* 37(4) October: 575–592.

Borras, S., Jr. 2010. 'The Politics of Transnational Agrarian Movements'. *Development and Change* 41(5): 771–803.

Brahmapurkar, K. P. 2019. 'High Under-Five Mortality Rate in Rural Madhya Pradesh, Time to Identify High-Risk Districts Using National Family Health Survey-4 Data with Comparison to Low Under-Five Mortality Rate in Rural Tamil Nadu, India.' *International Journal of Preventive Medicine* 10:33. https://doi.org/10.4103/ijpvm.IJPVM_157_17.

Brass, P. 2012. *An Indian Political Life: Charan Singh and Congress Politics, 1957–1967*. India: Sage Publications.

Brenner, N. 1999. 'Beyond State-Centrism? Space, Territoriality and Geographical Scale in Globalisation Studies'. *Theory and Society* 28: 39–57.

Brenner, N. and N. Theodore. 2007. 'Neoliberalism and the Regulation of "Environment"'. In *Neoliberal Environments, False Promises and Unnatural Consequences*, ed. N. Heynen, J. McCarthy, S. Prudham and P. Robbins, 153–160. London, New York: Routledge.

Brenner, R. 2006. 'What Is, and What Is Not, Imperialism?' *Historical Materialism* 14(4): 79–105.

Bromley, D. W. 1997. 'Constitutional Political Economy: Property Claims in a Dynamic World'. *Contemporary Economic Policy* 15(4): 43–54.

Bromley, Daniel. 2003. 'The Commons, Common Property and Environmental Policy'. In *Property Rights and Environmental Problems*, ed. B. Larson, vol. 1, 83–99. Burlington: Ashgate.

Bryman, A. 1988. *Quantity and Quality in Social Research*. London: Routledge.

Bunge, W. 1974. 'The Human Geography of Detroit'. In *La Crise Urbaine: A Challenge to Geographers*, ed. R. A. Roberge, 49–69. Ottawa: University of Ottawa Press.

———. 1977. 'The First Year of the Detroit Geographical Expedition: A Personal Report'. In *Radical Geography*, ed. R. Peet, 31–39. London: Methuen.

Byrman, A. 2008. *Social Research Methods*. 3rd edn. Oxford: Oxford University Press.

CAG (Comptroller and Auditor General). 2016. 'Report of the Comptroller and Auditor General of India on e-Auction of Coal Mines', Report No. 20 of 2016. New Delhi: Ministry of Coal, Union Government. Available at https://cag.gov.in/sites/default/files/audit_report_files/Union_Ministry_of_Coal_eAuction_of_Coal_Mines_Compliance_Audit_Report_No_20_of_2016.pdf. Accessed 1 April 2020.

Cannon, G. T. 1975. 'Geography and Underdevelopment'. *Area* 7(3): 212–216.

Caracelli, V. J. and J. C. Greene. 1993. 'Data Analysis Strategies for Mixed-Method Evaluation Designs'. *Educational Evaluation and Policy Analysis* 15(2): 195–207.

Carey, J. W. 1993. 'Linking Qualitative and Quantitative Methods: Integrating Cultural Factors into Public Health'. *Qualitative Health Research* 3(3): 298–318.

Casebeer, A. L. and M. J. Verhoef. 1997. 'Combining Qualitative and Quantitative Research Methods: Considering the Possibilities for Enhancing the Study of Chronic Diseases'. *Chronic Diseases in Canada* 18(3): 30–135.

Castells, M. 1977. *The Urban Question*. London: Edward Arnold.

Cernea, M. and H. Mathur. 2008. *Can Compensation Prevent Impoverishment? Reforming Resettlement through Investments and Benefit-Sharing*. New Delhi: Oxford University Press.

Cernea, M. M. 1999a. '"Development's Painful Social Costs": Introductory Study to S. Parasuraman'. *The Development Dilemma*, 1-31. Displacement in India. London: MacMillan Press and ISS.

———. 1999b. *The Economics of Involuntary Resettlement: Questions and Challenges*. Washington, DC: World Bank Publications.

———. 2000a. 'Involuntary Resettlement: Some Thoughts on Research Priorities'. *Eastern Anthropologist* 53(1–2): 3–12.

———. 2000b. 'Risks, Safeguards, and Reconstruction: A Model for Population Displacement and Resettlement'. In *Risks and Reconstruction: Experiences of Resettlers and Refugees*, ed. M. M. Cernea and C. McDowell, 1–11. Washington, DC: World Bank.

———. 2002. 'For a New Economics of Resettlement: A Sociological Critique of the Compensation Principle'. *An Exchange on the Compensation Principle in Resettlement*, ed. M. M. Cernea and R. Kanbur, 20–46. Ithaca, NY: Cornell University Press.

———. 2003. 'For a New Economics of Resettlement: A Sociological Critique of the Compensation Principle'. *International Journal of Social Science* 55:37–45.

———. 2005a. '"Restriction of Access" Is Displacement: A Broader Concept and Policy'. *Forced Migration Review* 23:48–49.

———. 2005b. '"The Ripple Effect' in Social Policy and Its Political Content: A Debate on Social Standards in Public and Private Development Projects'. In *Privatising*

Development: Transnational Law, Infrastructure and Human Rights, ed. B. M. Likosky, 65–101. Leiden and Boston, MA: Martinus Nijhoff.

———. 2007. 'Financing for Development: Benefit Sharing Mechanisms in Population Resettlement'. *Economic and Political Weekly* 42(12): 1033–1046.

———. 2008. 'Compensation and Benefit Sharing: Why Resettlement Policies and Practices Must Be Reformed'. *Water Science and Engineering* 1(1): 89–120.

Cernea, Michael M. 1988. 'Involuntary Resettlement in Development Projects: Policy Guidelines in World Bank-Financed Projects.' World Bank Technical Paper No. 80. World Bank, Washington, DC. Available at http://documents.worldbank.org/curated/en/699511468325205947/Involuntary-resettlement-in-development-projects-policy-guidelines-in-World-Bank-financed-projects. Accessed 1 April 2020.

———. 1995. 'Social Integration and Population Displacement: The Contribution of Social Science'. *International Social Science Journal* 143(1): 91–112.

Chacko, P. A., et al. 2003. *Enquiry Report: PUCL Dumka, Jharkhand Unit.* Available at http://www.pucl.org/Topics/Industries-envirn-resettlement/2003/ pachwara. Accessed 15 Octoober 2015.

Chakravorty, S. 2013. *The Price of Land: Acquisition, Conflict, Consequence.* New Delhi: Oxford University Press.

Chambers, R. 1994. 'Participatory Rural Appraisal (PRA): Analysis of Experience'. *World Development* 22(9): 1253–1268.

Chan, N. 2003. 'Land Acquisition Compensation in China: Problems and Answers'. *International Real Estate Review* 6(1): 136–152.

Chandhoke, N. 1994. 'Of State and Civil Societies'. In *Understanding the Post-Colonial World: Theory and Method*, ed. Neera Chandoke, 200–206. New Delhi: Sterling Publisher and Nehru Memorial Museum and Library.

Chandrasekhar, C. and J. Gosh. 2002. *The Market That Failed: Neoliberal Economic Reforms in India.* New Delhi: LeftWord Books.

Chapman, K. 1979. *People, Pattern and Process.* London: Arnold-Heinemann.

Chatterjee, Dev. 2014. 'Stalled Projects See a Sharp Decline'. *Business Standard.* Available at https://www.business-standard.com/article/economy-policy/stalled-projects-see-a-sharp-decline-115070301146_1.html. Accessed 17 May 2020.

Chatterjee, P. 2004. *The Politics of the Governed.* New York: Columbia University Press.

Chomsky, N. 1999. *Profit over People: Neoliberalism and Global Order.* New York: Seven Stories Press.

CII (Confederation of Indian Industry). 2014. Highlights and reports. Available at https://www.cii.in/Digital_Library_Details.aspx?enc=pZVQM37jtSRTHIkmBsithecTEGiGA0zVe4rr3c8fiU8YCyH5pjFgrbJkuBh8L+OC.

Clark, A. L. 2000. *Political, Economic and Administrative Decentralisation: Addressing the Distributional Effects of Mineral Sector Development in Asia.* UNCTAD Workshop on Growth and Diversification in Mineral Economics, 7–9 November 2000, Cape Town.

Clark, D. H. 1997. 'The Fiscal Transfer System in Canada'. In *Financing Decetralized Expenditures: An International Comparison of Grants*, ed. E. Ahmad, 292–333. UK: Edward Elgar Publishing.

———. 1997. 'The Fiscal Transfer System in Canada'. In *Financing Decentralized Expenditures: An International Comparison of Grants*, ed. Ehtisham Ahmad, 70–102. Cheltenham, PA: Edward Elgar Publishing.

Clarke, P. N. and P. S. Yaros. 1988. 'Research Blenders: Commentary and Response'. *Nursing Science Quarterly* 1: 147–151.

CMIE (Centre for Monitoring Indian Economy). 2012. 'Sharp Increase in Projects Getting Shelved'. Available at http://www.cmie.com/kommon/bin/ sr.php?kall= wclrdhtm.php&cmienvdt=20120704101759176 &pc=099000000000&type=INSIGHTS. Accessed 20 October 2012.

———. 2015. *Urbanomics*. Data computed from CMIE & Economic Survey. Available at http://gulzar05.blogspot.com/2015/05/restructuring-stalled-infrastructure.html. Accessed 7 April 2020.

Coal India. 2014. *2014-15: Annual Reports and Accounts*. Kolkata: Coal India. Available at https://www.coalindia.in/DesktopModules/DocumentList/documents/Annual_Report_&_Accounts_2014-15_Deluxe_version_In_English_03102015.pdf. Accessed 1 April 2020.

Collier, P. 2007. *The Bottom Billion: Why the Poorest Countries are Failing and What Can Be Done about It*. Oxford: Oxford University Press.

Collier, P. and A. Hoeffler. 1998. 'On Economic Causes of Civil War'. *Oxford Economic Papers* 50: 563–573.

———. 2000. 'Greed and Grievance as Causes of Civil War'. Paper presented to a conference on 'The Economics of Political Violence', 18–19 March, Centre of International Studies, Woodrow Wilson School of Public and International Affairs, Princeton University, and the Development Research Group, World Bank.

———. 2004. 'Greed and Grievance in Civil War'. *Oxford Economic Papers* 56: 563–595.

Commonwealth Human Rights Initiative (CHRI). 2015. *Not a Single Acquisition under Land Ordinance for Developmental Projects in Six Months*. New Delhi. Available at http://articles.economictimes.indiatimes.com/2015-07-30/news/65036713_1_land-ordinance-land-acquisition-13-central-acts. Accessed 15 November 2015.

Cooter, R. 2000. *The Strategic Constitution*. Princeton, NJ: Princeton University Press.

Corbridge, S. 1987. 'Perversity and Ethnoregionalism in Tribal India: The Politics of the Jharkhand'. *Political Geography Quarterly* 6(3) July: 225–240.

Corbridge, S. and J. Harriss. 2000. *Reinventing India*. Cambridge: Polity Press.

Corbridge, Stuart. 2009. 'The Political Economy of Development in India since Independence'. In *Routledge Handbook of South Asian Politics: India, Pakistan, Bangladesh, Sri Lanka, and Nepal*, ed. Paul Brass, 318–336. Abingdon: Routledge.

Council for Social Development. 2008. *India Social Development Report*. New Delhi: Oxford University Press.

Cox, K. 1984. 'Neighborhood Conflict and Urban Social Movements: Questions of Historicity, Class, and Social Change'. *Urban Geography* 5:343–355.

Creswell, J. W. 2009. *Research Design: Qualitative, Quantitative, and Mixed Methods Approaches*. 3rd edn. Thousand Oaks, CA: Sage Publications.

CSE (Centre for Science and Environment). 2011. *Sharing the Wealth of Minerals*. New Delhi: Centre for Science and Environment. Available at http://www.cseindia.org/userfiles/profit_ sharing.pdf. Accessed 12 June 2012.

———. 2017. 'People First: District Mineral Foundation (DMF)'. Available at https://www.cseindia.org/people-first-district-mineral-foundation-dmf--8893.

Dan, P. K., K. Guhathakurta and S. Gupta. 2008. 'Modelling for Land Acquisition for SEZ'. *e-Journal of Science & Technology* 3(2): 43–50.

Dana, C. 2003. 'Singrauli: An Unfulfilled Struggle for Justice'. In *Demanding Accountability: Civil Society Claims and the World Bank Inspection Panel*, ed. C. Dana, J. Fox and T. Kay, 167–190. Washington, DC: Rowman and Littlefield Publishers Inc.

Das, J. R. 1998. 'The Social and Spatial Character of the Indian State'. *Political Geography* 17(7): 787–808.

Das, V. 1992. *Jharkhand: Castle over Graves*. New Delhi: Inter-India Publications.

Davis, G. A. and J. E. Tilton. 2005. 'The Resource Curse'. *Natural Resource Forum* 29:233–242.

De Angelis, M. 2007. *The Beginning of History: Value Struggles and Global Capital*. London: Pluto Press.

De Soysa, I. 2000. 'The Resource Curse: Are Civil Wars Driven by Rapacity or Paucity?' In *Greed or Grievance: Economic Agendas in Civil Wars*, ed. M. Berdal and D. Malone, 113–136. Boulder, CO: Lynne Rienner Publishers.

Dear, M. and S. Flusty. 2001. 'The Banality of Interdiction: Surveillance, Control and the Displacement of Diversity'. *International Journal of Urban and Regional Research* 25:658–664.

Debnath, B. 2008. 'Land Acquisition and National Highways.' *Economic and Political Weekly* 43(31).

Deininger, K. (2003). 'Land Policies for Growth and Poverty Reduction'. *A World Bank Policy Research Report*. Washington, DC and Oxford: Oxford University Press and World Bank.

Denyer-Green, Barry. 1994. *Planning Law Report*. Amsterdam: Elsevier BV.

Denzin, N. K. andY. S. Lincoln. 1994. 'Introduction: Entering the field of Qualitative Research'. In *Handbook of Qualitative Research*, ed. N. K. Denzin and Y. S. Lincoln, 1–17. Thousand Oaks, CA: Sage Publications.

Desai, A. R. 1975. *State and Society in India: Essays in Dissent*. Bombay: Popular Prakashan.

Directorate of Census Operations. 2011. *District Census Handbook*: *Singrauli*. Directorate of Census Operations, Madhya Pradesh. Available at http://censusindia.gov.in/2011census/dchb/DCHB_A/23/2346_PART_A_DCHB_SINGRAULI.pdf. Accessed 1 April 2020.

Divan, S. and A. Rosencranz. 2002. *Environmental Law and Policy in India*. New Delhi: Oxford University Press.

Donald, J. H. 2006. *Uneven Development*. Stanford, CA: Stanford University. Available at www-econ.stanford.edu/faculty/workp//swp06007.pdf. Accessed 5 February 2012.

Downing, T. 1999. 'Mitigating Social Impoverishment When People Are Involuntarily Displaced'. In *Understanding Impoverishment: The Consequences of Development-Induced Population Displacement*, ed. C. McDowell, 132–216. Oxford: Berghahn Books.

Dreze, J. and A. Sen. 2002. *India: Development and Participation*. New Delhi: Oxford University Press.

———. 2013. *An Uncertain Glory: India and Its Contradictions*. Princeton, NJ: Princeton University Press.

Dutt, L., R. Krishanan and N. Ahmad. 2012. 'Land Acquisition and Dispossession: Private Coal Companies in Jharkhand'. *Economic and Political Weekly* 47(6): 39–45.

Dutta, R. P. 1970. *India Today*. Calcutta: Manisha.

Dwivedi, R. 2006. *Conflict and Collective Action: The Sardar Sarovar Project in India*. London: Routledge.

Easton, D. 1981. 'The Political System Besieged by the State'. *Political Theory* 9(3): 303–325.

EBMWG (Ecosystem Based Management Working Group). 2010. *Benefit Sharing Agreements in British Columbia: A Guide for First Nations, Business and Government*. Victoria, CA: Woodward & Company. Available at https://www.for.gov.bc.ca/ tasb/ slrp/lrmp/nanaimo/cencoast/ ebmwg_docs/hw03b_benefit_sharing_final_report.pdf. Accessed 10 January 2012.

Economic Times. 2015a. 'Can't Blame UPA Land Acquisition Bill for Stalled Projects: RTI'. New Delhi, 28 April. Available at https://economictimes.indiatimes.com/news/politics-and-nation/cant-blame-upa-land-acquisition-bill-for-stalled-projects-rti/articleshow/47077042.cms. Accessed 1 April 2020.

———. 2015b. 'Not a Single Acquisition under Land Ordinance for Developmental Projects in Six Months.' New Delhi, 30 July. Available at https://economictimes.indiatimes.com/news/politics-and-nation/not-a-single-acquisition-under-land-ordinance-for-developmental-projects-in-six-months/articleshow/48274659.cms. Accessed 1 April 2020.

EDF (Environmental Defense Fund). 1995. 'Environmental Study of Singrauli Area'. NTPC (National Thermal Power Corporation Limited), New Delhi.

EJAtlas. 2020. Maps and other data. EJAtlas, Institute of Environmental Science and Technology, Autonomous University of Barcelona. Available at https://ejatlas.org, https://ejatlas.org/country and https://ejatlas.org/country/india. Accessed 1 April 2020.

Elliot, C. M. 2003. *Civil Society and Democracy*. New Delhi: Oxford University Press.

England, K. V. L. 1994. 'Getting Personal: Reflexivity, Positionality and Feminist Research'. *Professional Geography* 46:80–89.

Epstein, R. 1985. *Takings: Private Property and the Power of Eminent Domain*. Cambridge, MA: Harvard University Press.

F. Nancy. 1990. 'Rethinking the Public Sphere: A Contribution to the Critique of Actually Existing Democracy'. *Social Text* 25 and 26:56–80.

Fact Finding Committee on the Sri Sailam Project. 1986. 'The Srisailam Resettlement Experience: The Untold Story'. In *Dams, Displacement, Policy and Law in India:*

Contributing Paper for WCD Thematic Review 1.3 Displacement, ed. R. Hemadri, H. Mander, and V. Nagaraj. Washington, DC: World Commission on Dams.

Fernandes, W. 2008. 'Sixty Years of Development-Induced Displacement in India'. In *India Social Development Report: Development and Displacement*, ed. Hari Mohan Mathur 89–102. New Delhi: Oxford University Press.

Fernandes, W. and G. E. Thukral. 1989. *Development, Displacement and Rehabilitation: Issues for National Debate*. New Delhi: Indian Social Institute.

Fernandes, Walter. 2000. 'Pawns in the "Development" Game'. In *India Disasters Report Human-Instigated Disasters*, ed. S. Parasuraman and P. V. Unnikrishnan, 276–279. New Delhi: Oxford University Press.

Finance Commission of India. 2004. *Twelfth Finance Commission Report, 2005–10*. New Delhi: Ministry of Finance, Government of India. Available at http://fincomindia.nic.in/pubsugg/memo_ori.pdf, http://fincomindia.nic.in/pubsugg/memo_jkhand.pdf and http://fincomindia.nic.in/pubsugg/memo_mp.pdf. All were accessed on 10 January 2012.

Fischel, W. 1995. *Regulatory Takings: Law, Economics, and Politics*. Cambridge, MA: Harvard University Press.

Frankel. F. 1978. *India's Political Economy 1947–77: The Gradual Revolution*. Princeton, NJ: Princeton University Press.

Fraser, N. 2007. 'Transnational Public Sphere: Transnationalizing the Public Sphere; On the Legitimacy and Efficacy of Public Opinion in a Post-Westphalian World' *Theory, Culture & Society* 24(4): 7–30.

Freeden, M. 1991. *Rights*. Milton Keynes: Open University Press.

Friedman, Milton. 1980. *Free to Choose*. New York and London: Harcourt Brace Jovanovich.

Gazette of India. 2013. 'The Right to Fair Compensation and Transparency in Land Acquisition, Rehabilitation and Resettlement Act, 2013, Part II, Section 1'. Legislative Department, Ministry of Law and Justice, Government of India, New Delhi, 27 September. Available at http://indiacode.nic.in/acts-in-pdf/302013.pdf. Accessed 15 October 2015.

Ghatwai, M. 2009. 'Another Land Acquisition Bid, another Protest'. *Indian Express* [Online], 10 January. Available at http://www.indianexpress.com/news/another-land-acquisition-bid-another-protes/408858/. Accessed 31 August 2009.

GHK/MRM International. 1994a. *Development and Environmental Strategy*. New Delhi: NTPC.

———. 1994b. *Report on Singrauli Development and Environmental Strategy: Displaced Peoples Action Plan*. Cyclostyled Report. GHK/MRM Mumbai.

Giddens, A. 1984. *The Continuation of Society: Outline of the Theory of Structuration*. Cambridge: Polity Press.

———. 1990. *The Consequences of Modernity*. Cambridge: Polity Press.

Giovann, A. 2004. *Capitalism, Socialism and Uneven Development* [Online]. Available at http://ricardo.ecn.wfu.edu/~cottrell/ope/archive/0410/0063.html. Accessed October 2010.

Glaser, B. G. and A. L. Strauss. 1967. *The Discovery of Grounded Theory: Strategies for Qualitative Research*. Hawthorne, NY: Aldine de Gruyter.

GRAIN (Genetic Resources Action International). 2008. *Seized: The 2008 Land Grab for Food and Financial Security*. Barcelona.

Granville, A. 1966. *The Indian Constitution: Cornerstone of a Nation*. New Delhi: Oxford University Press.

Greenpeace. 2011. 'Singrauli: The Coal Curse; A Fact Finding Report on the Impact of Coal Mining on the People and Environment of Singrauli'. Greenpeace, New Delhi. Available at https://www.greenpeace.org/india/en/publication/1006/singrauli-the-coal-curse/. Accessed 1 April 2020.

Gregory, D. 1978. 'Social Change and Spatial Structures'. In *Timing Space and Spacing Timing*, ed. T. Carlstein, D. Parkes and N. J. Thrift, 163–180. London: Macmillan.

Gregory, D. and J. Urry, eds. 1985. *Social Relations and Spatial Structures*. London: Macmillan.

Guba, G. E. and Y. S. Lincoln. 1989. *Fourth Generation Evaluation*. Newbury Park, CA: Sage Publications.

———. 1994. 'Competing Paradigms in Qualitative Research'. In *Handbook of Qualitative Research*, ed. N. K. Denzin and Y. S. Lincoln, 105–117. Thousand Oaks, CA: Sage.

Gubbi, S. 2006. 'Tiger Habitats and Integrated Conservation and Development Projects: A Case Study from Periyar Tiger Reserve, India'. MSc dissertation. University of Kent, Canterbury.

Guha, B. S. 1997. *Spatial Dynamics of International Capital*. Hyderabad: Orient Longman.

———. 2002. 'Critical Geographical Praxis: Globalisation and Socio-spatial Disorders'. *Economic and Political Weekly* 37(44–45): 4503–4509.

———. 2004. 'Space, Society and Geography: Investigating the Crisis of Postmodern Urban Space'. In *Space, Society and Geography*, ed. B. S. Guha 61–82. New Delhi: Rawat Publishers.

———. 2008. 'Space Relations of Capital and Significance of New Economic Enclaves: SEZs in India'. *Economic and Political Weekly* 43(47): 51–60.

Gunton, T. 2003. 'Natural Resources and Regional Development: An Assessment of Dependency and Comparative Advantage Paradigms'. *Economic Geography* 79(1): 67–94.

Haase, J. E. and S. T. Myers. 1988. 'Reconciling Paradigm Assumptions of Qualitative and Quantitative Research'. *Western Journal of Nursing Research* 10:128–137.

Habermas, J. 1962. *The Structural Transformation of the Public Sphere: An Inquiry into a Category of Bourgeois Society*. Cambridge: Polity Press.

Halarnkar, Samar. 2011. 'Powerless in Urjanchal'. *Hindustan Times*. 1 September. Available at https://www.hindustantimes.com/india/powerless-in-urjanchal/story-yoBkWlumapEcpagolk0fAP.html. Accessed 12 August 2020.

Handique, M. 2008. *30 Years of Destitution: India's Largest Energy Hub and the People of Singrauli, U.P.* [Online]. Available at http://sanhati.com/articles/1181/. Accessed 29 August 2009.

Hardikar, Jaideep. n.d. 'The Destruction of Development'. Available at htq)://infbdi^ / Other/Development - Dictionary/The-destruction. Accessed 26 June 2009.

Harvey, D. 1973. *Social Justice and the City*. London: Edward Arnold.

———. 1982. *The Limits to Capital*. New York: Basil Blackwell Oxford.

———. 1985. 'The Geoplitics of Capitalism in Social Relations and Spatial Structures'. In *Social Relations and Spatial Structures*, ed. D. Gregory and J. Urry, 128–163. London: Macmillan Publishers Ltd.

———. 1989. *The Condition of Post Modernity: An Enquiry into the Origins of Cultural Change*. Cambridge, MA: Blackwell.

———. 1996. *Justice, Nature and the Geography of Difference*. Oxford: Wiley Blackwell.

———. 2001. *Spaces of Capital towards a Critical Geography*. Edinburgh: Routledge and Edinburgh University Press.

———. 2003. *The New Imperialism*. New York: Oxford University Press.Harvey, D. 2006a. *Limits to Capital*. London: Verso.

———. 2006b. *Spaces of Global Capitalism*. London: Verso.

Hindu. 2007. 'Farmers' Interests Will Be Protected: CPI (M).' New Delhi, 10 January. Available at https://www.thehindu.com/todays-paper/tp-national/Farmers-interests-will-be-protected-CPI-M/article14704241.ece. Accessed 1 April 2020.

———. 2013. 'Odisha Govt. Completes Land Acquisition for POSCO'. Bhubaneshwar, 4 July.

Hindustan Times. 2009. *Singur to Singrauli*. Available at http://www.hindustantimes.com/News/india/Singur-to-Singrauli/Article1-362470.aspx. Accessed 29 August 2009.

Hoggart, K., L. C. Less and A. R. Davies. 2002. *Researching Human Geography*. London: Arnold Publishers.

Howe, K. R. 1988. 'Against the Quantitative-Qualitative Incompatibility Thesis or Dogmas Die Hard'. *Educational Researcher* 17:10–16.

Hummon, D. H. 1992. 'Community Attachment: Local Sentiment and Sense of Place'. In *Place Attachment*, ed. I. Altman and S. M. Low, 253–278. New York: Plenum Press.

IDFC (Infrastructure Development Finance Company). 2009. *India Infrastructure Report 2009: Land; A Critical Resource for Infrastructure, 3i Network*. New Delhi: Oxford University Press.

IIED (International Institute for Environment and Development) and WBCSD (World Business Council for Sustainable Development). 2002. *Breaking New Ground: Mining, Minerals and Sustainable Development*. London: Earthescan.

Impact Benefit Agreement. 2015. 'Impact Benefit Agreements Lab'. Available at https://www.sfu.ca/rem/planning/research/IBA.html. Accessed October 2015.

Indian Express. 2015. 'Land Acquisition: A New Capital City in Farmland'. 25 December 2015.

Jain, S. and M. Bala. 2006. *The Economics and Politics of Resettlement in India*. New Delhi: Pearson Longman.

Jan Lok Hit Samiti. n.d. *Report on 'Cost of Development: The Affect of Big Gigantic Projects in Singrauli*. Cyclostyled report. Singrauli.

Jenkins, R. 1999. *Democratic Politics and Economic Reform in India*. Cambridge: Cambridge University Press.

Jeremy, B. 1789. *An Introduction to the Principles of Morals and Legislation*. Oxford: Clarendon Press.

Jetli, K. 2011. *Mineral Resources and Policy in India*. Delhi: New Century Publication.

Jick, T. 1979. 'Mixing Qualitative and Quantitative Methods: Triangulation in Action'. *Administrative Science Quarterly* 24:602–611.

Jones, M. 1974. *The Government and Politics of India*. New Delhi: B. I. Publications.

Kakani, K. R., L. T. Raghu Ram and N. S. Tigga. 2008. *Insights into Land Acquisition Experiences of Private Businesses in India*. XLRI working paper, November.

Kaldor, M. 1999. *New and Old Wars: Organized Violence in a Global Era*. Stanford, CA: Stanford University Press.

Kasturi, K. 2007. 'Land Acquisition from Colonial Times to the Present'. *Ghadar Jari Hai* 2(1): 5–8. Available at http://www. ghadar.in/Vol.2 Issue 1 PDF/v2 I1 Cover Story pdf. Accessed 10 January 2010.

Kaviraj, S. and S. Khilnani. 2001. *Civil Society: History and Possibilities*. New Delhi: Cambridge University Press.

Keogh, J. 2001. 'The "Special Value" of Land in Compulsory Acquisition Cases.' Pacific Rim Real Estate Society Seventh Annual Conference, 21–24 January 2001, Adelaide.

King, G., R. O. Keohane and S. Verba. 1994. *Designing Social Inquiry: Scientific Inference in Qualitative Research*. Princeton, NJ: Princeton University Press.

Kitchin, R. and N. J. Tate. 2000. *Conducting Research into Human Geography: Theory, Methodology and Practice*. London: Prentice Hall.

Klare, M. T. 2001. *Resource Wars*. New York: Metropolitan Books.

Kochanek, S. 1974. *Business and Politics in India*. Berkeley, CA: University of California Press.

Kohli, A. 2012. *Poverty Amid Plenty in the New India*. Cambridge: Cambridge University Press.

Kohli, Atul. 2009. *Democracy and Development in India: From Socialism to Pro-business*. New Delhi: Oxford University Press.

Kohli, M. n.d. *Request for Inspection NTPC Power Generation Project Cr. 3632* [Internet]. Available at http://www.ciel.org/Publications/sing1.html. Accessed 29 August 2009.

Kothari, R. 1972. *Politics in India*. New Delhi: Orient Longman

———. 1987. *State against Democracy*. Delhi: Ajanta.

Kothari, S. 1996. 'Whose Nations? Displaced as Victims of Development'. *Economic and Political Weekly* 24(31) June: 1476–1486.

Kothari, Smithu. 1988. 'The Survival'. *Illustrated Weekly of India*, 24 April.

Krishnaswami, M. 2005. 'One Step Forward and, Two Steps Back'. *Economic and Political Weekly* 40(47): 4899.

Kujur, J. M. 2005. 'A Tribal Reading of the Resettlement and Rehabilitation Policy 2003'. *Social Action* 55(April–June): 138–151.

Kumar, C. 2007. 'The Displaced People of Rihand Dam and Their State of Rehabilitation'. *National Geographical Journal of India* 53(March–June): 117–128.

Kurien, M. 1975a. 'Class Character of the Indian State'. In *India, State and Society: A Marxist Approach*, ed. K. Mathew Kurien, 113. Madras: Orient Longman.

———. 1975b. *India – State and Society: A Marxian Approach*. Bombay: Orient Longman.

Lahiri-Dutt, K. 2001. 'From Gin Girls to Scavengers: Women in Ranigunj Collieries'. *Economic and Political Weekly* 36(44): 4213–4219.

Lalor, John J., ed. 1899. *Cyclopaedia of Political Science, Political Economy, and of the Political History of the United States by the Best American and European Authors.* Abdication-Duty, vol. 1. New York: Maynard, Merrill, & Co. Available at https://oll.libertyfund.org/titles/1679. Accessed 2 April 2020.

Land Conflict Watch. 2019. Available at https://www.landconflictwatch.org/#home. Accessed 1 April 2020.

Lassailly-Jacob, V. 2001. 'Land-Based Strategies in Dam-Related Resettlement Programmes in Africa'. In *Transforming Settlement in Southern Africa*, ed. C. J. De Wet and R. C. Fox, 242–267. Edinburgh: Edinburgh University Press.

Leelakrishnan P., ed. 2008. *Environmental Law in India.* 3rd edn. New Delhi: LexiNexis.

Lefebvre, H. 1974. *The Production of Space.* Oxford: Blackwell UK.

———. 1976. 'Reflections on the Politics of Space'. *Antipode* 8(2): 30–37.

———. 1991. *Production of Space*, trans. D. Nicholson-Smith. Malden, MA: Blackwell.

Leite, C. and J. Weidmann. 1999. 'Does Mother Nature Corrupt? Natural Resources, Corruption, and Economic Growth'. IMF Working Paper WP/99/85, International Monetary Fund, Washington, DC.

Levien, M. 2011. 'Special Economic Zones and Accumulation by Dispossession in India'. *Journal of Agrarian Change* 11(4): 454–483.

———. 2012. 'The Land Question: Special Economic Zones and the Political Economy of Dispossession in India'. *Journal of Peasant Studies* 39(3–4): 933–969.

———. 2013. 'Regimes of Dispossession: From Steel Towns to Special Economic Zones'. *Development and Change* 44(2): 381–407.

———. 2017. 'From Primitive Accumulation to Regimes of Dispossession: These on India's LAnd Question'. In *The Land Question in India: State, Dispossession, and Capitalist Transition*, ed. Anthony P. D'Costa and Achin Chakraborty, 49–75. New York: Oxford University Press.

Lewis, W. A. 1954. 'Economic Development with Unlimited Supplies of Labor'. *Manchester School of Economic and Social Studies* 22: 139–191.

LiveMint. 2010. 'Yamuna Expressway Case'. Available at http://www.livemint.com/2010/09/09223901/Public-purpose-redefined.html. Accessed 2 August 2012.

Lokayan. 1985. 'Vikas Ki Kimat: Problem of Displacement in Singrauli.' Setu Centre for Social Knowledge and Action, Ahmedabad.

Low, S. M. and I. Altman. 1992. 'Place Attachment: A Conceptual Inquiry'. In *Place Attachment*, ed. I. Altman and S. M. Low, 1–12. New York: Plenum Press.

Luke, D. 2002. 'Sustainable Development Framework for Coalbed Methane Development.' *Regulation and Development of Coalbed Methane*, Rocky Mountain Mineral Law Foundation Mineral Law Series, vol. 2002, no. 4, pt 9. Denver, CO: Pendergast Sarni Group LLC. Available at https://static1.squarespace.com/static/5bb24d3c9b8fe8421e87bbb6/t/5c3bd50d2b6a28e8ada533c7/1547425041654/A-Sustainable-Dev.-Framework-for-Coalbed-Methane-Development.pdf. Accessed 4 April 2020.

MacLeod, G. and G. Mark. 1999. 'Reconstructing an Urban and Regional Political Economy: On the State, Politics, Scale, and Explanation'. *Political Geography* 18:697–730.

Mahalingam, A. and A. Vyas. 2011. 'Comparative Evaluation of Land Acquisition and Compensation Processes across the World'. *Economic and Political Weekly* 46(32): 94–102.

Mahapatra, L. 1999. *Resettlement, Impoverishment and Reconstruction in India, Development for the Deprived*. New Delhi: Vikas Publications.

Manor, J. 1999. *The Political Economy of Decentralization*. Washington, DC: World Bank.

Martinez-Alier, J. 1999. 'The Socio-ecological Embeddedness of Economic Activity: The Emergence of Tran Disciplinary Field'. In *Sustainability and the Social Sciences*, ed. Egon Becker and Thomas Jahn, 112–139. New York: Zed Books.

Massey, D. 1973. 'Towards a Critique of Industrial Location Theory'. *Antipode* 5:33–39.

Mathur, H. 2006. *Managing Resettlement in India: Approaches, Issues, Experiences*. New Delhi: Oxford University Press.

———. 2011. *Resettling Displaced People: Policy and Practice in India*. New Delhi: Routledge.

———. 2013. *Displacement and Resettlement in India: The Human cost of development*. London: Routledge.

Mathur, Hari Mohan and David Marsden. 1998. 'Good Intentions or Policies Are Not Enough: Reducing Impoverishment Risks for the Tribal Oustees'. In *Development Projects and Impoverishment Risks: Resettling Project-Affected People in India*, ed. Hari Mohan Mathur and David Marsden, 216–236. New Delhi: Oxford University Press.

Mathur, Hari Mohan. 2005a. 'Involuntary Resettlement: A Review of Current Literature'. Prepared for the Government of Orissa UNDP/DFID Resettlement Policy Project (mimeo). Available at https://journals.sagepub.com/doi/abs/10.1177/004908570803800401.

———. 2005b. 'Resettlement Policies: International, National, and State; A Review'. Prepared for the Government of Orissa UNDP/DFID Resettlement Policy Project (mimeo). Available at https://journals.sagepub.com/doi/abs/10.1177/004908570803800401.

Mawdsley, E. 2002. *Redrawing the Body Politic: Federalism, Regionalism and the Creation of New States in India*. London: Birkbeck ePrints. Available athttp://eprints.bbk.ac.uk/ archive/00000216. Accessed 15 October 2012.

Maxwell, J. A. 1996. *Qualitative Research Design: An Interactive Approach*. London: Sage Publications.

McGregor, H. 1988. *McGregor on Damages*. London: Sweet & Maxwell.

McMahon, G. 1998a. 'Mining & the Community: Results of the Quito Conference.' World Bank, Washington, DC.

———. 1998b. 'The Natural Resource Curse: Myth or Reality?' World Bank Economic Development Institute, Washington, DC.

Merrill. T. 1986. The Economics of Public Use. *Cornell Law Review* 72:61–116.

Miceli, T. 1997. *Economics of the Law: Torts, Contracts, Property, Litigation*. New York: Oxford University Press.

Miles, M. and A. Huberman. 1984. 'Drawing Valid Meaning from Qualitative Data: Toward a Shared Craft'. *Educational Researcher* 13:20–30.

Milton, F. 1980. *Free to Choose*. London: Harcourt Brace Jovanovich.

Ministry of Commerce. 2017. *Special Economic Zones: Performance, Problems and Opportunities – A survey Based Empirical Study on SEZs in India*. Available at https://www.phdcci.in/wp-content/uploads/2018/11/Research-Study-on-Special-Economic-Zones-in-India-April-2017.pdf.

Ministry of Finance. 2015. *Economic Survey*. New Delhi: Oxford University Press.

Ministry of Mines. (2011). *Annual Report (2010–11)*. New Delhi: Ministry of Mines, Government of India.

Mitra, A. 1977. *Terms of Trade and Class Relations*. London: Frank Cass.

Morris, S. and A. Pandey. 2007. 'Towards Reform of Land Acquisition Framework in India'. Working Paper for Indian Institute of Management, Ahmedabad, India. Available at https://www.researchgate.net/publication/46437223_Towards_Reform_of_Land_Acquisition_Framework_in_India. Accessed 2 April 2020.

Mukerji, S. 2017. 'Land Acquisition in Contemporary India: The Growth Agenda, Legislation and Resistance'. *Indian Journal of Public Administration* 63(1): 85–103.

Mukherji, R. 2014. *Political Economy of Reforms in India*. New Delhi: Oxford University Press.

Myrdal, G. 1968. *Asian Drama: An Inquiry into the Poverty of Nations*. London: Allenlane and Penguin.

Nagaraj. R. 2000. 'Indian Economy since 1980: Virtuous Growth or Polarisation?' *Economic and Political Weekly 35*(32): 2831–2839. Available at from www.jstor.org/stable/4409590. Accessed 2 April 2020.

Nagaraj, R. and S. Motiram, eds. 2017. *Political Economy of Contemporary India*. New York: Cambridge University Press.

Nagpal, S .2014. 'Land Acquisition and Development? Exploring Narratives of Modernity at a Land Acquisition Site in Singrauli India'. Master's dissertation, unpublished, Central European University, Hungary.

Nayar, B. R. 1971. Business Attitudes towards Economic Planning in India. *Asian Survey* 11(9): 864.

———. 1989. *India's Mixed Economy: The Role of Ideology and Interest in Its Development*. Bombay: Popular Prakashan.

NCL (Northern Coalfields Limited) files. Hardcopy files accessed at NCL corporate office, Singrauli. Available at http://nclcil.in/page.php?pid=133.

Neumayer. 2004. 'Does the "Resource Curse" Hold for Growth in Genuine Income as Well?' *World Development* 32(10): 1627–1640. Available at https://doi.org/10.1016/j.worlddev.2004.05.005.

Nilsen, A. 2010. *Dispossession and Resistance in India: The River and the Rage*. New Delhi: Routledge.

NITI Aayog. 2019. 'Transforming Aspirational Districts in India: A Programme for New India; 2022'. NITI Aayog, Government of India, New Delhi.

Available at https://niti.gov.in/sites/default/files/2019-08/4_Presentation-for-PrincipalSecretariesPlanning.pdf. Accessed 1 April 2020.

Noronha, L. 2005. 'Assessing Quality of Life in the Mining Region'. *Economic and Political Weekly* 40(1) January: 72–78.

Noronha, L., N. Srivastava, D. Datt and P. V. Sridharan. 2009. 'Resource Federalism in India: The Case of Minerals'. *Economic and Political Weekly* 8(17) 21–27 February: 51–59.

NTPC (National Thermal Power Corporation) files. Hardcopy files accessed at NTPC corporate office, New Delhi. Available at https://www.ntpc.co.in/power-generation/coal-based-power-stations/vindhyachal.

O'Faircheallaigh, Ciaran and G. Ginger. 2010. *Negotiation and Implementation of Impact and Benefit Agreements*. Toronto: The Walter & Duncan Gordon Foundation. Available at https://www.afoa.ca/afoadocs/L3/L3a%20-%20IBA_ toolkit_March_2010_low_resolution.pdf. Accessed 10 September 2014.

O'Faircheallaigh, Ciaran. 2003a. 'Implementing Agreement between Indigenous People and Resource Developers in Australia and Canada'. Research Paper 13. Centre for Australian Public Sector Management, Australia. Available at https://www.griffith. edu.au/business-government/griffith-business-school/pdf/research-paper-2003-implementing-agreements.pdf. Accessed 12 June 2012.

———. 2003b. 'Financial Models for Agreements between Indigenous Peoples and Minin Companies'. Research Paper 12. Centre for Australian Public Sector Management, Australia. Available at https://www.griffith.edu.au/business-government/griffith-business-school/pdf/research-paper-2003-financial-models.pdf. Accessed 12 June 2012.

Office of the Registrar General and Census Commissioner. 2011. *Census of India 2011*. New Delhi: Office of the Registrar General and Census Commissioner, Ministry of Home Affairs, Government of India. Available at http://censusindia.gov.in/.

Olsen, W. K. 2004. 'Triangulation in Social Research: Qualitative and Quantitative Methods Can Really Be Mixed'. In *Developments in Sociology: An Annual Review*, ed. M. Holborn, 1–30. Ormskirk: Causeway Press.

Padel, F. and S. Das. 2008. 'Orissa Highland Clearances: The Reality Gap in R&R'. *Social Change* 38(4): 576–608.

Pahl, R. E. 1985. *The Restructuring of Capital, the Local Political Economy and Household Work Strategies*. London: Macmillan Publishers Ltd.

Palit, A. and S. Bhattacharjee. 2008. *Special Economic Zones in India: Myths and Realities*. New Delhi: Anthem Press.

Pandey, B. 1998. *Displaced Development: Impact of Open Cast Mining on Women*. New Delhi: Friedrich Ebert Stiftung.

———. 2000. 'Impoverishing Effects of Coal Mining Projects: A Case Study of Five Villages in Orissa'. In *Development Projects and Impoverishment Risk: Resettling Project Affected People*, ed. H. Mathur and D. Maesden, 1–30. Oxford: Oxford University Press.

Pandey, B. Kumar and B. Rout. 2004. *Development-Induced Displacement in India: Impact on Women*. New Delhi: National Commission for Women.

Parasuraman, S. 1996. 'Development Projects, Displacement and Outcomes for Displaced: Two Case Studies'. *Economic and Political Weekly* 31(24): 1529–1532.

———. 1999. *The Development Dilemma: Displacement in India*. London: MacMillan Press Ltd.

Patnaik, P. (1973). 'On the Political Economy of Underdevelopment'. *Economic and Political Weekly* 8(February): 197–212. Available at http://www.jstor.org/stable/4362292. Accessed 21 February 2012.

———. 1972. 'Imperialism and the Growth of Indian Capitalism'. In *Theories of Imperialism*, ed. R. Owen and R. B. Sutcliffe, 53–63. London: Longman.

———. 1979. 'Industrial Development in India Since Independence'. *Social Scientist* 7(11): 83, 3–19.

Patnaik, U. 2005. 'Ricardo's Fallacy: Mutual Benefit from Trade Based on Comparative Costs and Specialization?' In *The Pioneers of Development Economics*, ed. K. S. Jomo, 30–41. New Delhi: Tulika Publishers.

Peet, R. 1989. *New Models in Geography: The Political Economy Approach*. Ed. Nigel Thrift. London: Unwin Hyman.

———. 1999. *Theories of Development*. New York: Guilford Press.

———, ed. 1977. *Radical Geography: Alternative Viewpoints on Contemporary Social Issues*. Chicago, IL: Maaroufa Press.

Pickvance, C. J., ed. 1976. *Urban Sociology: Critical Essays*. London: Tavistock Publishers.

Planning Commission. 1962. *Report of Irrigation and Power Team on Rihand Project: Committee on Plan Projects*. New Delhi: Government of India. Available at http://cslrepository.nvli.in/bitstream/123456789/1841/2/2088.pdf. Accessed 14 August 2020.

———. 2006. 'National Mineral Policy, Report of the High Level Committee' (popularly known as 'Hoda Committee Report'). Government of India, New Delhi.

Porwal, V. and S. Singh.. 2011. 'Land Acquisition and Determination of Land Price: A Critical Appraisal of the Existing and Proposed Normative Framework as Applied in Singrauli District, Madhya Pradesh'. In *Development Induced Displacement, Rehabilitation and Resettlement in India: Current Issues and Challenges*, ed. S. Talwar and S. Saumyaji, 59–74. London: Routledge Publication.

Poulantzas, N. 1978. *State, Power, Socialism*. London: Verso.

Prakash, A. 2001. *Jharkhand: Politics of Development and Identity*. New Delhi: Orient Longman.

Raj, K. N. 1973. *The Politics and Economics of Intermediate Regimes*. Pune: Gokhale Institute of Politics and Economics.

Rajiv, B. 2004. *Jharkhand Matters: Essays on Ethnicity Regionalism and Development*. New Delhi: Konark Publishers.

Ramanathan, S. 1996. 'Displacement and the Law'. *Economic and Political Weekly* 31: 1486–1491.

Rao, G. and N. Singh. 2005. *Political Economy of Federalism in India*. New Delhi: Oxford University Press.

Rawls, J. 1993. 'Distributive Justice'. In *Justice*, ed. A. Ryan, 73–94. Oxford: Oxford University Press.

———. 2001. 'Justice as Fairness'. In *A Restatement*, ed. E. Kelly, 164–194. Cambridge, MA: Harvard University Press.

Rawls, John. 1971. *A Theory of Justice*. Cambridge, MA: Harvard University Press.

Ray, S. and S. Patra. 2009. 'Evolution of Political Economy of Land Acquisition'. *India Infrastructure Report 2009*, 41–43. New Delhi: Oxford University Press.

Rebecca, S. R. and E. Jacque. 1992. 'Uneven Development and Tragedy of the Commons'. *Economic Geography* 68(3) July: 249–271. Available at http://www.jstor.org/ discover/10.2307/144185?uid=3738256&uid=2129&uid=2&uid=70&uid=4&sid=21101182149407. Accessed 30 January 2012.

Reddy, I. U. B. 1994. *Industrial Development and the Problems of the Uprooted*. New Delhi: Rawat Publications.

Reichardt, C. S. and S. F. Rallis. 1994. 'Qualitative and Quantitative Inquiries Are Not Incompatible: A Call for a New Partnership'. *New Directions for Program Evaluation* 61: 85–91.

RFCTLARR (Right to Fair Compensation and Transparency in Land Acquisition and Resettlement and Rehabilitation). 2013. *Gazette of India, Extraordinary*, Part II. Ministry of Law and Justice, Government of India, 27 September.

Robinson, R. J. 1990. *Compulsory Purchase and Compensation: The Law in Scotland*. Edinburgh: W. Green.

Rosencranz, A. 2002. *Environmental Law and Policy in India: Cases, Materials and Statutes*. New Delhi: Oxford University Press.

Ross, M. 2003a. *How Does Mineral Wealth Affect Poor?* [Internet]. Available at http://www.polisci.ucla.edu/faculty/ross/minpoor.pdf. Accessed 8 July 2012.

———. 2003b. 'Oil, Drugs and Diamonds: The Varying Role of Natural Resources in Civil War'. In *The Political Economy of Armed Conflict: Beyond Greed and Grievance*, ed. K. Ballentine and J. Sherman, 47–70. Boulder: Lynne Rienner Publishers.

———. 2004. 'What Do We Know about Natural Resources and Civil War?' *Journal of Peace Research* 41: 337–356.

Ross, M. L. 1999. 'The Political Economy of the Resource Curse'. *World Politics* 51:297–322.

Rosser, A. 2006. 'The Political Economy of the Resource Curse: A Literature Survey'. IDS (Institute of Development Studies) Working Paper 268, Brighton.

Rost, R. O. and G. H. Collins. 1984. *Land Valuation and Compensation in Australia*. Sydney: Australian Institute of Valuers.

Rowan-Robinson, J. 1990. *Compulsory Purchase and Compensation: The Law in Scotland*. Edinburgh: W-Green.

Roy, A. 1999. 'The Greater Common Good'. *Frontline* 16(11), 22 May–4 June.

Roy, P. 1995. *Coal Mining with Sustainable Development: Report on a Project in Hazaribagh and Chatra Districts of Bihar*. Ranchi: People's Union of Civil Liberties.

———. 2007. 'Social Implications of Mining in the Northern Karnapura Valley'. In *Managing the Social and Environmental Consequences of Coal Mining in India*, ed.

Gurdeep Singh, David Laurence and Kuntala Lahiri Dutt, 151–160. Dhanbad: Indian School of Mines in association with University of South Wales and The Australian National University.

RRI (Rights and Resources Initiative). 2016. 'Land Disputes and Stalled Investments in India'. Rights and Resources Initiatives, Washington, DC. Available at http://rightsandresources.org/wp-content/uploads/2016/11/Land-Disputes-and-Stalled-Investments-in-India_November-2016.pdf. Accessed 1 April 2020.

Rudolph, L. and S. Rudolph. 1977. *In Pursuit of Lakshmi: The Political Economy of the Indian State.* Hyderabad: Orient Longman.

———. 2001. 'Iconisation of Chandrababu: Sharing Sovereignty in India's Federal Market Economy'. *Economic and Political Weekly* 36(18): 1541–1552.

———. 1987. *In Pursuit of Lakshmi: The Political Economy of the Indian State.* Chicago, IL: University of Chicago Press.

Sachs, J. D. and A. M. Warner. 1995. 'Natural Resource Abundance and Economic Growth'. NBER Working Paper Vol. 5398, National Bureau of Economic Research, Cambridge.

Sampat. P. 2013. 'Limits to Absolute Power: Eminent Domain and the Right to Land in India'. *Economic and Political Weekly* 8(19): 40–52.

Saunders, P. 1985. *Space City and the Urban Sociology.* London: Macmillan Publishers Ltd.

Sax, J. 1970. 'Public Trust Doctrine in Natural Resource Law: Effective Judicial Intervention'. *Michigan Law Review* 68(3): 471–566.

Schultz, Theodore W. 1964. *Transforming Traditional Agriculture.* New Haven, CT: Yale University Press.

Scudder, T. 1982. *From Welfare to Development: A Conceptual Framework for the Analysis of Dislocated People.* Boulder City, NV: Westview Press.

Scudder, Thayer. 1997a. 'Social Impacts'. In *Water Resources: Environmental Planning, Management and Development*, ed. Asit K. Biswas, 623–664. New York: McGraw Hill.

———. 1997b. 'Resettlement'. In *Water Resources: Environmental Planning, Management and Development*, ed. Asit K. Biswas, 667–709. New York: McGraw Hill.

———. 2005. *The Future of Large Dams.* London: Earthscan Publications.

Segerson. K., ed. 2002. *Economics and Liability for Environmental Problems.* Aldershot: Ashgate.

Sen, A. 2009. *The Idea of Justice.* London: Penguin Allen Lane.

Sen, M. 1977. *Social Revolution in India: Path and Problems.* New Delhi: People's Publishing House.

Sen, R. 1975. 'Capitalism, Imperialism and Underdevelopment'. *Economic and Political Weekly* 33/35(10) August: 1263–1276.

Shah, G., ed. 2002. *Social Movements in India: A Review of Literature.* New Delhi: Sage Publications.

Sharma, B. D. 2002. 'Rights of Tribals'. *Journal of National Human Rights Commission* 1:79.

Sharma, R. N. 2003. 'Involuntary Displacement: A Few Encounters'. *Economic and Political Weekly* 9, no. 38 (March): 907–912.

———. 2009. 'Displacement for Special Economic Zones (SEZs) and Real Estate Business'. In *Beyond Relocation: The Imperative of Sustainable Resettlement*, ed. R. Modi, 199–217. London and New York: Sage Publications.

Sharma, R. N. and S. Singh. 2009. 'Displacement in Singrauli Region: Entitlements and Rehabilitation'. *Economic and Political Weekly* 14(51) December: 62–69.

Singh, C. 1991. *Water Rights and Principles of Water Resource Management*. Mumbai: N. M. Tripathi Pvt Ltd.

Singh, J. 2004. 'Constituting Property: The Deconstruction of the "Right to Property" in India'. CSLG Working Paper Series CSLG/WP/04-05, Jawaharlal Nehru University, New Delhi.

———. 2006. 'Separation of Powers and the Erosion of the "Right to Property" in India'. *Springer* [Internet] 17:303–324. Available at http://rd.springer.com/article/ 10.1007/s10602-006-9008-7?state=cookieless. Accessed 14 October 2010.

Singh, K. S. 2005. *Inside Jharkhand*. Ranchi: Crown Publications.

Singh, M. P. 2004. 'Federal Division of Responsibilities in India'. *Indian Journal of Federal Studies* 1(9): 109–111.

Singh, S. 2009. 'People and Public Sphere in India'. *Social Change* 39(2): 270–280.

———. 2017. 'Political Economy of Land Acquisition and Resource Development in India'. In *India's Contemporary Political Economy*, ed. R. Nagraj and M. Sripad, 279–306. New Delhi: Cambridge University Press.

Singh, Shashi Ratnaker. 2015. 'Political Economy of Land Acquisition and Resource Development in India'. Doctoral thesis, unpublished, University of Cambridge, UK.

Smith, G. and M. Sweeney. 2006. 'The Public Trust Doctrine and Natural Law: Emanations within a Penumbra'. *Boston College Environmental Affairs Law Review* 33(2): 307–344.

Smith, J. K. 1983. 'Quantitative versus Qualitative Research: An Attempt to Clarify the Issue'. *Educational Researcher* 12: 6–13.

Smith, N. 1982. 'Gentrification and Uneven Development'. *Economic Geography* 58(2) April: 139–155. Available at http://www.jstor.org/stable/143793. Accessed 21 February 2012.

———. 1993. 'Homeless/Global: Scaling Places'. In *Mapping the Futures: Local Cultures, Global Change*, ed. J. Bird, B. Curtis, T. Putnam, L. Tickner, 87–119. London: Routledge.

Smith, Neil. 1984. *Uneven Development: Nature, Capital and the Production of Space*' Oxford: Basil Blackwell Publisher Ltd.

Soja, E. 1989. *Postmodern Geographies: The Reassertion of Space in Critical Social Theory*. London: Verso.

Sonak, Ishani. 2018. 'State Govts Acquire Land by Subverting Rights and Bending the Law'. *Down to Earth*. Available at https://www.downtoearth.org.in/news/agriculture/-state-govts-acquire-land-by-subverting-rights-and-bending-the-law--62463.

Springer, S. 2010. 'Neoliberalism and Geography: Expansions, Variegations, Formations'. *Geography Compass* 4(8): 1025–1038.

State Planning Commission. 2010. 'District Wise Poverty Estimates for Madhya Pradesh.' State Planning Commission, Madhya Pradesh. Available at http://mpplanningcommission.gov.in/international-aided-projects/pmpsu/District%20Wise%20Poverty%20Estimates.pdf. Accessed 1 April 2020.

———. 2012. 'Poverty Monitoring and Policy Support Unit.' State Planning Commission, Madhya Pradesh. Available at http://mpplanningcommission.gov.in/international-aided projects/pmpsu/Rural_Electrification.pdf.

Statesman. 2015. 'Tribals Protest against Vedanta Aluminium Refinery'. Bhubaneshwar, 18 June 2015.

Steckler, A., K. R. McLeroy, R. M. Goodman, S. T. Bird and L. McCormick. 1992. 'Toward Integrating Qualitative and Quantitative Methods: An Introduction'. *Health Education Quarterly* 19:1–8.

Steele, F. 1981. *The Sense of Place*. Boston, MA: CBI Publishing.

Sundar, N. 2005a. 'Custom and Democracy in Jharkhand'. *Economic and Political Weekly* 11(41) October: 4430–4434.

———. 2005b. 'Laws, Policies and Practices in Jharkhand'. *Economic and Political Weekly* 40(41) October: 4459–4462.

Temper, L., D. Del Bene and J. Martinez-Alier. 2015. 'Mapping the Frontiers and Front Lines of Global Environmental Justice: The EJAtlas'. *Journal of Political Ecology* 22(1): 255–278.

TERI (The Energy and Resources Institute). 2007. *Study of Compensation to Resource Bearing States*. New Delhi: TERI. Available at http://www.teriin.org/upfiles/projects/ES/2006RD21formatted_ 20080922133649.pdf. Accessed 8 June 2012.

———. 2012. *The Energy and Resource Institute (TERI) Energy Data Directory and Year Book (TEDDY) 2009/10*. New Delhi: TERI Press.

Thukral, E. G. 1996. 'Development, Displacement and Rehabilitation Locating Gender'. *Economic and Political Weekly* 31(24): 1500–1503.

Tillin, L. 2013. *Remapping India: New States and Their Political Origin*. New York: Oxford University Press.

Tripathi, Purnima S. 2007. 'Road to Success'. *Frontline*. 13 July. Available at https://frontline.thehindu.com/other/advertorial/article30192067.ece. Accessed 5 January 2015.

Tuan, Y. F. 1977. *Space and Place: The Perspectives of Experience*. St. Paul, MN: University of Minnesota Press.

Turner, R. K. 1999. 'The Place of Economic Values in Environmental Valuation in Valuing Environmental Preferences'. In *Valuing Environmental Preferences*, ed. I. J. Bateman and K. G. Willis, 17–41. Oxford: Oxford University Press.

Ulen, Thomas S. 1992. 'The Public Use of Private Property: A Dual Constraint Theory of Efficient Government Takings'. In *Taking Property and Just Compensation: Law and Economics Perspectives of the Takings Issue*, ed. N. Mercuro, 163–198. Boston, MA: Kluwer Academic Publishers. Available at doi: 10.1007/978-94-011-2958-9_6.

UNDP (United Nations Development Programme). 2011. 'Recognition of Community Rights under Forest Rights Act in Madhya Pradesh and Chhattisgarh: Challenges and Way Forward'. UNDP, New Delhi. Available at https://www.undp.org/content/

dam/india/docs/DG/recognition-of-community-rights-under-forest-rights-act-in-madhya-pradesh-and-chhattisgarh-challenges-and-way-forward.pdf. Accessed 1 April 2020.

Upadhya, S., et al. 2006. *Estimating the Economic Value of Forest Land: The Legal Perspective*. New Delhi: Institute of Economic Growth.

Upadhyay, V. 2000. 'Changing Judicial Power: Courts on Infrastructure Projects and Environment'. *Economic and Political Weekly* 35(43/44) October–November: 3789–3792.

Upadhyaya, C. 2005. 'Community Rights in Land in Jharkhand'. *Economic and Political Weekly* 40(41): 4435–4442.

Valdivia, G. 2008. 'Governing Relations between People and Things: Citizenship, Territory, and the Political Economy of Petroleum in Ecuador'. *Political Geography* 27: 456–477.

Valuation Office Agency. 2000. *Land Compensation Manual*. London: Crown Copyright.

Verma, M. K. 2004. *Development Displacement and Resettlement*. New Delhi: Rawat Publications.

Vira, B. 2001. 'Claiming Legitimacy: Analysing Conflict in the Environmental Policy Process'. *EPC: Government and Policy* 19:637–650.

Virginius, X. 1999. 'Tribes as Indigenous People of India'. *Economic and Political Weekly* 34(51): 3589.

Vishwanath, C. K. 1997. 'Adivasis: Protesting Land Alienation'. *Economic and Political Weekly* 32(32): 2016.

Waldron, J., ed. 1984. *Theories of Rights*. Oxford: Oxford University Press.

Warhurst, A. and N. Hughes. 1998. 'Liberalisation, Globalisation and Regulation in the Mining Industry: The Case of Latin America'. MERN Working Paper No. 154, Latin American Studies Association.

Weiner, M. 1962. *The Politics of Scarcity*. Chicago, IL: University of Chicago Press.

———. 1967. *Party Building in a New Nation: The Indian National Congress*. Chicago, IL: University of Chicago Press.

Welsch, H. 2008. 'Resource Abundance and Internal Armed Conflict: Types of Natural Resources and the Incidence of "New Wars"'. *Ecological Economics* 67:503–513.

Wheare, K. C. 1963. 'Federal Government'. Heidelberg Papers in South Asian and Comparative Politics, Working Paper No. 27,. Clarendon Press, Oxford.

Wheeler, D. 1984. 'Sources of Stagnation in sub-Saharan Africa'. *World Development* 12(1): 1–23.

Whitehead, J. 2010. *Development and Dispossession in the Narmada Valley*. New Delhi: Pearson.

World Bank. 2001. *Operational Policies 4.12. Involuntary Resettlement*. Washington, DC: World Bank.

———. 2004. *Involuntary Resettlement Sourcebook: Planning and Implementation in Development Projects*. Washington, DC: World Bank.

Xaxa, Virginius. 1999. 'Transformation of Tribes in India: Terms of Discourse'. *Economic and Political Weekly* 34(24): 1519–1524. Available at www.jstor.org/stable/4408077. Accessed 20 February 2020.

Zimmermann, E. 1951. *World Resources and Industries: A Functional Appraisal of the Availability of Agricultural and Industrial Resources.* New York: Harper & Brothers.

Zoomers, A. 2010. 'Globalisation and the Foreignisation of Space: Seven Processes Driving the Current Global Land Grab'. *Journal of Peasant Studies* 37(2) April: 429–447.

Laws and Policies

- Australian Expropriation Law
- Constitution of Brazil, Article 153
- Constitution of Cambodia, Article 44
- Constitution of Japan, Article 49
- Constitution of the Philippines, Article III
- Constitution of the United States, Amendment V
- Expropriations Law of 1936, Mexico
- Land Administration Law of 1988, Peoples Republic of China
- Singapore Land Acquisition Act of 1996
- UK Town and Country Planning Act of 1990

List of Acts

- Coal Bearing Act
- Commonwealth Australia Act
- Constitution of the USA (5th Amendment)
- Environment Protection Act
- Forest Conservation Act
- French Civil Code (Article 545)
- Land Acquisition Act
- Mineral Concession Rules
- Mines and Minerals (Development and Regulation) Act
- Panchayat Extension to Scheduled Areas Act

Index